OTHER BOOKS BY DOUGLAS C. JONES

The Treaty of Medicine Lodge

The Court-martial of George Armstrong Custer

Arrest Sitting Bull

A Creek Called Wounded Knee

Winding Stair

Elkhorn Tavern

Weedy Rough

The Barefoot Brigade

Season of Yellow Leaf

Gone the Dreams and Dancing

Roman

Hickory Cured

Remember Santiago

Come Winter

THE
SEARCH
FOR
TEMPERANCE
MOON

DOUGLAS C. JONES

A Donald Hutter Book
HENRY HOLT AND COMPANY
NEW YORK

Copyright © 1991 by Douglas C. Jones
All rights reserved, including the right to reproduce
this book or portions thereof in any form.
Published by Henry Holt and Company, Inc.,
115 West 18th Street, New York, New York 10011.
Published in Canada by Fitzhenry & Whiteside Limited,
195 Allstate Parkway, Markham, Ontario L3R 4T8.

Library of Congress Cataloging-in-Publication Data
Jones, Douglas C. (Douglas Clyde), 1924–
    The search for Temperance Moon / Douglas C. Jones.—1st ed.
       p.   cm.
    "A Donald Hutter book."
    ISBN 0-8050-1387-3
    I. Title.
PS3560.0478S38   1991
813'.54—dc20   90-25134
                                                          CIP

Henry Holt books are available at special discounts for bulk purchases
for sales promotions, premiums, fund-raising, or educational use.
Special editions or book excerpts can also be created to specification.

For details contact:
Special Sales Director, Henry Holt and Company, Inc.,
115 West 18th Street, New York, New York 10011.

First Edition

DESIGNED BY KATY RIEGEL

Printed in the United States of America
Recognizing the importance of preserving the written word,
Henry Holt and Company, Inc.,
by policy, prints all of its first editions on acid-free paper.∞

10 9 8 7 6 5 4 3 2 1

AUTHOR'S NOTE

The trials and tribulations of many real people have provided inspiration for the scenes that follow. However, actors in the tale are entirely fictitious excepting a few actual persons, Judge Isaac Charles Parker chief among them, who play minor supporting roles. There is no claim here that any old historical mysteries have been solved.

But if the players are imaginary, their social milieu is not. It was there as portrayed on the last wild border of the United States of America, and some of it still is there, although sometimes hard to find or to recognize when found.

This effort is dedicated to my children, a band of incorrigibles that has, despite its fiercely maintained freedom of mind, shown great patience in listening to the same Indian Territory stories over and over and over again. And usually without interruption, illustrating a wisdom beyond their ages in the business of avoiding thumps on the head from the patriarch.

So to them I say, maybe in these pages you will find a few things you have not heard before.

If not, remember. No interruptions!

Douglas C. Jones
Fayetteville, Arkansas

1 It was a large dapple-gray gelding gentle as violets. Having become so perhaps when the expert knife of a Creek Indian horse breeder had taken away forever any inclination or reason to snort and prance and impress the mares. Riding him along a narrow road muddy from recent rain was a woman. Sidesaddle. Easily. Her head up. Shoulders back, reins held loosely in one suede-gloved hand. Riding as though she had ridden many times before and knew how to do it well.

She was a woman of indeterminate age. Maybe old. Maybe young. She was not beautiful but except for a thin mouth turned down rather sharply at the corners, not ugly either. She wore a long woolen dress, fastened collar to hem with black bone buttons. The one exposed shoe in the stirrup was black and highly polished. On her head was a small box hat with a white plume that trailed out behind and bobbed up and down as the gelding moved. Her hair was the color of copper, probably dyed, and swept back from ears pierced and each showing at the lobe a milky pearl that gleamed in the late-afternoon sun.

As they went along, the gelding at a slow walk, the rider sang a hymn. Not really sang. Not the words. Just the tune, humming, as though it were something come to her from a long time ago, a little unfamiliar yet impossible to forget. The sound of it seemed to please the horse and he shook his head and danced a little as they came into a grove of jack oak and young hickory, trees close on either side of the trace.

But there, she pulled up the horse and looked back, and listened, and almost started again, then stopped.

"Who is it?" she called.

There were blackbirds in the high limbs of this thicket, and when the explosion came, they flew off screaming. And the gray gelding, single stirrup flapping, ran on toward home or safety or someplace, and the woman, having felt the impact of the shot, was down in the muddy road and rolling there and trying to pull the pistol from her shoulder-strap purse, a pistol that was always there, but couldn't, and then face up in the mud, unable to free the pistol from the purse, saw the figure move from the trees toward her, come close, and bend down.

"You?" she said.

"Yes."

And then the second blast, the other barrel of a ten-gauge shotgun directly into her face. And then the assassin stooping to take the pearls from the ears of what was left of her head.

冱 冱 冱 It wasn't winter yet but it was snowing, the fat flakes drifting to ground wetly instead of falling like snow is supposed to, a cotton-white fluff under the gray dome of sky where all wind, all breath of air was stilled.

Snow in November was one of those climactic quirks of nature endemic to the country of the Arkansas River's middle reaches, as here in Fort Smith on the border of the Indian Nations during the presidency of people like Grover Cleveland and Benjamin Harrison. Of course, it made no difference who was president, Democrat or Republican, because they were no more capable than anybody else of predicting early snow or of doing anything about it once it came. Even had they wanted to. Even had they cared one way or the other.

The locals who had to put up with the cold mush were not much more concerned about early snow than were those powerful men in faraway places. They knew it was never a sure bet to come but never a surprise when it did. After all, they said, you could ride a good horse due west for two days and be in the high plains of the Indian Territory where sometimes an April blue norther could blow in and freeze cattle's feet to the ground.

So sudden and unexpected changes in weather were not uncommon in any month of the year, sometimes having dramatic effect as in the case of tornadoes and sometimes being little more than a pain-in-the-arse nuisance. As with early snow.

The citizens of Fort Smith handled this particular snowfall as they did all November blusterings. They refused to take it seriously. They knew the river-bottom sultry heat would be back with a vengeance in a few days for one last suffocating whack at them before real winter arrived. So in their bullheaded rebuttal of the fact that it was cold and wet and slippery underfoot, the men went along Garrison Avenue in summer duck jackets or rumpled seersucker suits, brims of July's straw hats turned down over calm brows, hurrying along whitened sidewalks to the next saloon or standing hunch-shouldered at streetcar stops or holding black umbrellas for their women, who despite all evils of the elements continued to go from hat shop to meat market to bookstore to bank.

And there was still the influx of outlanders, the people from surrounding countryside and closeby towns like Greenwood and Braden and Bloomer. Into the city with a wagon drawn by a span of mules, or maybe just one mule, buying the things they couldn't grow. Like salt or black pepper or boots or red hair ribbon. And before the day was finished most of these farmers would go along Rogers Avenue to the site of old Fort Smith. Nothing there was now left of the army except one large building which once served as an officers' quarters but had been a federal district court and jail for over a decade. So on this snowy November as in sunshine, they went to what was called the Federal Compound, the father rushing along at the head of the column, dragging by the hand his most recalcitrant offspring, and the wife and mother to this towhead platoon bringing up the rear, wearing an ankle-length gingham dress, off-white waist apron, and sunbonnet. All of them stood finally for a reverent moment before the symbol of the court's power and authority so that someday the kids could tell their grandchildren they had actually seen the gallows upon which Judge Isaac Charles Parker had hanged almost eighty men.

After all, the fathers would say, you don't pass up the chance to see such an inspirational thing even in foul weather.

To some Sebastian County folk, these early snows were taken as a pleasant harbinger of the Yuletide just ahead. They could be heard to exclaim that it was like standing in the middle of a ten-cent Christmas card to be on Garrison Avenue looking east to where the white frame Catholic church stood and behind that above the trees the crosses of other churches rising toward the gray heavens. In this city of some twenty thousand souls in the late nineteenth century there were many churches, sometimes standing almost side by side in harmony and good fellowship, for these were a people who could respect the proposition that somebody else might have a few ideas of their own now and then, ideas to be tolerated with good grace. So long as they were not pushed down one's throat.

Mostly they were Protestant Scots or Welsh or English or German or Swiss. But there were a number of mid-European Jews and a smattering of Greeks and a sizable community of Irish and Italian Catholics.

Hence it could be completely usual for a member of the Methodist church board of stewards whose heritage went back to the mines of Cornwall to admire the cross of a Roman temple rising as he stood in the snow and then walk to Towson Avenue and have a slice of chocolate cake in a Jewish café where he called the owner by his first name and then perhaps to B Street to pay a dollar for a pair of boots resoled by a black man who had been a slave and was now a Baptist and then perhaps to a cellar on 1st Street to retrieve a pistol left for repair for a faulty sear and there visit for some hour or so with the artisan who had cured the pistol's sickness with a knowledge of clearances and whetstones and who was a completely pagan Creek Indian in town only from time to time when he was sober or else not wanted by various authorities for committing offenses against the peace and dignity of the United States of America.

At the end of that lightless day, all to their homes. The ones who had come in mule wagons going along rutted roads to milk cows and slop hogs and throw corn to the chickens. The townspeople walking or maybe taking the trams, as some of them, especially the English-lineage ones, called the streetcars, and then in warm, well-lighted kitchens reading the *Fort Smith Elevator*, a newspaper that took the pulse of city and county but which would never, in years ahead, be recognized or even known by any of the authorities in great eastern and northern universities who made their reputations on the history of the press.

Then all, city citizen and outlander alike, sitting down to a table of fried pork and white gravy, or some such thing, and perhaps in their grace thanking the Lord that they were a part of such a wonderful Anglo-Saxon civilization, few of them realizing that a large percentage had no Anglo-Saxon blood at all but were almost pure Celtic.

So they lived. So they died.

In Fort Smith nobody put it into so many words, but to most in the lovely pre-winter snow, as in all times, God for them stood toward the east along the Avenue. The east, where all the holy legends lived. Those songs of a birth under a star in the east. Always in the east. So it was appropriate that the highest-reaching crosses were toward the east of Garrison Avenue.

At the other end of the street, where it ended at the river, there was no edifice of piety. At the other end of the Avenue, alongside the river, were the railyards. The Missouri Pacific. The St. Louis–San Francisco. The Kansas City Southern. A massive grid of steel tracks and crossties. And standing between those tracks like a dike between them and the river, beside the main line, beside the spurs, beside the paddle-shaped signal flags on tall pylons, beside all the silent standing boxcars, the switch engines with their bells and steam whistles and yellow headlamps, beside all that was the Fort Smith tenderloin.

Perhaps, per capita, it was the most impressive collection of intentionally-ignored-by-the-law quality bordellos in all of Christendom's cities and maybe even most of those cities controlled by the Turks. Or anybody else.

And the snow falling throughout that November night shrouded the spires of the church at one end of the Avenue and so also laid its blanket of purity over the heads of the daughters of joy at the other. Most of whom, by the way, were having a restful sleep, because bad weather always meant slow business.

As on any other night, the streetcars made their last run at ten o'clock. Thirty minutes later, all the gaslight streetlamps along Garrison Avenue were extinguished. Two Fort Smith policemen began their march along the Avenue, one on either side of the street, testing each door to ensure that it was locked. There was one last tremble of life at exactly seventeen minutes before midnight when the Frisco red-ball freight from Monett, Missouri, to Paris, Texas, went through. Then serene sleep.

Until the pre-dawn when bakers rose to stoke their ovens. Outlying dairymen tended their cows, bottled the milk, drove small panel wagons drawn by gentle horses past the doors where the dairymen left the glass quarts and pints, the pure cream already risen to the top like yellow honey, in the cold pushing against the bottle stoppers. The agent for the Missouri Pacific opened his cage to sell tickets to those bound for Little Rock on the 5:00 A.M. Limited. The black cooks at the Southern Hotel were up and making fires in hickory-burning kitchen ranges and blending the dough for biscuits.

And at the city and county jails, last night's drunks were being turned out shivering into the streets in order that the chief of police and the county sheriff would not be burdened with feeding them breakfast, even though each would submit vouchers for reimbursement testifying that he had.

Everything was as it always was, except that on this particular snowy November morning, because it was still snowing and with more intensity now, there was in at least one place something more than thought of daily routine. There was the thought of murder.

≈ ≈ ≈ She sat beside a front window with a cup of hot chocolate beside her hand, the steaming brew in a hand-painted Meissen china cup in its appropriate saucer on a highly polished round table of teakwood. Beside the cup and saucer was a deep cut-glass ashtray where a black cigarillo lifted a column of blue smoke toward the ceiling. From time to time, as she watched the gray dawn come, she smoked, inhaling with a little gasp. She did not drink the hot chocolate. And as soon as the vapor ceased to rise from the cup, a slender black girl appeared, a slender black girl who might have been seventeen years old or thirty-seven, and took away the cold cup and then replaced it with another hot one. Throughout this little ceremony no word was spoken nor any glance exchanged between them.

The black girl's name was Nasturtium. The white woman's name was Jewel Moon, or so she claimed.

Although she looked toward the heart of the city, there was little evidence that any city was there. The closest buildings were low, box-shaped warehouses of brick and stone seen only as soft shapes in the falling snow, the nearest of them about one hundred yards away. Across the intervening space were the railroad tracks. Frosted steel laced back and forth, the farthest of which was the Frisco main line, the nearest a siding less than twenty paces from the front door of this Commerce Railroad Hotel.

Of course, it was not a hotel at all. It was recorded in the

Sebastian County courthouse as such, but everybody knew it was not a hotel. Even the circuit clerk who was responsible for keeping the records of real estate. Everybody referred to it as Miss Jewel's Society Parlor. Which was a euphemism for bordello. People across the river, in Indian Territory, where things were more basic, called it a whorehouse.

For eight years it had stood, since the time Miss Jewel had bought the lot and contracted its construction. She had not come out of New Orleans or Louisville or other such places whence whorehouse builders generally came, but out of the Indian Nations. She was not an Indian, but so far as Fort Smith was concerned, she was a creature of the Territory.

She had not done it alone.

There had been, and still were, two silent partners. Who provided the money. Abram Jacobson, who owned among other things a pawnshop on 2nd Street, and Herkimer Warson, senior vice-president of the First City Bank. Only a few people in Arkansas and none in the Indian Territory were aware of this association. Neither of the gentlemen had ever come forward to claim any part of it, and certainly Miss Jewel had never divulged the extent of her involvement with them.

In fact, at the time the deal was struck it had been made abundantly clear that were she ever to reveal her silent partners she would immediately be indicted for public lewdness, her assets confiscated, her name vilified in the newspapers, her little daughter placed as a ward of the state in some orphan asylum, and other unpleasant things. Like the definite possibility that Miss Jewel herself might end as catfish fodder in the Poteau River.

Miss Jewel suffered no illusions. She knew her business partners had the ability to do all these things, being as they were outstanding and law-abiding citizens on the best of terms with police officials, judges, aldermen, state legislators, governors, and United States Senators. And although Miss Jewel retained in her entourage a certain amount of muscle in the form of bouncers and general handymen, she was aware that her business associates had all the means necessary to hire whoever was needed for less-than-legal proceedings if they felt so inclined.

Hence, most effective of all the strictures on her revealing business connections was the part about catfish in the Poteau River.

As it developed, Messrs. Jacobson and Warson found nothing

about which to complain. The so-called Commerce Railroad Hotel had been a lucrative venture from the beginning. Jewel Moon quickly demonstrated that she was an entrepreneur of extraordinary talent in the business of lust. Capable of hiring and retaining the most industrious and attractive employees, she controlled them with the iron hand and profane mouth of a regular army sergeant major. Sometimes, certain of her clients who had served in the army said that when a drink was spilled or a blouse slipped too far down a shoulder in dining room or bar, Miss Jewel, assuming her sudden role as disciplinarian, even *looked* like a regular army sergeant major.

Well, after all, they said, she weighs about two hundred and fifty pounds and no ounce of fat in all of that meat, although none of those with such opinions had ever dared touch Miss Jewel's body to actually determine its consistency. For although she was in the business of flesh against flesh, she never herself became involved in such sweating foolishness, as she put it, confining herself to the command and logistics of the regiment. And she had not only the best troops. She had the best kitchen in town and the best-stocked bar short of Little Rock and the best mattresses west of Memphis and the best and most frequent medical inspections anywhere.

All these things Miss Jewel did and did well. And at the proper time, every two weeks, she counted the money and deposited the profits in Mr. Warson's bank. She did that well, too. Skimming only a little bit now and again so that even a senior vice-president of a bank would not discover it and begin thinking about catfish in the Poteau River.

Sometimes, Miss Jewel said to Nasturtium, "We live in a brutal world, honey."

And Nasturtium would say, "Yes ma'am." Knowing much of brutal worlds but not the one about which Miss Jewel was speaking.

So without the vaguest notion of the internal workings of this organization, outside observers appraised the only part they could. Its surface.

Switch-engine engineers and firemen and boxcar and caboose brakemen and section gangs working the crossties and rails had come to accept Miss Jewel's, along with less elegant structures at scattered intervals to Miss Jewel's left and right, as part of the Fort Smith scenery. Just houses, with fronts on the yards and backs almost against the willows, locust, and scrub timber along the river's edge. Accepting them all for places of fun and frolic when payday came and boards of directors in St. Louis or some such place were kind enough to give them a few hours' freedom, even though most of the yard people never had enough money to frequent Miss Jewel's. The only railroad people who ever passed that door were main-line engineers or conductors. The rest just supposed.

But they knew. Miss Jewel's was the class of Fort Smith sin. Hell, the building itself proclaimed it.

It was baroque Victorian, green clapboard with cream trim, two stories of operating space and a third floor behind eye-of-the-ox dormer windows. Here on the top level, Miss Jewel and her ladies lived in tiny individual rooms. On the middle floor were larger rooms and larger beds, where the ladies worked. At ground level was the dining and drinking area, where the ladies demurely socialized and made themselves as seductive as possible within the limits of Miss Jewel's rather puritanical dress codes—which below the second floor did not allow much more exposed flesh than nose and ears, according to complaints by the more vivacious ladies.

Of course, such complaints were never uttered when Miss Jewel was within hearing. Mostly they were heard only when Miss Jewel was visiting her seven-year-old daughter on a hill farm Miss Jewel owned in the Ozark hamlet of Weedy Rough. Or else when she visited her mother in Creek Nation in that time before Temperance Moon came to a not completely unexpected and violent end. Since which time, about two months before the November snowfall, Miss Jewel had seldom left the Commerce Railroad Hotel except for an occasional hour spent at the greengrocer on 3rd Street, for although she generally allowed her chief cook, Clarence, to stock larder and icebox, she enjoyed a day now and then fingering the celery and radishes and heads of cabbage and perhaps even having some satisfaction from the covert glances decent matrons gave her, who despite the affront of having to shop for grub alongside a madam, could not help but admire her expensive frocks and hats. Not to mention her garish double handful of precious-stone rings.

Complaints by employees included Miss Jewel's policy of setting prices on everything herself, from a beefsteak dinner to a full night with Venus. But none of this had any deleterious effect on how the place was perceived by passing citizen or patron alike.

A few cosmopolitan locals said Miss Jewel's was like a cottage at Newport where Jay Gould or Hamilton Fish or Jim Brady might bring two or three dozen rich New York friends for a weekend party. Less cosmopolitan locals always asked where the hell was Newport.

In fact, the building itself looked as though it didn't belong there in the smoke and soot of coal-fired locomotives and only a short swim to the Cherokee Nation. But it was there and famous enough to be talked about, sometimes with envy, by people who had only seen it from the outside but who had listened to those who had been inside. So its floor plan was more widely known than that of any other whorehouse on the Row.

From the massive front door facing onto the tracks, a wide entry and reception hall extended the length of the building. On the left were two dining rooms, elegantly furnished and with red-and-gold velvet wallpaper. Across the hall was the saloon, done in black walnut paneling with tables, captain's chairs, and bar to match. Next that was the stairwell to the levels above, and at the rear, the kitchen with a dumbwaiter to the top floors.

In the back dining room was a player piano, the only one in Fort Smith. And all about were peacock feathers in floor vases. There were framed and matted lithographs of street scenes from Paris, France, and Toledo, Ohio, and other exotic places.

On the working level, it had the appearance of any well-kept hotel. Except that over each of the dozen room doors was a leaded-glass transom with the name of the lady who worked inside etched in the glass. This sometimes created confusion among clients who had been too long at the bar, because as ladies retired, got married, went to St. Louis, were discharged by Miss Jewel for infraction of rules, or died, a new lady was immediately hired to occupy the vacated bed. Hence, because it was more economical to rename the lady than to re-etch the transom, there were over a period of years as many as ten Julips, seventeen Samanthas, and twenty-six Natashas. There seemed to be an inordinate turnover of Natashas.

So on that 1892 snowy morning, Miss Jewel sat as queen in her realm beside the Arkansas, smoking, not drinking the hot chocolate Nasturtium brought, and watching the whitening railyard. But silent no more after the northbound Frisco freight had just pulled out and through the black smoke of the locomotive still lying like a smudge on the snow she observed a small man in a palmetto hat and a cotton duster coming toward the Commerce Railroad Hotel, head down so that the brim of his hat covered his face. But Miss Jewel knew whose face it was, and she called Nasturtium.

"Open the front door for the gentleman," Miss Jewel said. "Then stay out unless I call. And tell everybody else to stay out, too."

"Yes ma'am."

In the short time it took for the man to pick his way across the tracks and come to her, Miss Jewel had in her mind the image that had come so frequently over the past two months. The image of her mother, Temperance Moon, riding a woodland road in Creek Nation with the sun striking brilliant colors in her hair. She could imagine the first loud blast, and the second, obliterating all features of the face. And the gloves. Miss Jewel always thought of the gloves her mother wore, gray suede with dark stitching across the backs. And the pearls, always the pearls. Milky globes, which she somehow was sure in her very first memory of her mother were the thing her baby hands reached for but could never touch.

"Come on in outa that snow, Mister Marshal," she heard Nasturtium say from the front hall. "Miss Jewel waitin' in the front room, you come on in now, stomp off them feet now, Miss Jewel don't lak no snow on her rugs, come on now. It's cole out there."

₪ ₪ ₪ When he came to the door of the dining room where Miss Jewel waited, he paused and his pale eyes moved quickly behind thick, steel-rimmed glasses, giving her the impression that in a single second he had seen every detail of the place and registered it in his mind. Like neat figures on the columns of a ledger book.

"Good morning, Marshal Schiller," Miss Jewel said. "Take off your coat and make yourself at home."

His spectacles were steaming over in the heat of the room, and still standing in the doorway he took them off, produced a handkerchief from some pocket in his duck jacket, and wiped the lenses. Then with the glasses back in place he slipped out of his duster and hung it on a clothes tree just inside the hallway door, and as he did his jacket opened at the front enough for Miss Jewel to see the butt of a very large, nickel-plated pistol under his left arm.

Actually, it was not an unusually large pistol but seemed so in contrast to the man's size. He was small. Thin almost to frailness, as though he had suffered a long time from consumption or some such thing, and his sallow complexion added to this illusion. For it was only an illusion.

"You can forget the marshal part," he said, and the voice was as unmusical as sandstone pebbles grinding together.

Seating himself opposite Miss Jewel at the table, he took his hat off and dropped it on the floor. The head thus revealed was round, and the hair was almost the same color as the pink scalp flesh it was brushed straight across but too sparse to conceal.

"I see that even though you've had your badge taken away you still go armed," Miss Jewel said, looking directly into his blue eyes with her own deep brown ones and with no sign of friendship on her face. Yet none of real hostility, either.

"There are people," he said, his thin lips hardly moving, "walking free now who I sent to prison in various places and they might enjoy doing me harm. So far, the local police have not seen fit to arrest me for carrying a concealed weapon."

"I was surprised to hear that you became suddenly unemployed," she said. "I'd be interested in hearing about it."

"Is that why you sent one of your people to tell me you wanted a little talk? To get the details on why Judge Parker's marshal revoked my commission?"

There was no edge to his voice, but he sat well back from the table, hands on thighs, appearing ready to leap up at any moment.

"No," she said. She took a small glass bottle with a cork stopper from a pocket of her white dress. It was a dress that started with a tight collar at her throat and went without frills to a hem just above her ankles. She placed the little bottle on the table. "I have business I need to discuss, and the nature of it, as I think you will understand, makes it better if I know about your standing as a United States Deputy Marshal."

He looked at the bottle. It was a bottle that would normally hold about three fluid ounces. But there was no fluid in it now. Only a fine white powder.

"I have no place in the Parker court now. They revoked my commission. Which I'm sure you know."

He bent forward and took the bottle, uncorked it, smelled it, then reached inside his jacket to the pocket of a gray cotton collarless shirt and produced a common wooden kitchen match. He wet the match in his mouth and dipped it into the white powder and placed the match in his mouth, rolling it from side to side with his tongue.

"Hmmmm," he said.

"It is the best money can buy," Miss Jewel said. "At least in Fort Smith, where it is not always easy to buy good cocaine."

He thrust the wet match into the bottle again. Put it in his mouth, leaned back in his chair, and sucked on it. Behind his thick glasses, his eyes seemed to throw off small sparks as he looked at Miss Jewel.

"Well," he said. "I had supposed there was an arrangement with a certain party in McAlester. On a particular night, she said otherwise and locked her door to me."

Miss Jewel suddenly laughed. A short, bubbly sort of laugh coming from deep.

"So you took that cannon of yours and tried to shoot down the door," she said. "And I heard you were drunk. My God, Oscar, I thought you didn't use hard spirits."

"It was the first time since the war," he said. "A long time ago. A part of being locked out, I would expect. But at least nobody was killed by the flying bullets."

She laughed again.

"My God, Oscar, you're too damned old to be running around waving a six-shooter and trying to break into the room of some cheap doxy in a McAlester whorehouse."

A slight smile seemed about to break from the corner of his mouth where the match was, but it didn't.

"Jewel, I am still young enough to have some juice left in me," he said. And shook his head. "But old enough so that it flows pretty thick most of the time."

They both understood that now the preliminaries were adequately fulfilled. Oscar Schiller pulled his chair closer and put his elbows on the table. Miss Jewel called Nasturtium and when the girl arrived, gave her instruction.

"Bring Marshal Schiller his breakfast. Half a dozen eggs, sunny side up, some ham, grits, biscuits, and a pot of coffee."

"Yes ma'am."

"And tell Clarence I don't want it at noon. I want it right now, you hear?"

"Yes ma'am."

When Nasturtium had gone, Miss Jewel spoke softly, but urgently, leaning across the table.

"Oscar, I need help," she said and took from the pocket of her dress a stack of yellow-backed bank notes tied with a twine string. She held the bundle of money in one hand, but she didn't look at it. She looked directly into Oscar Schiller's eyes and he didn't look at the money either, except for just long enough to see the top bill was a fifty and the bundle was about three inches deep. From the rear, there were the kitchen sounds of plates rattling and a stove warming-oven slamming shut and sudden, loud laughing as the ladies there for their breakfast found something amusing. A freight yard switch engine went past close by the building and the windows rattled with a faint sound as though it might have started snowing tiny shards of crystal. After what Oscar Schiller thought was a long time during which he figured she might be measuring his reaction, she spoke again.

"I need help."

She placed the money on the table beside the small bottle of cocaine.

"I'd suppose it's enough there to buy a lot of help," he said.

"Put it in your pocket. And mum's the word, you understand?"

"Yes," he said, and took the stack of bills and put them in some pocket beneath the pistol. Just in time, because Nasturtium was coming back with a platter of food.

"All right, honey, get the hell out of here now," Miss Jewel said.

"Yes ma'am."

Miss Jewel poured coffee from the large pot into a cup. Oscar Schiller, beginning with his fingers, was already tearing the ham in small pieces, dipping the pieces into the egg yolks, eating silently and furiously. Miss Jewel watched him and said nothing, letting him finish. It didn't take long. The only thing left on the platter was the small mound of grits.

"I never come to a taste for hominy," he said.

He wiped his mouth with the linen napkin that had been brought on the tray. Then took the small bottle and poured some of the white powder into the coffee, stirred it, and sat back in his chair and sipped.

"I can use the money," he said.

"That's why I offered it."

"You understand I don't hire out as an assassin."

"You don't have to shoot anybody," she said. Her full face had taken on a hard, square look, like the end of an oak railroad crosstie. "You just have to find them."

Oscar Schiller watched her face over the cup as he sipped. He waited until the cup was empty before he spoke again, and she seemed willing to wait, showing no impatience, only intensity.

"Do I get the proper sense of things here? Are we going to talk about your mother directly?"

He pronounced it "drekly." Only two syllables instead of three.

"Not directly," she said, and pronounced it the same. "Now. About who shot her. That's what we're going to talk about."

"Jewel, when Temperance Moon was murdered I knew the men who worked that case," Oscar Schiller said. He was speaking slowly, deliberately. "There were two suspects. One was arrested and brought to Fort Smith. The United States Commissioner, Mr. Claude Bains, didn't even remand him to the grand jury because the evidence wasn't there. You know that."

She poured him another cup of coffee and he laced it with the white powder, stirring with one of the famous Commerce Hotel sterling silver spoons. Miss Jewel watched him sip, her massive face not at all soft. Her gaze never left Oscar Schiller's face.

"The other one, Toby Jupiter. You know about him. Being he was the brother of your mother's last husband. Brother to Styles Jupiter, who they say ran off to California. Toby was named in a warrant issued on strong suspicion of his doing the murder. It wasn't my case, but everybody knew right away we were looking for him. Before anybody could apprehend him, they found him shot dead on an old farm alongside the Canadian."

"Good riddance."

"Maybe. I never knew him too good. Arrested him once in Wealaka, Creek Nation, for stealing a white woman's goat. Years back. He was just a tough Indian kid then. He spent a year in the federal jail, one of the first prisoners in the new wing they added to the courthouse building."

"Good riddance."

"Well, they found him dead. So it was a closed case as far as Parker's court was concerned."

"It's not closed as far as I'm concerned."

"Jewel," Oscar Schiller said, "Toby Jupiter ran with a very mean crowd. And I guess he got to be the meanest of the lot. And I also understand there was no love lost between him and your mother. And as you also know, your mother ran with that same crowd."

"I never took no pride in it."

"Hell, Jewel, you ran with that crowd, too, until you came over here and got into a legitimate business," Oscar Schiller said.

"And I tried to get her to come with me, but she wouldn't."

"Well, at least she financed you."

Jewel Moon stared at Oscar Schiller for a long time, her eyes dancing fire.

"She never put a penny into this place."

"Oh," said Oscar Schiller. "Everybody thought she had. If not her, who? I can't really picture you having enough to start this place."

"That's none of your business, Oscar," she said.

Oscar Schiller drummed his fingers on the white tablecloth, not looking into Jewel Moon's face. Looking into the empty cup before him.

"Jewel," he said finally, "you said you need to know where I am before we deal. I need the same from you. It's only right."

Now, for the first time, Jewel Moon lifted her gaze from Oscar Schiller's face. She looked at the delicate white curtains on the window. She looked at the red-and-gold wallpaper of the room. She looked at the peacock feathers in floor vases at each corner of the room. She looked at the framed and matted color prints of exotic places on the walls. At last, as though having assured herself that all of these things were still there, she looked again into Oscar Schiller's face.

"Oscar, I'll only tell you it was a Jew businessman and a bank man. But that's as mum as you can make it," she said.

"I understand," Oscar Schiller said, and his face showed no expression of surprise, no indication that a long-held opinion was now destroyed. "How much money?"

"How much money what?"

"To start this place."

"A lot. That's all I'll tell you. What's any of this got to do with what we're talkin' about?"

"Probably no more than you knowing I tried to break down that door in McAlester. But you know me. Mum's the word you say, mum it will be."

"All right," said Miss Jewel. "Now she was my mother, don't make a damn about our differences. And some bastard shoots her, I want to know who."

"Well, I understand that, too, but Jewel, you understand that your mother was no Baptist church choir director. On three occasions she was arrested by officers of the federal court. Always somebody else, never me somehow. I had nothing to do with any action against your mother. All I know is what I hear from the other deputies."

"I understand that."

"Your mother always had a lot of help from very impressive defense counsel. She was brought in three times, suspended twice, but there was that time she spent two years in the federal house of correction in Detroit for stealing horses."

"I know all that. My mother was a good woman."

Oscar Schiller shrugged. He took off his glasses and wiped them again with the handkerchief he took from some hidden pocket. Then placed them back on his nose, adjusting them, then looking into Jewel Moon's face.

"Let's not worry about the good or bad with your mother," he said. "Let's worry about what you want me to do."

"You're sure you want it?"

"It's better than anything I'm doing now."

She didn't pour him any more coffee. It was cold now anyway. She moved the coffeepot aside with her hand, casually, but yet somehow making an absolute end to all they had said so far.

"I'm not sure of your loyalty, Oscar."

"I'm not sure of yours," he said. "In this kind of game, things can come to a sudden stop. And they'd be planting me in the ground."

"I'm not wanting that, Oscar."

"All right."

"Do you think Toby killed her?"

"It's as good a guess as any."

"I'm not interested in guesses," Miss Jewel said. "I don't think you are, either, Oscar. I want to know who. And why."

Oscar Schiller looked through the window, through the film of white curtain into the film of white snow across the railyards. He shrugged, the most elaborate response he could think to make.

"You really do think Toby killed her, don't you?" Miss Jewel asked.

"As little as I know about the case, I'd have to say it's a strong possibility."

"All right," she said. "Even if you're gonna take that bullheaded law opinion of it, at least I want to know why."

Oscar Schiller shook his head, and still did not look at her, still watched the switch engines working in the snow.

"Jewel, maybe the only person who could answer that is under the headstone I heard you put up in Creek Nation, over your mother's head. Maybe even she didn't know."

And now he looked at her, his eyes behind the thick glasses glinting.

"Why is the *why* so important to you? What's done is done."

"You never rested on that before," Miss Jewel said. "And besides, bein' truthful with one another as we are here, and mum's the word again, I may have more than passing interest in the why."

"Well," said Oscar Schiller, "maybe it was just somebody that got put out with something your mother did. Like we both know, your mother knew men who didn't enjoy being put out."

"Sure, maybe. But maybe not."

"You're willing to lay down considerable money on maybe, aren't you?"

"It's my money."

And then Miss Jewel Moon yelled for Nasturtium, who appeared quickly, as though she had not been far away.

"Clear all this out, honey," said Miss Jewel, and Nasturtium took the tray of Oscar Schiller's breakfast and quickly disappeared into the back of the building.

"I don't know how you expect me to dig this out," Oscar Schiller said. "I can't talk to anybody in the Nations who don't know I was a federal officer. You think they'll tell me anything?"

"Oscar," she said, "I got confidence in you. You'll find a way. No matter what kind of foolishness you got into at McAlester, everybody knows you were one of Parker's best deputies. You're like a bulldog. With his teeth locked in a cow's nose. You won't let go. Maybe because you're stubborn. Maybe because you're just as mean and vicious as them you take in after."

"Hmmm," he said, watching a Missouri Pacific switch engine working boxcars in the snow. "It's the nicest thing anybody has said about me since they took my badge. But if it works, we're going to have to spread around a lot of money."

"I'll take care of that."

Oscar Schiller drew a deep breath and expelled it suddenly like a cough.

"All right. I'll take the job."

"Good. I expected you would."

"Have you got any more of that good sugar?"

She laughed again, and the rock-square face turned soft, almost schoolgirl young and pretty.

"I happen to," she said, and from the obviously large dress pocket took another bottle of cocaine and pushed it across the table. "I don't know why you use that stuff."

"It's good for the toothache."

"You got the toothache?"

"No. But just in case."

She laughed, and it was a soft counterpoint to the sound of the locomotive bell from the railyard, soft too, its ringing muffled by the still-falling snow.

2 Everybody knew the snow would stop by noon. Because there was growing light under the clouds to the west, and sure enough, the snow did stop and the clouds all ran off to the east, toward Mississippi or Tennessee, and the sun came out and within the space of two hours the white winter fairyland was gone and bricks that paved Garrison Avenue were slicked with muddy water, which was the usual thing, but everybody understood that by sunset the water would run off, leaving everything as it has been in the drought weeks of August.

In this new sun, Oscar Schiller walked along Rogers Avenue still wearing his long duster. He was en route to a German sweet bakery, but not for the apple strudel. On the second floor of this establishment was the courtroom of United States Commissioner Claude Bains, the man who dealt with minor offenses against the statutes in force, but more important, the man who decided if any suspected felon who came before him should be remanded to the grand jury. Hence to a petit jury in Parker's court. Hence, maybe, to the rope.

So Claude Bains was a powerful man. Soon, the Congress of the United States of America would change his title to magistrate, but for now he was the commissioner, and conducting a hearing which was of considerable interest to Oscar Schiller.

As he walked, Oscar Schiller was thinking that sometimes things fell into place like the pieces on one of these new jigsaw puzzles. Sometimes they didn't. But maybe this was one of the times he might find a piece that fit. Here he was, just commissioned by the richest madam between St. Louis and Fort Worth to discover certain facts. And on this very day, at this very hour, there was appearing before Claude Bains a man who might, just might, be useful. Provided, of course, that the commissioner didn't send him on the path to Parker's court.

The man in question was Candy Redstripe, citizen of Creek Nation, who had presented himself to the federal judiciary relative to the assault and battery of a white man. And this Candy Redstripe was a man of some stature in the Indian Territory and perhaps in a position to assist in satisfying Miss Jewel Moon's curiosity in regard to her mother's demise.

In his present game, as in the game of five-card stud, Oscar Schiller needed to see all the pips, and maybe Candy Redstripe could help him look. It was an advantage that Oscar Schiller knew this Candy Redstripe from past associations, all satisfactory. And knew Candy Redstripe's wife as well.

As he hurried across Garrison Avenue, avoiding the horses and mule-drawn vehicles, he caught himself in a greenhorn kind of musing, saying to himself, "I know Indians." Then snorted and stopped such foolish thinking. Hell, there was no such thing as "Indians," all alike as tadpoles in a pool. There were so many different kinds it would take a lifetime to identify them all and another lifetime to understand half of them.

In the moment his mind went to Indians, he frowned, thinking of the woman who had raised him. Well, at least any raising he ever considered he'd had what with his mother working and who knew what else in the Menger Brewery and Hotel in San Antonio de Bexar before the war. In Oscar Schiller's beginning. His mother had moved to San Antonio from the German settlement in New Braunfels when Oscar was a diaper babe. They left Oscar's Grandfather Waldenberg's house, which apparently suited Grandfather Waldenberg just fine, because he never made any effort later to come the forty miles south to the city for a look at his only grandson. Well, maybe once, the old man just passing through and drunk. Oscar wasn't sure. He had no memory of the old man's face.

They left Oscar's father behind, too. Only Oscar never knew exactly who his father was, and he figured his mother wasn't too sure herself.

His mother had picked up the name Schiller from a husband

acquired aboard ship when they came to America, part of a colonizing party organized by old Prince Carl of Solms-Braunfels. They were going to put down some German roots in the Republic of Texas, and they did. Only by the time they did, it was the state of Texas. And Herr Schiller was gone, lost to the cholera almost as soon as his feet hit the dock in Galveston. It was a long spell later before Oscar was born, and he got the dead husband's name, for his mother had kept it, finding certain advantages in being the Widow Schiller. Likely because there wasn't much encouragement for the Widow Schiller to hang about the German settlement at New Braunfels with a little bastard on her hands, she moved to San Antonio and hired an Indian woman to wet-nurse the boy and kept her on as a kind of watchdog afterward.

The squaw did a lot more than keep Oscar out of the streets and saloons of the city. She taught him how to sing and dance and made him read his books that he studied in the German Lutheran school (although she had no idea what was in them) and told him stories about buffalo and sat on his bed and held his hand during thunderstorms.

Her name was Gill. At least that's what she said. She was a Tonkawah, that tribe of tall, handsome Texas aboriginals the Comanches said were cannibals. She and Oscar were together for a long time. She left him when he was in his early teens. Her leaving him was the primary cause of his running away toward the east and eventually becoming one of those sixteen-year-old boys enlisted in a Confederate regiment of infantry during the Civil War.

Well, he always figured, maybe Gill didn't really run away from him. Maybe she'd been out picking bluebonnets on the prairie and wandered too far away from town and got picked up by a wandering Comanche war party. Comanches hated Tonks almost as much as they did Apaches. Maybe, Oscar Schiller thought, because sometimes Tonks scouted for the Texas Rangers. And maybe Comanches hated Texas Rangers most of all. You never could tell about Comanches.

To Oscar Schiller, pretty much deserted by blood kin, what little there had been of it, that Tonk squaw stuck in memory as a special thing, not like a person but more like a Greek church icon or something. And to Oscar Schiller, the most comely woman he'd ever seen, until recently.

Yes sir, Oscar Schiller thought, that Tonk was beautiful and smart and kind. Now he was hurrying to see another Indian woman even more beautiful and probably smarter. It remained to be seen whether she was kind. She was no Tonkawah. She was a Creek. Perhaps thirty years old and with walnut-wood color on her face that was calm in sunlight but seemed to glow with inner fire in the lamp-shine of night, and with great, black eyes and full lips. Oscar Schiller was a man who did not spend a lot of his thinking on the beauty of women, but he knew that this woman was beautiful beyond any beauty he had ever known.

Her name was Tishacomsie, and she was known from Muskogee to Durant as Tish. And when Oscar Schiller let himself in at the rear door or Commissioner Bain's court, she was testifying on the witness stand as her husband sat on the front row fighting sleep.

ᛈ ᛈ ᛈ   "And on this evening in the question before the court," Commissioner Bains was saying. "What happened?"

"My husband had gone. To Honey Springs, Creek Nation. There was supposed to be horse racing there. I expected he'd be home in a day or two. It was raining, and Mr. Clark came to my door."

"Mr. Clark, the friend of your husband?"

"They were always going to races together. Then coming to my house and we'd have supper together. Mr. Clark was always a nice man."

Tishacomsie spoke a fluid, flowing English, having been educated in such things at Mrs. Sawyer's Ladies' Seminary in the city of Fayetteville, Arkansas, a place where many prosperous fathers of the Nations sent their daughters to learn the mysteries of Arabic numbers and the proper relationship of verbs to nouns.

"So you knew Mr. Clark?" the commissioner asked.

"Yes. He's been in the Nations a long time on legal papers. He's a section foreman for the KATY line."

"The Missouri, Kansas, and Texas Railroad?"

"Yes. He knocked at my door. It was raining. Did I say that already?"

"It doesn't matter. Please go on, Mrs. Redstripe."

"I told him to come in and that I was frying hominy and in a minute we'd have supper. Mr. Clark was very drunk."

"Please go on, Mrs. Redstripe."

"I had some pork chops. I put a few of them in the skillet with the hominy. Mr. Clark was talking. Then, while I was cooking, he jumped up and tore my dress down the back and put his hands on me."

"Where did he put his hands on you?"

"Here," she said and touched her breasts. "And other places."

"What did you do then?"

"I hit Mr. Clark with the cast-iron skillet I was using to fry the meat and the hominy. I hit Mr. Clark in the head and there was hominy and meat scattered all over the floor of my kitchen. I hit him twice, I think it was, but it took no effect. He threw me down and then picked up the hatchet we use to cut kindling. Mr. Clark had started to talk very dirty."

"What did Mr. Clark say?"

"I wouldn't say the words."

"Very well. And then."

"Mr. Clark started to wave the hatchet around and say all the things he was about to do to me."

"What sort of things?"

"Carnal things. I wouldn't say his exact words."

"Very well, go on, Mrs. Redstripe."

"I was thinking how I could get to our sleeping room, where there was a loaded shotgun. But Mr. Clark was in the way. He hit my kitchen table with the hatchet and he was laughing and talking very dirty. I asked him why he was being so mean when he was such a good friend to my husband and had been to our home so many times to have supper. He laughed and broke my sugar bowl with the hatchet. That's when my husband came in the door."

"Did Mr. Clark say anything to your husband?"

"Yes. He said, 'Well hello, I thought you was at a horse race.' And my husband said, 'I come home because it was raining and there wasn't no horse race. What are you doing with that hatchet?' And Mr. Clark said, 'I'm fixin' to brain you with it.' That's when my husband took a stick of firewood from the woodbox and hit Mr. Clark."

"How many times did your husband hit Mr. Clark?"

"I don't know. Maybe four licks. All in the head. Mr. Clark fell down in front of my kitchen stove and there was blood all over the place. You know how head wounds bleed."

"Yes. So?"

"So my husband got me up and put a slicker over me and he

got Mr. Clark up and we went to Eufaula. We left our racing ponies for our horse boy to take care of and put in the sheds. We went to the Creek Light Horse Police and said my husband had just hit a white man pretty hard with a stick of wood and he might die so maybe the federal deputy should come because being as Mr. Clark was a white man, it was something for here in Fort Smith.

"So the Light Horse took Mr. Clark to Dr. Elmer Purtry, who is there in Eufaula, and he said Mr. Clark would probably not die but was going to have a pretty good headache, and Deputy Nason Breedlove came and after a while we all got horses and rode into Fort Smith."

"You didn't take the train?"

"No, we figured there wasn't any hurry and Deputy Nason Breedlove didn't think so either. The rain had stopped. We had a nice ride and I bought some ham and pickles and we had a good night on the trip camped close to Sallisaw in Cherokee Nation and Deputy Breedlove and my husband told stories about the old days."

"Then you swear to your god that you say the truth here in this official chamber that said Mr. Clark did offer lewd advances unwanted by you and did threaten your husband with a hatchet."

"I do. And that Mr. Clark said just before my husband come in that he would screw me to the floor and other things he said he'd do that I cannot repeat."

"And do you file a criminal complaint?"

"No. We heard the railroad has fired him and we expect that's punishment enough."

"Very well. This case is obviously one of self-defense of home, property, and person. And the man Mr. Clark be noted on the record as a mischief maker apprehended and dissuaded while in commission of violations of just statutes and tradition transgressing the peace and dignity of all things and persons concerned and those responsible for terminating said atrocities are absolved of any crime or guilt before the laws of the United States of America. Mrs. Redstripe. That means you can go home."

"I sure do appreciate that, your honor!"

₪ ₪ ₪ Mr. Clement Hake had a home on North 7th and B streets in a residential area called the Belle Grove District. It was a district of considerable magnificence spaced for several blocks around a nucleus of the massive brick Belle Grove School, which gave the place its name. Perhaps some visitors thought the homes there incongruous considering the proximity of the Indian Nations, for they were in the style of Victorian Renaissance, Second Empire, Eastlake, Baroque, Queen Anne Cottage, and a lot of other structures the less well-to-do citizens of Fort Smith made no attempt to classify. All of these homes, they said in the saloons along Towson Avenue, were crapper-in-the-house rich.

Mr. Hake claimed Greek Revival architecture as mode for his house, with white columns in front. Nobody disputed him. Least of all his tenant of ten years in the basement furnace room, Oscar Schiller.

Mr. Hake had built this tribute to the classical pagan period of history from the profits of his business, which was a scissors factory on the north edge of town. It was there, among his various cutters, that Mr. Hake had first met Oscar Schiller when the latter came to him after appointment to Judge Parker's court as deputy marshal and asked if maybe Mr. Hake could nickelplate a pistol, a process Mr. Hake used on all his highest-quality scissors.

It happened, whether Oscar Schiller knew it or not and most likely he did, that there were things other than good scissors which aroused Mr. Hake's enthusiasm. Like the Fort Smith fire department, whose uniforms Mr. Hake always helped purchase; like the local Baptist Boys' Orphanage, which Mr. Hake had founded and on whose board of directors he served for over twenty years; like sidearms, of which he was a collector. Among his most prized weapons was one which he claimed had belonged to King Charles I of England. A pistol, by the way, which most citizens of Fort Smith found amusing because being a matchlock it was useless in the rain. And because it was a single-shot muzzle-loader, and once it had been charged and successfully fired, the process of reloading required more time than it would take a three-legged dog to run from one end of Garrison Avenue to the other. Besides which, they said, with such a pistol nobody could be expected to hit any target smaller than a Frisco freight train.

But Oscar Schiller had admired the weapon where it reposed on blue velvet in a glass case beside the door of Mr. Hake's office at the scissors factory, and so because of such appreciation Mr. Hake nickeled Oscar Schiller's pistol free of charge.

Well, maybe not, the cynics said. It had to be more than Oscar Schiller's admiration for a useless pistol. It had to be more than Mr. Hake's saying he was fascinated with Oscar Schiller's pistol, which was a single-action revolver chambered for Winchester .38-40 ammunition and with a seven-and-a-half-inch barrel, all set on a Colt .45 frame. It had to be something that meant profit. And sure enough, within a week of his having served as a new member of Judge Parker's court, Mr. Hake began to run advertisements in the *Fort Smith Elevator* to the effect that any white man of sound mind who was not a minor could bring his sidearm to the Hake Scissors Factory and have a finish chemically applied to it that would make it appear sterling silver and avoid thereafter the problem of rust and discoloration associated with aging blued-steel pistols.

As a result, Mr. Hake made a wagonload of money, because such a proposition was something understood by a generally well-armed male population. It created not only profits. It created a community respect for Mr. Hake that had never been there before, because now it was obvious that he knew more about sidearms than everybody had supposed, thinking of that pallet-bedded matchlock useless pistol that had belonged to some English king, a weapon that wasn't worth a damn and hadn't done a thing to save the king's head from Cromwell's ax.

So Mr. Hake not only nickeled Oscar Schiller's gun, he rented him living space in the basement of the Greek classical house on North 7th and B streets. And even after the childish escapade in the McAlester bordello, Mr. Hake did not throw Oscar Schiller out into the street, as everyone expected Mr. Hake to do, he being highly moral and against such things as dancing and fornication in daylight and people being happy for any reason whatsoever. Not only did Mr. Hake allow Oscar Schiller to remain in the basement of the house, he gave the disgraced deputy marshal a job of night watchman at the scissors factory with enough salary to keep mind and body together, as they said, but not enough to purchase even the least snort of the white powder which Oscar Schiller had used since the War Between the States.

There were people in Fort Smith who knew that Oscar Schiller used cocaine, which was not against the law. And these people, mostly policemen on the city force, had many chuckles thinking about it and suggesting that if Mr. Hake suspected what his basement tenant was doing to his coffee and with those matchsticks,

Mr. Hake would have been so mortified and embarrassed that he likely would have sold his scissors factory and moved to New Bedford, Massachusetts, where his wife's family had made a fortune during the war selling the Union Army shoes that promptly fell apart in the first rainstorm.

These were all little jokes that Oscar Schiller could endure, his knowing about them of course, so long as nobody laughed at him to his face. And nobody did. Because there was not an informed man in Sebastian County and not many in the Indian Territory either who was not aware of the danger involved.

So on that November afternoon following the session in the court of the United States Commissioner, Oscar Schiller went to his subterranean room. A Spartan room. There was a bed with a lumpy straw mattress and a few blankets. A small table with three straight-back chairs, a clothes closet, and a dry sink with pitcher and washbowl. Just outside the door, which was at the rear of the house facing the alley, was a rain barrel and a well. Although upstairs there were two modern water closets, the basement tenant used an old-fashioned one-hole privy on the alley for his requirements of regularity. Which were irregular to say the least, Oscar Schiller having suffered since his youth from constipation, which in his maturity he fought with a daily swig from a bottle of Brown's Indian Root Tonic Elixir, which was about one part water, one part grain alcohol, one part opium, and the rest calomel, all of which did little to assist Oscar Schiller's clogged colon but at least led him to believe he was doing everything about it that he could. Plus, on those occasions when he took more than one swig, made him feel that he didn't give a damn one way or the other.

When electricity came to Fort Smith, Mr. Hake wired his house. But he had seen no reason to wire the basement, so Oscar Schiller's light was as it had always been. Kerosene lamps.

As a result, the place smelled of coal oil. It smelled of more than that, for changing his underwear was a thing Oscar Schiller did not consider particularly important, and when he did the pink flannel garments were thrown into a cardboard box next to the door and there remained for some considerable time until Oscar Schiller decided to haul them off to the steam laundry on 7th Street. Which didn't happen very often.

Having heard all he needed to hear in the commissioner's court, Oscar Schiller stood in this room and did the things he normally did there. He lit a lamp because even in sunlit day the place was twilight dim. He carefully positioned the two bottles of white powder taken from Miss Jewel Moon's hand on the table beside the lamp. And beside the open box of matches which were always there, matches from Ohio, where Oscar Schiller had observed that the best matches were made, either to strike fire or for sucking. Then he took off duster and duck jacket and the shoulder holster harness with the nickel-plated pistol and tossed it all on the bed. Then sat. And took from his pocket a small notebook and lead pencil and prepared to write, as he always did at the beginning of each case.

But before beginning that, he looked to the dark corner beside the clothes closet to see that he had not been robbed in his absence and saw that he had not been. The two large-bore rifles were still there. Lever-action. Neither one of which he had ever used himself, but only passed along to assistants in his cases. And looking at them recalled that he had arrested men in the Nations who now used Winchester semiautomatic magazine rifles. And thought of the stories he had heard of European semiautomatic pistols. And all of these things were to Oscar Schiller an abomination.

In fact, had Oscar Schiller had his secret way everyone would be armed with only lances and clubs and bowie knives. So that in flare-ups of temper innocent bystanders would not be killed or maimed by flying bullets. And just as important to him, with such weapons, when a man came facing another man it would be a true test of strength and not simply a matter of courage measured by the use of some machinist's patent.

But in a world he did not control, Oscar Schiller knew at least himself. He knew that he would never, if he could avoid it, be the man who stood against another with deadly force in his hand. But he knew as well that in such contests, even though he was not personally involved, he would be the one who controlled those who were and, arriving at his ends, would employ anyone to his service so long as he had the requisite qualities, first among which had to be the cool, controlled, deliberate fury of an attacking shark.

Thus knowing himself and little more on that November afternoon, Oscar Schiller sat with the cobwebs above his head weaving a pattern of smoke in the lifting heat of his coal-oil lamp, sucking the wetted matches coated with the white powder, writing his little notes concerning the husband of the Creek woman Tishacomsie. And above him, landlord Hake home early from the scissors factory explaining to his wife a new scheme for nickel-plating garden trowels for old ladies and perhaps even kindling hatchets.

"My dear," said Mr. Hake, "we owe a great deal to Mr. Schiller, who first suggested my process on things other than scissors."

"Indeed we do, Mr. Hake," she said.

And thinking that tomorrow she would go downstairs and tell Oscar Schiller the great things he had wrought, but of course only after Clement had gone to the scissors factory and the children off to school and then bracing herself for the vile smell of that basement room. But bad odor or not, Mrs. Hake always told herself, there were more than adequate compensations to be found on the lumpy straw mattress.

℘ ℘ ℘ When they came it was past light of day, as Oscar Schiller had suggested they come in a note he had written in the commissioner's court. Because he was not interested in anyone knowing that he was in some sort of concert with them. Or with anybody else. So best to have them arrive after dark.

They came into his basement lodging with confidence and assurance, maybe with a little arrogance showing as well, not at all like most Nations Indians, who were hangdog at the prospect of entering a white man's lodge. But they'd been here before, during times when Oscar Schiller was a United States Deputy Marshal and working on a case in Creek country and needed a little conference.

"Hello, Oscar," Candy Redstripe said. His voice was soft and well modulated.

"Hello, Marshal," said Tishacomsie, and her eyes were bold as a man's looking directly into Oscar Schiller's face.

"Sit," Oscar Schiller said. They took the chairs he indicated, without his having risen from his own, and they all begun to eat the supper Oscar Schiller had provided from the Tula Grocery & Meat Market on 6th Street near the fire station, a place where he had stopped on the way from the commissioner's court and a place where Oscar Schiller had a charge account of long standing, an account of such long standing that by now Mr. Tula had even stopped adding up what Oscar Schiller owed him at the end of each month. It was a recognized system of frontier mercantile business survival that such services were done for peace officers who desired them.

There were peaches, taken from the open can with fingers, and yellow cheese torn into grainy chunks by the same sticky fingers, and a tin of sardines rolled open with a long key and filling the room with the smell of faraway fisheries.

"I like these oily little fish," said the man.

That was the only conversation as they ate. And Tishacomsie took the food to her mouth with delicate fingers as surely as did the men, without reserve, without any thought that she was different from them, and all the while her dark gaze fastened on Oscar Schiller's face like a cat looking at a caged bird. In fact, both Indians sized up the white man, and Oscar Schiller reciprocated in kind. With intense curiosity on both sides to ensure that everything was as it had been in the past, that there was still trust between them.

These two were not dressed as some eastern newspaper writers might have reported that Indians dressed. She was in flowered gingham and wore a small bonnet discreetly ribboned in pink silk. The man in a light woolen suit, the vest buttoned over a white cotton shirt with no collar, and a narrow-brimmed felt hat and low-heeled boots. At a distance they could be mistaken for a well-to-do couple of European lineage, but at closer inspection such an illusion would disappear. There were the high, solid cheekbones, the black eyes, the short-cropped raven hair. And the finely sculpted lips, his always seeming about to smile and reveal a rank of teeth as perfectly aligned as a regiment of white uniformed French infantry in those days when his people had seen such soldiers in distant places where the war had been fought between France and the British to decide who was boss on the North American continent, a decade before the American Revolution.

As they ate, Oscar Schiller reviewed in his mind the notes he had made in his little book, now secreted again in a shirt pocket. And thought of a great deal more besides concerning these guests of his. Because Oscar Schiller had always been a man who believed in research and had sometimes gone to such lengths that his fellow deputies on Parker's court had made fun of it.

Had gone so far, in fact, as to solicit historical information in the library of the St. Agnes Academy until after a while the Franciscan nuns there came to know him and suspect that he was really a Catholic and that due to great adversity or else insanity was unable to partake of the Eucharist or other holy sacraments. And prayed for him.

Most of Oscar Schiller's associates at the Federal Compound, had they known of it, would have said these prayers were wasted.

So Oscar Schiller, as he sat having supper with his Creek Nation guests in the basement of Mr. Hake's house, watched them and knew a great deal about them. And they knew he knew. And they were not disturbed that he knew and Oscar Schiller was aware that they were not disturbed.

Therefore, even though it was never said in so many words, there was a bond between them all. A bond they recognized and one that went back a long way. A bond as obvious as the string to the bow, a bow now in repose but ready to be drawn if there was a requirement. And each of them realizing that with such a meeting as this, there was the strong likelihood of a few arrows let loose.

But in what direction, they had no idea.

ℵ ℵ ℵ   After their little supper, Oscar Schiller rose and taking a coffeepot from the lower reaches of the dry sink went to the furnace and opened a spigot at the steam safety valve to take about a quart of hot water. Then into that pot placed a clean sock filled with a handful of coffee beans crushed earlier with the butt of his Hake Scissors Factory nickeled pistol. In the dry sink, too, were tin cups and a quart mason fruit jar of sugar. And spoons. So as the Indians sweetened their coffee from the mason jar so did Oscar Schiller sweeten his with the white powder from one of the small bottles from Miss Jewel Moon.

There was a distinctive taste to the coffee due to rust and other residue in the pipes of the furnace heating system.

From his shirt pocket, Oscar Schiller took little black cigars that Miss Jewel Moon smoked and kept in a four-ounce shot glass on a table in her entry hall as a sign of hospitality. When he'd left the Commerce Railroad Hotel that same morning Oscar Schiller had taken a handful. Now he passed these to his guests and lighted them with one of his Ohio-manufactured matches and so all sipped their furnace-flavored coffee and drew deeply on Miss Jewel Moon's cigarillos and the smoke turned the basement room into a blue gauze cave, secure from all outside influence. A situation which Oscar Schiller not only noted but had tried to create.

Knowing as well as anyone that Indians enjoyed having a little conversation of no consequence whatsoever before coming to serious business, but believing their supper together had fulfilled that requirement, Oscar Schiller looked at the man and came directly and brutally to the point.

"Candy," he said. "Who killed Temperance Moon?"

There was no change of expression on either of the Indian faces. Oscar Schiller had the impression that there would have been no change in expression had he told them their coffee was poisoned or that a tornado was about to take off the entire house where they were sitting.

"Is that why we're here for this little powwow?" the man asked.

"Yes."

"You could have saved yourself trouble and expense," the man said. "Everybody knows Toby Jupiter killed her."

"Some in Parker's court said as much," said Tishacomsie.

"I'm not talking about Parker's court," he said. "I'm talking about what happened in Creek Nation."

"Everybody knows Toby killed her," said Tishacomsie.

"All right, even if I accept that," said Oscar Schiller. "The next question, and the important one, is why?"

"I don't know. And I don't care."

"Start caring," Oscar Schiller said. And took from his trouser pocket the bundle of bank notes Miss Jewel Moon had given him, untied the twine string, counted off a number of bills, laid them on the table, and pushed them toward the man.

The man and his wife looked at the stack of bills. They had watched as Oscar Schiller counted them out and knew that there was about two hundred dollars there. A lot of money.

"I've started to care," the man said, and without further instructions and everybody knowing there was no need for details, took the money and quickly slipped it into an inner coat pocket.

"Good," said Oscar Schiller. "So with Toby, it wasn't love."

Tishacomsie laughed.

"Maybe of all the men Temperance had around," she said, "Toby didn't have a place in her bed. And didn't want one."

"Sure," said Oscar Schiller. "But he was brother to Temperance Moon's husband of the moment."

"Sure, Oscar," the man said. "But you know as well as me that

Toby's brother Styles, old Temperance Moon's husband then, hadn't been around for over a year. And besides that, Toby and Styles didn't like one another at all, and part of it was that Toby was a crazy bastard, and he wanted nothing but whiskey. Or to go fishing. He didn't want Temperance Moon."

"Well, Candy, these people have been your neighbors for a long time," said Oscar Schiller. "So I reckon you know them better than me. And can talk to them better than me."

"That's likely true."

Oscar Schiller rose from his chair abruptly, and the other two realized the powwow was finished.

"Think about the why of it," Oscar Schiller said. "And I'll be in touch somewhere down the line. I may send a man. To ask things I can't ask. You keep him alive. And look around. You understand, Candy?"

"I understand the money." And his wife laughed.

"I'll send somebody because I can't ask questions over there and get true answers, and you know that," Oscar Schiller said. "Meanwhile, buy a few drinks of whiskey for people and do a lot of listening."

"I always do a lot of listening," the man said, and the fine lips parted in a small smile and the teeth brightened the room. "But whiskey is illegal in Creek Nation."

"Sure," said Oscar Schiller. "Just like it's illegal for you to come into a United States Commissioner's court with that Smith and Wesson .44 double-action pistol you got. And you had it today, didn't you?"

"I never did any such thing," the man said, and his smile was very large now.

"You oughta know better than that, Marshal," Tishacomsie said. Taking a last, deep draw on her black cigarette. "My husband never took any weapon into that court."

As they went to the door, Tishacomsie turned and smiled and said, "I had the pistol in my purse."

Then was gone into the darkness, and the man shrugged.

"What the hell can you do with a strong-willed woman?" he asked. Then turned to leave but paused and looked back, and the rows of white teeth were shining. "Oscar, I'll talk around Creek Nation on what you want. And we thank you for a good feed. I sure like them little oily fish. But that coffee you got. That's real goat shit, you know that, Oscar?"

ℕ ℕ ℕ Gazing at the yellow arrowhead of flame in his coal-oil lamp, Oscar Schiller sat for a long time after his guests had gone thinking about their journey home. They'd pick up their saddle horses from whichever livery they'd used. These were the kind of people who seldom traveled by wagon. Then south out of town to ford the Poteau, then along the south banks of the Arkansas and Canadian rivers in Choctaw Nation, finally to the Missouri, Kansas, and Texas Railroad trestle just south of Eufaula, which they'd use to cross over to the other side of the river, and then close along the north bank of the main fork of the Canadian to their farm. More than sixty miles, so he reckoned they'd be home in two days.

In the meantime, he thought, what have we got here? What we've got here, he answered himself, is the start of the little game which will make Jewel Moon happy she put so much of her money into the pot. Maybe. He had been in this kind of business long enough to understand that simplicity was the last thing in the world to expect.

"Cold trails have a way of twisting out from under you," he said aloud. He gave another match the cocaine treatment and put it in his mouth.

Oscar Schiller was acutely aware that neither of his guests had mentioned the fact that Toby Jupiter had come to the violent end of his wicked life less than a week after Temperance Moon was murdered. Had it been him, with their situations reversed, Oscar Schiller would have pointed out that there might be a connection. Everybody in Creek Nation must have been aware that after Temperance Moon's body had been found in the mud of that road, Parker's deputies were going to bring Toby to Fort Smith as soon as they could find him.

They found him, all right. With multiple gunshot wounds, the body lying in that corncrib shack or whatever it was, not five miles upstream from the very property to which Oscar Schiller's just-departed guests were now riding.

But neither of the two Indians had mentioned it. And Oscar Schiller hadn't really expected them to, even though he was dead sure it was something heavy on their minds as soon as he'd started talking about Jewel Moon's mama.

He dipped a fresh matchstick into one of Jewel Moon's little bottles and looked closely at how the white powder clung to the wetted wood. Then slipped it into his mouth and thought of the notes he'd made in his book, but didn't take the book from his pocket, because he knew everything that was written there. And he knew everything that was written on the pages in his head that might have something to do with this case. For although Oscar Schiller no longer wore one of Parker's badges, it was still a case to him.

Those guests of his! Those Indians! Tishacomsie. And Candy Redstripe.

Redstripe was a Delaware, so he claimed. Redstripe being the closest he could come to any understandable English translation of his real name. The Candy part had been added by white men, the kind of white men who spent a lot of time in saloons and domino parlors and thought about such things. And the Indian had accepted it with that little half-smile because he couldn't change it. And besides, maybe he saw some irony in it, just as Oscar Schiller did. Candy, sweet and toothsome, but anybody trying to bite into this particular piece would find a completely different flavor.

Delaware. The only Indians of whom Oscar Schiller had ever heard known by an English name. A tall and stately people who had fought both with and against white men beginning in the states of New Jersey and New York a long time before either one of those places was even a state. A people who had seen the red coats of British infantry and the white coats of the French and the butternut of Scots-Irish settlers moving up the wooded valleys from the seacoast who carried rifled muskets, deadly at over a hundred paces.

Eventually, in about 1867, some of those Delawares left had been removed by the federal government to a small northern section of Cherokee Nation. After the Civil War. Because during that war, a lot of Cherokees had fought for the South, and so the politicians whose predecessors had promised all that land to the Cherokees in perpetuity now had the excuse of rebellion to cancel all previous undertakings and hence use Indian Territory as an official dumping ground for peoples they had no other place to hide.

Of course, Oscar Schiller knew all this, even though having labored so long and hard for that same federal government against which he had fought as a boy in what he called the War Between the States. And knew as well that Candy Redstripe's people had been moved onto Cherokee land after the Cherokees had agreed to it, but along with forceful implication that the Cherokees had no other choice in the matter.

Illustrating, Oscar Schiller thought, that land tenure in the Nations after the war would damn well be decided by the white man. And that was the only perpetuity involved.

Anyway, he thought, a man has to play the cards he's dealt, like it or not. Candy Redstripe's daddy had been elected to the Cherokee National Council and sat making laws in Tahlequah when old Chief Ross had still been alive. But by then the son was off in Texas scouting for Ranald S. Mackenzie before that complex man had gone mad. Scouting against the Comanches in the Red River War, and when the last of Quannah Parker's people had been subdued, primarily through destruction of their pony herds, Candy Redstripe had been an interpreter at the Comanche-Kiowa agency, Fort Sill, I.T.

And Oscar Schiller knew all that agency business had bored Candy Redstripe simple, so he left and returned to his daddy's farm on the Neosho River in Cherokee Nation, bringing with him a string of the most disreputable Indian ponies anybody had ever seen and a short, squat, bowlegged, moon-faced Comanche youth whom he called Toad. To ride the disreputable horses.

There was some talk that Candy Redstripe had come away from Fort Sill with all those horses without bothering to pay for them. Nobody ever proved anything. Primarily because no Comanche with any sense at all was going to come east of the Crossed Timbers and into green country to accuse somebody of stealing anything. Because among the Civilized Tribes, folks like the Comanches and Kiowas were considered outright savages and beneath contempt.

Of course, nobody among the Civilized Tribes ever went west of Crossed Timbers to Comanche and Kiowa country to say such a thing to their faces. After all, Oscar Schiller always said, these people in the Nations may be Indians but they're not crazy.

But then there he was, Candy Redstripe, back on his daddy's farm with a bunch of little ponies and a Toad who could talk horse to them. Oscar Schiller had heard Candy Redstripe say many times that only High Plains Indians could speak with their horses and both sides understand what was being said.

For whatever reason, Candy Redstripe began racing those ponies, Toad riding them. In the only known races in the Nations. Quarter of a mile, full out from the starting gun. And the Comanche ponies made Cherokee and Choctaw and Creek racehorses look like drays that should have been hitched to wagons. At least in the first four hundred yards. Maybe, Oscar Schiller thought, those terrible-looking ponies Candy Redstripe had brought from Fort Sill had some inherited will to race from ancestors who had become a distinctive part of Comanche and Kiowa culture because they could run down any buffalo that ever lived on Llano Estacado. And sometimes, Oscar Schiller had heard, if used in relays even run down pronghorn antelope.

Those horse races, as the Comanche boy Toad rode the ponies, won a hell of a lot of money for Candy Redstripe. Because those Comanche ponies could come out of a crouch from dead still to dead full-out run more like a cat than a horse. So Candy Redstripe kept bringing in gold to his pockets, betting on those races. Which, in the Nations, attracted a lot of attention. Particularly the attention of certain types of men, red, white, and black, who had shown from evidence taken against some of them in Parker's court that they were more than willing to kill a man or a boy or a woman just for the shoes on the victim's feet.

So even in his youth, Candy Redstripe had become a marked man in the Nations. The kind of marked man whose feet might be held to the fire until he told where the money was hidden and then dispatched with an ax. An ax, as the records of Parker's court showed, seemed to be a favorite weapon of such men in that place.

And at the thought of it, Oscar Schiller laughed aloud. For he knew of the time when Candy Redstripe had been at Vinita horse races and on the way home offered to share his campsite with three men. A hospitality returned by the three when they rose just before dawn, one with an ax of course, and came to Candy Redstripe's bedroll. Two of the three men were never found. Having obviously run off into the woods and died of wounds and provided meals for buzzards.

The third was found lying beside the ashes of the campfire, both cold by the time Candy Redstripe brought the Cherokee Light Horse Police to the scene to observe the effect of a .45 caliber slug entering the head at a left upper incisor and coming out with exploding fury where normal men had a bald spot.

Self-defense, the Cherokee court had said. In fact, after that case, Oscar Schiller had heard a member of the Cherokee Supreme Court say that Candy Redstripe should be subsidized for his ammunition in order that the Nations might be rid of its vermin more efficiently.

But there were other things. Like the persistent rumor that Candy Redstripe always had more money than one would expect a man to make just from betting races, even betting on those wild Comanche ponies. Soon, Candy Redstripe began to stand in bad odor with the Cherokee police, and they watched him so closely and dogged his father with so many questions that Candy Redstripe became very irritated and finally gathered up his Comanche ponies and his Comanche rider Toad and departed, coming to rest in Creek Nation. Where he married Tishacomsie, who had just come to full bloom and was considered the prize catch for any man within fifty miles of Eufaula in all directions.

About the only thing anybody knew about that romance was that Tishacomsie's father had been violently opposed to any union, but union it was, and the couple settled on a part of the land that was Tishacomsie's heritage, a farm with a house in sight of the main fork of the Canadian River, where Toad proved that even if he was a barbarian Comanche he was pretty good with hammer and saw and so began improvements to the house and the barn and other outbuildings.

It was good bottomland but they didn't farm it. They leased it out to various people, because Candy Redstripe's hands would never fit a plow any more than would the Comanche's. Besides, there was still the racing, year-round, and they went all over the eastern end of the Nations to run their ponies, and sometimes even into northern Texas and sometimes into western Arkansas. After a time, Tishacomsie accompanied her husband and Toad and the ponies less frequently, staying at home just like any other housewife and planting petunias.

It became a nice-looking house, clapboard in a land of log and mud chinking, surrounded by woodlands and the fields cultivated by somebody else, all no more than ten miles from Eufaula along the Canadian. And no more than ten miles south of another farm that stood on a branch of the North Canadian called Mud Creek, a farm where there were mostly scrub oak hills and fallow fields grown up in sassafras, a farm where various men gathered to what purpose nobody knew, a farm never farmed at all and with a four-room log house with a dogtrot between the two rooms on either side, a breezeway easterners might call it.

This other place was called Fawley Farm and shown on the

property record books in the Creek couthouse at Eufaula as owned by one Temperance Moon Turtle, come by through legal marriage of said Temperance Moon to Tom Turtle, a Creek Indian whose family had been on that land since the removals in the 1830s. And now that Temperance Moon Turtle was dead, the property was owned by her brother-in-law Langston Turtle, who lived there among some of those same strange men who had been hanging about even while Temperance was still alive.

Oscar Schiller's ruminations were interrupted by a knock on the door at the head of the stairs leading to the Hake kitchen above.

"Damn," he whispered, then shouted, "Come in."

Meribelle Hake came down the stairway tentatively, carrying a plate with a large slice of coconut cream pie. She was always tentative, even in her constant little plump smile. But she was not unattractive. In fact, she was rather pretty in a children's balloon sort of way.

"Mrs. Hake," said Oscar Schiller, rising.

"Mr. Schiller. I thought you might enjoy a slice of pie," she said, smiling tentatively. "Mr. Hake was in such a rush to get off to his political meeting that he only ate one slice, and the children have been so bad I put them to bed without any. So I have so much left. It doesn't keep very well."

"Please come and sit down," said Oscar Schiller, knowing he would now be subjected to her vapid conversation about her husband's business and political activities. But it was worth it, because Mrs. Hake always provided delicious pie and cake. Among other things.

"Maybe for just a little while," she said, smiling. "This old house is so lonely when I'm here by myself."

So they sat at the small table and Mrs. Hake watched as Oscar Schiller ate the pie. And as he expected, she talked without pause.

"Mr. Hake is such a supporter of Herkimer Warson, you know at the bank, and Herkimer Warson just won election again to the state legislature and Mr. Hake said that Herkimer Warson wants to be in the Senate. Of the United States. I certainly wouldn't vote for Herkimer Warson, even if I could vote."

"Well, Mrs. Hake, you needn't worry. None of us can vote for a senator of the United States Congress. These people are selected by the state legislatures."

"I know. Mrs. Warson sent me some iris bulbs and I suppose I need to plant them. But I don't like her husband. And that evil-looking man he always keeps about."

"Creighton LaRue," said Oscar Schiller, finishing the last bite of pie. "Well, I suppose a man in Mr. Warson's position needs an associate of that type. Everyone on the Avenue calls Creighton Muley, did you know that?"

"Yes. I don't know why."

"Neither do I, Mrs. Hake," Oscar Schiller said, rising and wiping his mouth with the tips of his fingers. "Would you like to sit with me on the bed and talk?"

"Well," Mrs. Hake said, smiling, "maybe for just a little while."

Oscar Schiller took off his glasses. He could hear the clock that overhung the Garrison Avenue sidewalk in front of the City Bank striking ten.

ᛝ ᛝ ᛝ Muley LaRue heard the clock strike as well, only the sound was much louder in his ear, for he was only a short block from the source. The horse shed was just off Rogers Avenue, in the alley beside the bank, and Muley LaRue was there in the dim light of a single hanging lantern saddling his bay. His employer, City Bank senior vice-president Herkimer Warson, was involved in one of his meetings in the second-story boardroom, and Muley LaRue, being no part of what was proceeding, was homebound. Because on this particular night, Mr. Warson had no further need for his services.

Nobody except perhaps Mr. Warson himself knew precisely what those services were except that Muley LaRue appeared to be some sort of bodyguard and loan collector for Mr. Warson when Mr. Warson was in Fort Smith acting like a banker and some sort of personal companion and handyman when Mr. Warson was in Little Rock acting like a state legislator. Maybe a bodyguard there, everybody said, what with all the instances of one legislator attacking another on the floor of their capitol building chamber. With a cane or a riding whip, and once, not long ago, with a bowie knife, and one of the people's representatives expired on the carpet of the room where he had been elected to pass those statutes proving that Arkansas was a civilized place and not a den of barbarians.

It was a story that delighted citizens liked to keep alive so long as the expired legislator was not their own.

Muley LaRue didn't look like a bodyguard. He was slightly built, his face rather handsome in an oily sort of way, with a tiny mustache and moist black eyes. People remarked on the coats that Muley LaRue wore, always longer than the normal style, which they all said was likely the result of Muley LaRue having come originally from New Orleans and who the hell could tell what those crazy Creoles might wear next.

The kind of bodyguarding that Muley LaRue did was not associated with physical strength, so his size didn't matter. His kind of bodyguarding was associated with the two Remington double-barreled derringer pistols he always carried. Rimfire and .41 caliber, a vicious little weapon, everybody said. This arrangement of personal armament was perfectly legal, because the city police authorities had approved once Mr. Warson convinced them that anybody to be effective as a hedge against harm befalling a banker and his vaults needed to be prepared for swift and decisive action. Whether Mr. Warson had made the same arrangements with the Little Rock police nobody knew, except for Mr. Warson and Muley LaRue.

Those citizens who had had face-to-face experience with Muley LaRue in his capacity as loan collector could vouch for the fact that he was indeed swift and decisive. To the point of being deadly, but nobody could vouch for that because nobody had ever pushed Muley LaRue to such a point.

On this night, Muley LaRue, saddling his horse in the bank's shed, heard someone approaching along the alley from the front of the bank. It was too late for casual strollers in the city's alleyways, and Muley LaRue moved into deep shadow and placed his hands in coat pockets, where the pistols were.

But it was only George, the black man who did the bank's janitor work. He didn't see Muley at first, and when he did, he gave a startled little jump.

"Lordy, Mist' LaRue, I never seed you there," he said. "Somebody done drop this note in the letter slot at the front door."

George passed a folded piece of paper to Muley LaRue, and Muley LaRue opened it and read. There was a rather delicate pencil scrawl. "Jewel Moon and Oscar Schiller are interested in the Moon killings."

"You read this, George?" asked Muley.

"You know I can't read, Mist' LaRue."

After the black man had gone, Muley crumpled the paper and stuffed it in a coat pocket, then stood thinking for a long time. He knew he'd been there for a quarter hour, almost motionless in the horse shed, when he heard the clock on Garrison Avenue strike again. Then he mounted and reined along the alley toward Rogers Avenue and home.

Creighton Muley LaRue rather enjoyed the late-evening ride home through the streets of Fort Smith. It gave him the feeling of looking down from some lofty height, maybe even a somewhat sacred perch in the saddle above the passing pedestrians on the sidewalks. There was little traffic on Rogers except for the people on foot, most of them bakery workers just off late shift when the loaves were taken from the ovens. He could smell the bakery from the bank alley almost all the way home, past the last of the streetlights and past all the shop windows, some of these already dark. There was a superior swell of pride as he rode, shadowed and silent, past the noisy bakery crews with their white aprons showing in the darkness and their voices coming to him clearly through the night. As though he could see them but they had no notion of his being there. He gave the impression of riding without looking right or left, disdainful, haughty, his head held as immobile as the small plaster saints in the niches at either side of the doors of the Catholic church at the head of Garrison Avenue. But his eyes moved constantly, and he passed nothing on his way without notice.

Creighton Muley LaRue had made a life work of seeing everything that went on around him without always giving notice that he saw. He was like a tightly tuned piano wire, silent but waiting to vibrate with the slightest touch of the mallet. It was only at the end, when he turned the horse into his own residential street and there were only window lights through naked branches of dogwood trees in yards and no more walkers and the only sounds an occasional yard dog somewhere sounding protest of a cat or another dog, the wire tension eased, because he was coming to the little cubicle of Louisiana he had structured in this barbarous land, where his children waited in French bows, where his wife stood beside a table ready with old wine and oyster stew perhaps, or maybe ale with red beans and rice. Any part of Louisiana was good, French Quarter or bayou boathouse.

As he moved to the small shed behind his house and dismounted and rubbed the horse, for just an instant the piano wire went taut again, vibrating soundlessly. Somebody is interested again in Temperance Moon!

But then he shrugged and unsaddled the horse, stalled him, locked the shed door, and went in to the smell of gumbo.

3 In 1892, the Kansas City stockyards were not as large as they would become but large enough to create their own special blend of fragrances undiminished even with the windows closed against November chill. At least with the cold autumn winds blowing off the Kansas plains it was better than summertime, when the humidity where the Kaw and the Missouri rivers merged clamped a moist lid on any movement of air and the stench became as substantial as the walls of the brick buildings that sat in block rows all around the holding pens and slaughter sheds.

But the smell did not concern the young man who walked into his third-story one-room flat that fall evening, a flat with a window looking directly down into the yards, where there was at this point a large building displaying an electric sign that spelled out "Armour." For he had other concerns more important than the scent of manure and meat processing. He had the letter. From Fort Smith, Arkansas, and the sense of something unusual because he seldom received a letter from Fort Smith, Arkansas. In fact, this was the first he had ever received from that quarter.

He was a deliberate man for all his youth, being only twenty-five years old. Perhaps his controlled impetuosity was his major asset, although there were some who would have argued that a greater one was his expertise with the British Webley revolver he always carried in a holster under his left arm. After he'd come into the room, he removed his overcoat and suit coat and the bowler hat, placing the latter on his night table beside the bed and alongside that the .45 pistol. He did not remove the vest with the silver badge on it, a shield which on close inspection would indicate that he was a detective on the Kansas City metropolitan police force. He finally took the letter from a hip pants pocket and laid it on the table, too.

He went to the sink, as he always did on arrival in his flat, ran water from the cold tap and splashed some in his face, then patted his face and the thick black mustache dry with a small hand towel. He looked closely at his reflection in a wall mirror, and the eyes that looked back at him were light gray in an otherwise swarthy terrain. Black brows, black hair, olive skin pockmarked along the cheeks. And as he always did, staring at himself in the mirror, he said aloud, "Sand nigger!"

For he was a Syrian whose name had once been Musa Ibn Mustafa in Damascus before his family came to America, he at the time only twelve years old. Unlike many Arab Muslim immigrants to the place where the streets were paved with gold, the Mustafa family had been Christians for three generations. So maybe for that reason, or maybe to help integrate more smoothly into the United States of America, the old man had changed the family name. From Mustafa to Masada. He liked the musical sound of that name, Masada. Besides, he had always disliked Mustafa, because it was an Arabic name shared with many Turks. And he hated Turks.

So the boy Musa Ibn Mustafa became Moses Ben Masada, because Ibn was only an Arabic indicator of parentage, meaning "son of." So changed to Ben, a common name among Anglos. And Musa meant descendant of Moses, a man even English speakers had heard of, so therefore Moses Ben Masada.

Soon, the Ben was dropped completely. Hence, Moses Masada.

It required some explanation by the old man to a lot of non-Semitic peoples in this new land. That his son's name was a good Syrian one and did not mark him as a Jew, and the confusion, the old man always said, was because a lot of people, especially those who spoke English, did not know that Arabic and Hebrew were closely related Semitic languages.

The boy Moses Masada was not long in realizing the irony of his father's making a name change to escape that Mustafa handle and ending with one most perceived as Hebrew. The irony being that the old man hated Jews almost as much as he did Turks.

And as he grew older, Moses Masada thought of it all as he

might if observing the men of the Middle East dancing together. If one was not an expert, it was impossible to tell, watching those arm-intertwined, intricately kicking men, whether they were Armenian or Persian or Arab or Turk or Jew or even Greek. Only that in their dancing there was a universal joy, yet at the same time a sadness in the recognition that a new conqueror would soon arrive and say the old ways would now be abolished.

So Moses Masada accepted the slight irritation that there were those who thought he was a Jew. It was, he reckoned, a small price to pay for becoming a citizen of the United States of America, where the soldiers did not come to stop the dancing!

His father had brought the family to Detroit, where in 1879 there was already a small but growing Arab community. There the senior Masada operated a vegetable pushcart and later established a greengrocery. But the boy Moses Masada was never particularly enthusiastic about either pushcarts or vegetables and began to hang about on the streets.

He had his first experience with a neighborhood police station when he threw a brick through the window of an Armenian pawnshop. His father came and got him out, and paid for the window. Moses Masada paid with welts across his back and a bloody nose. The former from the belt of his father, the latter from the fist of the Irish policeman who had caught him.

There was a fascination with any organization which had the kind of power that could break his nose and make his father pay for a window that deserved to be broken, the young Moses Masada thought. So he began hanging about police stations and soon became a street informer. He had a quiet but cheerful intensity that appealed to certain instincts of peace officers and before long Moses Masada was encouraged to become a policeman himself.

Soon, pushcarts and greengroceries and father and mother and sisters and brothers and all else related to the old country were left behind. With no backward look. With no regrets. He worked for the Pinkertons, then became a railway detective, and then a member of the Kansas City police force.

Moses Masada was an asset to any such group. Primarily because he did not look like a policeman, most of whom at the time were Anglo-Irish, so he could go to places they could not and listen to conversations silenced when a normal lawman appeared. He spoke not only Arabic but Polish, thanks to his street years in Detroit, and French, thanks to his own self-education, and flawless English. He had no entangling family ties, substituting an occasional visit to some handy bordello for any form of accepted conjugal bliss. And he was ruthless.

Twice in the past, Moses Masada had worked with United States Deputy Marshal Oscar Schiller. To mutual advantage. Meaning that felons had been apprehended and hauled before appropriate magistrates for their crimes. So the letter was not a complete surprise. And being the good detective that he was, Moses Masada knew a great deal without opening the letter. Just from the envelope.

The return address was "Schiller, General Delivery, Fort Smith, Arkansas." No indication of any connection with the federal court system. And the stamp had been canceled on a Missouri Pacific mail car, which told Moses Masada that Schiller wanted no personally known post office employee in Fort Smith in the position to say that there had been a letter posted to the Kansas City police department. Hence, Schiller was writing as a private citizen and he wanted some secrecy about it.

"My Dear Detective Masada." Moses Masada smiled at the formal salutation. "There may be in the offing an opportunity to make some money." Implying that Moses Masada did not make much money with the Kansas City police department. Which was true.

"All in line with bringing criminals to justice, we can hope."

There followed an outline of what Oscar Schiller knew of the case. Names. Locations. Background. Specific missions required. More general missions involving an undercover role in the Five Civilized Tribes Nations.

"Perhaps you might pose as an Indian. You could easily do so. Perhaps a Mohawk. Not many of those here. You could call yourself Joe Moses."

Then, if Moses Masada decided to take the challenge, to contact the former deputy marshal in roundabout ways. Whatever that meant. Then the name of Candy Redstripe, and with a contact there to identify himself only with the cryptic message "I am from Oscar."

Bring field gear, Oscar Schiller said, and for God's sake, no lace boots or bowler hats. Moses Masada laughed aloud.

"I know you have never operated in the Nations, but that could be advantageous. However, I cannot emphasize too strongly that in those environs, you must protect yourself at all times. And buy a large-bore Winchester rifle, even though I understand you are unaccustomed to using such a weapon. Appearance alone is sometimes a deterrent."

Included, too, were Frisco railroad passes, a lot of them, and a railway money order in the amount of three hundred dollars. ". . . in the event that you should take up this gauntlet. Advise by return mail."

He was a little surprised that Oscar Schiller was contacting him as a private citizen. In their two previous encounters, Moses Masada had seen that this little man was intensely proud of his badge and happy for the power it brought him. The detective side of Masada's brain told him that Oscar Schiller was no longer a peace officer, and he suspected that an overexuberance in the discharge of official duties had put him at odds with his superiors and cost him his position. Moses Masada, in his line of work, was not unfamiliar with such a situation.

Purely a guess, of course. Masada knew almost nothing about Schiller except that he had served in an Arkansas volunteer regiment during the war, a very young man at that time. Moses Masada found it difficult to imagine Oscar Schiller as a young man. And he realized for the first time that he wasn't even aware of which army Schiller had served, Union or rebel.

Well, it didn't matter. Masada had seen enough to know that Oscar Schiller was a methodical man and trustworthy and not often wrong in his hunches, and that he knew where to find an extra dollar here and there. That was enough for now.

Moses Masada carefully folded the letter and placed it on the table beside the British Webley pistol. The darkness outside his window was harshly interrupted by Armour's electric sign, and for a moment he looked out across the gas-lit pens of the stockyards. But only for a moment.

From beneath his bed he drew a wicker suitcase and packed it quickly, pausing only long enough to write a note to his chief of police that he was called away on urgent family business. The note was written on a postal card, of which he always kept a few in his breast pocket. His movements now were not deliberate, once his mind had been set on what he would do, but a sort of frenzy. It didn't take long before he was out on the street, in the cold, drizzling darkness, going at almost a run along the five blocks of sidewalk from his own flat building to the *Kansas City News Beacon* newspaper.

It was a massive sandstone structure, and now, because the newspaper was a morning one, the great Hoe rotary presses in the basement were doing the first run, the home edition, of the next day's news. The building and the entire block around it quivered and hummed with the power of the running presses, as though there was a small earthquake.

In the basement of that building, separated from the press room by a solid concrete wall, was the morgue. The place where all the history of the ages was stored, at least according to the *News Beacon*. Moses Masada had been there many times before, and as he went down the narrow stairway the odor of newsprint and ink was not new to him. At the door to the morgue, as always, was Angus, an ancient black man who claimed he was the first man of color in the state of Missouri who could read. He looked at Moses Masada and the suitcase in Moses Masada's hand.

"You goin' somewheres, Mr. *Po*-lice-man?"

"Maybe," said the Syrian, passing a dollar greenback to the keeper of records. Whose only real duty was to ensure that no fire broke out in the files of newspapers on racks within his sanctuary.

"What date?" asked Angus.

"Try September 20. And go on from there. I don't know how far, just go on from there."

So, grumbling at the weight of the large folders that held the old issues, Angus pulled a few of them down, knowing exactly where September 20 was, and placed them on a small table under a dim electric light bulb.

"There some," he said. "You want more, Mr. *Po*-lice-man, you tell me."

And went back to his chair at the door.

It didn't take long. September 30, a Friday, on the third page, the first two pages then still being devoted to advertising. A single-column story on an eight-column page, but under a deck of half a dozen boldfaced headlines.

BANDIT WOMAN SLAIN

FOUND SHOT DEAD IN
INDIAN TERRITORY

MISSOURI'S DAUGHTER

KILLER COMES TO HIS END

HER FARM HAVEN FOR
DESPERATE MEN

LUST AND MURDER

Correspondence and press association telegraphs have arrived telling of the murder of Temperance Tilly Moon, the infamous Outlaw Queen of the Indian Territory. She was a onetime resident of Joplin in the family home of her father, a minister of the gospel. It was from there that she began her lurid and degenerate career as a creature of lust and mayhem among the barbaric peoples who are neighbors of the sovereign state of Arkansas only just south of us.

It has been remarked that there is no Sunday west of Kansas City and no God west of Fort Smith. From our own knowledge of her nefarious, nay felonious activities, it is safe to say that Temperance Tilly Moon was in large part responsible for such comments.

Now the decent citizens of her area lie down to rest at night more secure in knowing that she is dead.

Her body was found lying in vile mud, shredded head to foot with shotgun pellets. The Retribution of the Just had found her out!

Not since the cruel and bloodthirsty John Wesley Hardin of Texas has there been an issue from proud Baptist parents of such degeneracy. And Temperance Tilly Moon, as did John Wesley Hardin, sowed the wind and reaped the whirlwind. Her murderer was sought in vain by peace officers. He was found slain himself before he could be apprehended. All of it a barbarian play so often reported to us by our correspondence with those in the Indian Territory.

Temperance Tilly Moon was the unwed mother of a child some say was fathered by the renegade Fawley, who was shot dead not fifty miles from our own fair city when he attempted to rob an express office of the esteemed August Bainbridge, builder of railroads and well known in Kansas City and a civic-minded man when vindictive Democrat politicians created the trumped-up charges of fraud against him and with the aid of corrupt judges placed him in servitude at Lansing, Kansas, the state penitentiary.

Letters to this newspaper have indicated that Temperance Tilly Moon had a number of husbands as well as gentleman intimates, her being obviously an advocate of the growing sect of free love which is the movement that opens our children to the ravages of sin and depravity. Her first husband was a Joplin man named Charles Moon, who died shortly after their nuptials of causes mysterious.

It is known from our correspondence that Temperance Tilly Moon married at least two red Indians, one a Cherokee who was hanged for murder and a Creek named Turtle who gave her his family farmland and was shortly thereafter shot dead in Arkansas.

There is no evidence here that Temperance Tilly Moon will be mourned on her wild frontier. Like the prophet of old, she was despised in her own country.

By last report, she is survived by her illegitimate daughter, who operates a den of iniquity in the wild border town of Fort Smith, and a brother who still lives in Joplin.

As he left, Moses Masada passed another bill to Angus, who said. "You good, Mr. *Po*-lice-man. Come back and see us."

"In time, maybe in time."

He walked along Kansas City's dark streets, the wind biting him, coming after six blocks to the passenger depot of the Kansas City Southern. And there converted a fistful of Oscar Schiller's railroad passes to a one-way ticket south on the KCS Southern Flyer to Joplin. Then waiting for his train used another of his postal cards, writing with his suitcase on his legs like a desk, addressing it to O. Schiller, General Delivery, Fort Smith, Arkansas, with the message: Masada is coming!

੨ ੨ ੨ Barbers in southern Missouri were much like those in more northern cities from whom Moses Masada had often obtained valued information. Not under any sort of duress or even direct interrogation but only in the normal, casual tonsorial exchanges that took place especially when none of the barbers were aware that a customer in one of the chairs was a policeman.

It was true, of course, that barbers knew more than anybody else about the comings and goings of men, women, children, and good dogs in their communities, being as they were the stewards of talcum-powder-and-bay-rum enclaves where male gossip was as much a part of the environment as razors and scissors. Better than bartenders, because even though bartenders might know as much as barbers, they were very suspicious people and sometimes downright tight-lipped about revealing all the wonderful things they undoubtedly knew.

So the second step in the mission assigned by Oscar Schiller's letter involved nothing more than paying for a haircut in a Joplin Main Street barbershop, the usual kind of barbershop with a lot of mirrors and a black shoeshine man, and distinctive only in that on one wall there was a map of the area west of Joplin where all the lead mines were marked with a red pencil.

After the usual and almost ceremonial discussions of the weather and how nobody had figured out how to do anything about it, and then the revelation by Moses Masada that he was a traveling barbed-wire salesman en route to various places along the line of the Kansas City Southern Railroad, he made the comment that he was glad to be in Joplin because it was such a famous city.

"How's that?" his barber asked, clicking his scissors.

"Why, it has been my understanding from reading the newspapers in Illinois and such places," said Masada, "that the infamous outlaw queen Temperance Moon was born right here in Joplin."

"They write that in them northern papers. They call her the outlaw queen?"

"They certainly do."

"I'll be damned! Well, Temperance wasn't born here. She was born someplace in Illinois. Ain't that right, Floyd?"

Floyd, the barber at the next chair shaving a client, said, "That's right. My daddy said when Reverend Tilly come down here just before the war, the girl was about seventeen, eighteen years old."

"Floyd's daddy, he was a barber, too."

"Said that girl was already wild as an acorn-fed boar hog," said Floyd.

"Yeah," Moses Masada's barber said, clicking his scissors. "A terrible thing, that girl. Her daddy a good man. Baptist minister for so long. I guess that girl broke his heart."

"Does he still preach?"

"Oh no, Reverend Tilly passed on. Let's see. What was it, Floyd, fifteen years ago?"

"About that," Floyd said. "Same year Pearson's feed barn burned."

"Yeah, about fifteen years ago. Passed away. Broken heart, I'd say. People die of broken hearts, you know."

"Last of the line, then," said Moses Masada.

"No, the Reverend's son Lucas is still alive. Floyd, ain't Lucas still alive?"

"Lives in the old Tilly place on Elm Street," Floyd said, scraping the jowls of his customer with a straight razor. "All by his own self out there."

"Mean old son of a bitch, too," said Floyd's customer.

"Right there in the same house where Temperance Moon lived," said Moses Masada.

"That's right. Old place all fallin' down now. I 'member when I was a kid, go out that way and it was a pretty house, all yellow with white trim. Fallin' to rack and ruin. Screens broke."

"Weeds in the yard," said Floyd.

"Yeah, and all them empty tin cans Lucas throws in the backyard," Floyd's client said. "And his chickens runnin' all over the neighborhood."

"There's another one, too. That daughter Temperance had. Only she don't live here," Moses Masada's barber said.

"Yeah," said Floyd. "Caney, you want me to cut that hair out of your nose?"

"I reckon so."

"Yeah," Moses Masada's barber said. "That daughter Temperance had, she's down in Arkansas or the Indian Territory or someplace. Now *she* was born out there in that Elm Street house all right. Sends a little money, I guess, to her uncle Lucas, through the mails."

"Once a month, regular," said Floyd.

"Floyd's got a cousin's a clerk at the post office." Masada's barber was shaving his neck now.

"Once a month, regular."

"I don't recall," Moses Masada said, "reading anywhere that Temperance Moon's daddy was a preacher of the gospel."

"Oh yeah, poor old Reverend Tilly, likely spinnin' in his grave from what all his daughter's did. And right there beside of him at Oak Grove Cemetery is Charles Moon, that girl's husband. Both died of broken hearts, I'd guess."

"Charlie died because he drank too much bad whiskey," said Floyd, wrapping a hot towel around his customer's face. "He was already half dead when him and Temperance slipped off to Carthage that time and got married. Right before Temperance birthed that girl of hers. Daddy told me all that. It was before my time."

"Yeah," Moses Masada's barber said, sweeping the hair-catch cloth off like a matador teasing a bull. "Floyd's daddy was a barber, too. All finished, sir. That'll be two bits."

卍 卍 卍 The old Tilly house wasn't hard to find and only a half-mile walk from the center of town, the kind of exercise ideal for gusty autumn days with the dead elm and oak leaves blowing across the streets like brittle brown mice looking for their holes, making skittering sounds with their little feet. The Tilly house was as the barbers had described it. Fallen into forlorn disrepair and the yard all around a forest of tall grass, mostly grown gray now, and whispering in the wind.

Although Moses Masada was not a particularly large man, he was solidly built, and as he walked across the front porch to the door he felt the old planks beneath his feet bending under his weight. It was a long time after his knock before there was any response and he was sure that someone was inspecting him from behind the tattered curtains of the windows.

In his hands, Moses Masada held what he hoped would be the tickets of his admittance to this place. A quart bottle of the very best sour-mash whiskey and the latest edition of the *Police Gazette*, with a tinted engraving on the front page of a fully formed lady in pink tights above the caption "Forbidden Love Under the Bigtop!" And from a treasure trove of such things he always carried in his pocketbook, a card identifying him as Carlo Vapo, representative, writer, and editorial adviser to that same *Police Gazette*.

At last the door opened. A small crack of openness, but enough to reveal a pinched brown face, wrinkled, sparse black hair on a dome of skull, large brown eyes, and stains of old snuff juice at the corners of a wide mouth.

"Yeah?" It was a harsh voice, creaking from lack of use.

"Mr. Lucas Tilly? As you can see, I represent the *Police Ga-*

zette," said Moses Masada, passing the card to the man, a clawlike hand coming out to take it. "I have our latest edition for you, in case you have never seen our magazine before."

Lucas Tilly took the magazine, too, and glanced at it with his large eyes.

"I seen it before," he said. "But I ain't buyin' nothin'."

"No, no," said Moses Masada. "I'm not here to sell you anything. I'm writing an article about your sister and supposed you might help me."

"My sister? She's dead."

"I know. But she was a very fascinating person. And a story about her will be worth a lot of money."

The brown eyes studied Moses Masada's face. Then his clothes. Then his shoes. And then back to the face again.

"I don't know nothin' about her."

"I'm sure you could help me," said Moses Masada, smiling broadly. "I'd be willing to advance you some money just to talk awhile."

Lucas Tilly blinked rapidly. He looked at the *Police Gazette* again, and the business card.

"Funny name," he said.

"I'm Italian," said Moses Masada. "As you can see, I am very much an Italian."

"Yeah, I can see that. I ain't ever talked to no Italians. How much money?"

"I was thinking that now, just to talk awhile, oh, let's say fifty dollars. More, naturally, when the article is published."

Now smiling really broadly, Moses Masada produced the quart of sour-mash whiskey.

"I'd hoped we could cut the chill of this cold day with a few sips as we talked."

The brown eyes grew wider and there was a great deal of rapid blinking. Lucas Tilly stared fascinated at the amber liquid in the glass bottle. Moses Masada felt that he could hear the mind of Lucas Tilly meshing its gears slowly. Laboriously.

"All right," said Tilly. "Come on in."

And opened the door to the smell of old snuff, burning oak wood in his fireplace, and mildewed furniture of Civil War vintage.

"I am much obliged," said Moses Masada.

卍 卍 卍 "Cap'n Quantrill was over yonder in the Indian Territory, first year of the war. War Between the States," Lucas Tilly said. "You know about that war, I guess."

"Yes," said Moses Masada Carlo Vapo, and knowing the ground upon which he trod, lied with a straight face as all good policemen can lie when the occasion demands it. "My daddy fought with General Lee."

"Good, good," said Lucas Tilly, his eyes bulging in appreciation. "Wanta hear all about that here. We was always agin them Free-Soilers. Hated them Free-Soilers, me and Papa."

Lucas Tilly was slouched in an armchair that might have needed repairs during the administration of Martin Van Buren but had got none and now chair and man seemed to melt into one another like a single worn-out shoe cast aside and being outlined and given its only life by the flickering light of the fireplace.

Lucas Tilly held a white china cup in his hand, half full of sour-mash whiskey. The bottle was on the floor beside him, almost empty. And only now, after spending a lot of time explaining his various physical disabilities, had he begun to talk in the direction for which Moses Masada had come.

"Cap'n Quantrill and his men. They was always people comin' in here from the Territory, tellin' stuff. So we knowed they was there." Lucas Tilly's voice was by now a gurgling slur, like cold syrup coming from a small-necked jug. "Papa wanted to help all he could, so he sent me over yonder with two mules, loaded with beans and sides of bacon. Gawd, we had beans and bacon. Gawd, Papa hated them Free-Soilers."

Lucas Tilly took a swallow from the china cup, smacked his lips, and blinked, like an owl, looking for mice in the night. And it was almost night by now, the windows showing the last dim light of a sun already set.

"So I taken out for the Verdigris River. And by Gawd, Temperance come with me."

"Your sister?"

"Sure."

"How old was she then?"

"Hell, Mr. Vapo, I don't know. She was full-growed. And she could ride as good as any man I ever seen. Sidesaddle. Always said it wasn't ladylike to ride astride."

"Your father allowed her to go?"

Lucas Tilly's bony chest under an old sweater heaved up and down as he cackled in what Moses Masada assumed was supposed to be a laugh. When Lucas Tilly's mirth was under control, he wiped his eyes with the back of one hand, took another drink, and shook his head.

"Hell, Papa never had nothin' to say about what Temperance done. She done what she damn well pleased. Papa'd take in to whippin' her with a razor strap and get her on her knees so he could pray for her soul. Then she'd go right on doin' what she damn well pleased anyway.

"Well, we never had no task findin' Cap'n Quantrill. Ever' Cherokee savage Indian we seen knew where he was at. So we found 'em and they was a fine bunch of men. I even talked to the James boys. Good Gawd-fearin' boys, it seemed to me. Temperance, she found this man named Tyne Fawley and she took up with him. She never made no bones about it. She always said he was the daddy of her baby."

"Her baby?"

"Sure, little Jewel. We was in the Territory maybe two weeks, with Cap'n Quantrill, and then him and his boys rode off north somewheres. And we come home."

"Did this man, what's-his-name, come with you?"

"What man?"

"This daddy of the baby."

"Oh, Tyne Fawley. No, no, he went off with Cap'n Quantrill. We never seen him again. Temperance never seen him again, and a long time after, after the war was over, I heard that he was shot dead when he was tryin' to rob some express company in Kansas somewheres. I don't know much about that."

Lucas Tilly took a long drink from his cup, then bent to lift the bottle and shook it and glared with his bulging eyes at the low level of liquid.

"You don't want no more?" he asked.

"No, my stomach is very tender."

"By Gawd, mine ain't," Lucas Tilly said. "My whole insides is stout as that cast-arn cookstove out yonder in the kitchen."

He drank again.

"Right after we come home, Mama knew Temperance was with child. Hell, I don't know. Maybe Temperance told her. It never took long, though, to see it for yourself, the way her belly started puffin' up, and Papa was almost crazy knowin' his girl was in a family way and no husband.

"And you know, Mr. Vapo, maybe Temperance felt sorry for Papa or something like that, 'cause she went and married Charlie Moon. Old Charlie, Papa had been tryin' ever sinct we come down here from Illinois to save Charlie from perdition and demon rum. But by Gawd, Temperance run off with him and married him and they come back here to live and Temperance never let old Charlie into her bedroom as far as I know but at least he give that baby a name."

Lucas Tilly began to stare into the fire. His jaw slack. His eyes showing a vacant glare.

"Mr. Tilly. What ever happened to him?"

"To who?" Lucas Tilly said, looking around with a start as though just waking from sleep.

"Charlie Moon."

"Oh, him. Why hell, Mr. Vapo, not long after little Jewel was birthed right in yonder in that front bedroom, old Charlie was down at Joe Fentry's billiard hall and got drunk and went out back to get sick and nobody thought too much about it because old Charlie was always goin' out to get sick, and they found him next mornin' in the alley, dead as a doornail. It wasn't long then before Temperance run off."

"When was that?"

"Well, lemme see. We heerd about Cap'n Quantrill burnin' Lawrence, Kansas, I remember that. But Papa couldn't take much pleasure from it with Temperance tellin' Papa now that if he ever hit her with that razor strap again she'd shoot him right in the head with this little Remington pistol she'd got somewheres. Papa beat hell out of me, tryin' to get me to find out where Temperance ever got that pistol, but I never did find out."

"But when Temperance ran away. When was that?"

"Who?"

"Temperance. When did she run away?"

"Oh. Temperance. Well, lemme see. I guess little Jewel was about three years old. It was right after the war was over and this circus come through here and they had a tiger cat in a cage and this man who could ride a bicycle on a rope strung over Main Street, up high in the air, you see, and it was the damnedest thing I ever seen. So when that circus left town, Temperance run off with 'em."

"And left the baby here?"

"Why you damn tootin' she did, left little Jewel for us to raise, and that was the most hellish little booger you ever seen. I guess it was tryin' to get along with that child that sent Mama off to an early grave, I don't know, and then Papa come down with a stroke. That was around '78 I think. I don't know for certain. And Papa told me he wanted to see his little girl one more time before he passed to the Lord."

"Wanted to see Temperance."

"Who?"

"Temperance. Your papa's little girl, only she's a woman now."

"Oh yeah, yeah. That's it. So some of the church folks come in to nurse him and I taken out for the Indian Territory again because we'd heard a lot of times about Temperance bein' over there somewheres. And by Gawd, Jewel up and went with me."

"The child."

"Hell, she was the biggest damned child you ever seen. Fifteen, sixteen years old. I don't know. But by Gawd, Mr. Vapo, just like her mother. Do what she damn well pleased. So she come and we went off lookin' for Temperance."

Lucas Tilly took the last sip of whiskey from the china cup and shook his head.

"Good. Good. I like good whiskey, even if Papa always told me what a demon it was," he said.

"Mr. Tilly. Did you find your sister?"

"Oh, yeah. A place called Catoosa. On the Arkansas. Wildest place I ever seen. Temperance was there. Gettin' paid by men to dance with her. I don't know, Mr. Vapo, what else they mighta been payin' her for. But I wouldn't be surprised.

"Temperance never acted like she was overjoyed to see me and Jewel. But Jewel, she taken right into that place. We was only there a couple weeks, me gettin' acquainted and all, you know, and I tell you, them men thought Jewel was the best thang they ever seen, big, healthy girl like she was, and I could see right off that Temperance wasn't too overjoyed with that, either.

"I'd knowed Jewel was like her mama many ways, strong-headed and all. But different, too."

Lucas Tilly lapsed into a slack-jawed, open-eyed sleep, and was brought back to reality with a question.

"How was she different, Mr. Tilly?"

"Huh? Oh! Jewel. She was standoffish. Now Temperance, she

was always handlin' and pawin' anybody come near. Except maybe poor old Charlie Moon. But Jewel, she laughed at 'em and led 'em on and turned 'em away. I figured Temperance was a hot-blood woman. I come to that in Catoosa. And Jewel, mother's child, she was colder than a woodyard wedge in winter."

The jaw dropped again, the eyes became glassy, staring into the fire.

"Catoosa. Mr. Tilly?"

"What? Oh yeah. Catoosa. Wild. Too many Indians and black niggers. Hell, Temperance was married to some man named Hogan Birdsong, a savage of some fashion. I don't know. But I didn't like that place. So. I come on home."

Lucas Tilly paused, still staring into the fire, his eyes looking not at the flames but into some past years, Moses Masada guessed, and the spell broken one more time by the Syrian's voice.

"Did Jewel come with you? Back home?"

Lucas Tilly stared into the fire.

"Who?"

"Jewel. Your niece. Did she come home with you?"

"Her? Hell no. She stayed with her mama. And I don't think Temperance was too overjoyed over that, either. When I got home, Papa was already in the ground. He'd died two days after me and Jewel left for the Indian Territory. God, I hate that Indian Territory."

"So your father never saw his daughter again, after all?"

"No." Lucas Tilly tried to focus his eyes on Moses Masada, but the room was completely dark now and all he could manage was a vacant stare into the fireplace, where it had all gone down to red embers. "I never seen her again."

"Did you see Jewel again?"

"Who?"

"Jewel. Your niece."

"Jewel, my niece. Sure, she sends me money. She bought this place in some Arkansas hill burg, where she could keep her little daughter, send her little daughter to school there. Where nobody knew her. And right off, it got to be a place where friends of my sister would come to lay around on their ass and play cards and not worry about the law."

"Little girl? You said little girl. Who was that?"

"Why, hell. My own beloved little niece her ownself. Jewel sent me a ticket and I went down there to this place and seen her and her daughter, my little niece. She's about six years old now, I reckon. Sweet little thang. Then after me and Jewel talked for a while one night, Jewel give me some money and I come on home. Sweet little niece. Well, you can figure it out, can't you. My grandniece. Never thought I'd have a grandniece."

Lucas lifted the empty sour-mash bottle, shook it, his eyes bulging, then dropped the bottle on the floor. Then spoke once more, now with some tone of tenderness in his voice, so Moses Masada thought.

"Great-uncle Lucas," he said. "Never thought I'd be a great-uncle. That poor little girl. Little bastard. Like her mother. Wonders who her daddy is."

"I had heard that Jewel Moon was married," said Moses Masada.

Lucas Tilly gave a start, a sudden jerk as though surprised that someone else was in the dark room.

"Oh hell, Jewel got married. But that was three or four years after that little girl was born."

"Who'd she marry?"

"Damned if I know. I seen him at Weedy Rough."

"Mr. Tilly, what's that little girl's name? You haven't mentioned it."

Lucas Tilly's eyes, hooded, tried to find the figure of Moses Masada in the dark room.

"Little girl's name? Damned if I can recall."

"Well, there's one other thing, Mr. Tilly," said Moses Masada. "What ever happened to your sister's husband?"

"Which one?"

"The one you met in Catoosa. Hogan something-or-other."

"Oh. Hogan Birdsong. Listen, Mr. Vapo, I used to read the newspaper ever' day. And they was always pieces in the newspaper about that court down in Arkansas where they got this mean judge. And one day I seen that Hogan Birdsong was there and they hanged him for killin' a white man."

"Why, I'd heard Temperance Moon's husband was shot dead during a bank robbery down here in Harrison, Arkansas," said Moses Masada.

Lucas Tilly blinked rapidly. The firelight danced across his face and suddenly he laughed, that cackle, his chest heaving.

"Oh him," Lucas Tilly said. "That was Tom Turtle. Another one of them Gawd damned heathen Indians. He was Temperance's third husband. The one after Birdsong. I think. Hell, I don't know. It's mostly just what I hear around town. Gawd damned Temperance never told me nothin'."

His head drooped. His chin rested on the front of the frayed sweater.

"It sounds as though men who took up with your sister always bought a lot of bad luck," said Moses Masada.

"Yeah," said Lucas Tilly. "I don't give a damn. I'm glad she's dead. I wish it'd happened a long time ago. Before poor ole Papa . . ."

He was asleep.

Before he left, Moses Masada put another chunk of oak on the fire, looked at the fifty dollars still lying on the small table near Lucas Tilly's chair, thought of putting down more, decided against that, and went out into the cold night.

It was a bad walk to the center of town and the Kansas City Southern Railroad depot. But there were thoughts to take his mind off the wind.

This Temperance Moon, even more surely than Oscar Schiller had been able to suggest in his letter, had apparently spent her life jumping into a new bed before the sheets of the last one were cold. And being the police officer that he was, Moses Masada knew that where there was nymphomania you would surely find upset men. And the kind of men with whom Temperance Moon associated, he had come to realize, were not ones it was wise to upset. So he had begun to suspect that half the male population of the Indian Nations might have supposed themselves to have had a motive for blowing her head off.

4 Langston Turtle was a Creek Indian. In his fortieth year running to fat. He didn't care. Sometimes, he had observed, women seemed to enjoy the fact that his breasts were larger than theirs. It was amazing to him that little things frequently added to the excitement of life. Even the blue-and-red design of tattoos on his forearms, which didn't do anything except lie there like colored smoke, and yet a satisfaction and reminder of his heritage.

And now, a man of property! Real property, that had been his family land before he was even born. Now his, unencumbered by the claims of others. Maybe, he thought, he owed it all to Tom, his older brother.

Tom. A slim man. A light-skinned man, so light-skinned that there were those who thought he was not even Creek. Tom, a man full of energy, and a part of that energy running about the countryside showing how wild he could be, and once showing how wild he could be in a place called Harrison, Arkansas, where the white citizens became so incensed about Tom's trying to rob their bank that they shot him dead in the street.

It left an indelible impression on the mind of Langston Turtle. That no matter how wonderful and energetic a man might be, he did not go into Arkansas and try to rob banks. Maybe stealing a few horses in Choctaw Nation or even taking money from an express car on the railroads was acceptable, but one never, never went into Arkansas and exposed himself to that wild bunch of citizens who seemed to enjoy shooting anything that came out of the Indian Nations, whether wolf or crow or chicken hawk or man with tattoos on his arms.

So Tom shot to pieces in the dust of some small hamlet. But that same man, Langston Turtle's brother, married to Temperance Moon. And so, according to Creek law, as Tom Turtle's wife, sharing the real estate with him. And from the moment she came, Tom's wife, with the arrogance to call the place Fawley Farm. In honor of the daddy of her illegitimate daughter. And keeping the name of some long-forgotten husband whose name was Moon, because she took that label to place her out of the regular world, above all the rest around her. Or for some such reason. Even in the teeth of what might have been her husband's opposition.

But audacity, that's what it was, and everybody loved it. Even her husband, Tom Turtle, whose marriage to her had given her legal, Creek-law claim to the land. Because of all the men she knew, they were willing to concede to her what she wanted. The husbands, the lovers, the one-night fornicators taken on the spur of the moment. There was a power in her eyes. There was a witch in her touch. And a man could not resist her, even though, as Langston Turtle freely conceded to himself, there were times when she was as ugly as a mud fence. But even at those times, the magnet of a flame for moths.

He hated her. No! He loved her. No! He did not sense where he stood in relation to Temperance Moon. He knew where he stood in regard to his tattoos. But in regard to Temperance Moon, he did not know. He did know that she had been a great deal more than tattoos.

Well, the Moon had set. The great white queen of Fawley Farm was gone and now this land was Turtle family land again. Not that he felt any escape from slavery. She had always treated him well. In fact, she had come near to pampering him, as one scratches the head of the best hound in the pack more often than the others. Yet Langston Turtle knew he was not the best hound in the pack. Even though he had been in her sexual embrace two or three times. Maybe four, and then when he was drunk and she as well, and it had always lasted for only a short, sweaty time. So he knew her attraction for men. He had felt it himself, in many ways.

His thinking thus always brought to mind Toby Jupiter. Toby Jupiter, brother to Temperance Moon's last husband, the one who stole that horse and rode away to California or some such place.

Dear, stupid Toby, wanting only whiskey and the chance to go fishing when he pleased, and for some reason hating Temperance Moon yet unable to stay away from Fawley Farm, always hanging about, he and the queen screaming obscenities at one another.

To Toby Jupiter, she had not been the queen but rather That Old Bitch.

No doubt but that she was queen to all the others. She called the dance. She was smart. There was always money to hire lawyers when one of the men got himself into trouble with the law, either Creek or in Fort Smith. It was always her with the little plan in the back rooms of her mind that could be brought out when she pleased, little plans for stealing horses or cattle in various places or even plans not so little, not so little because they involved robbing an express car or a crossroads store. Always far distant, in some other part of the Nations.

Sometimes she would ride with the men to fulfill one of these plans. Sometimes not. It didn't matter, because when they returned to Fawley Farm, she took the lion's share of whatever the loot might be. Not against their wills, either. Booty given to her freely. Because they knew she was the queen and called the dance.

Langston Turtle couldn't do that. He knew it, and so did all the men who came to Fawley Farm. But he didn't care. For now the land belonged to him. Turtle family land. Because Temperance Moon was dead.

It made him sad to think about Temperance Moon. She had in many ways been as his own sister might have been, instead of only wife of his brother who was killed in the streets. It made him sad thinking about her dying, even though he always thought in his sadness that she was getting pretty old anyway. Because it made him sad, he tried not to think of her. Instead, he thought about his land, as he did now, on this windy November day, doing something he had seldom done before. Riding about the countryside on a saddle horse. One of Temperance Moon's saddle horses. He loved to look at his land. He wanted often to dismount and touch the earth with his hands but didn't because getting off and on the horse was painfully awkward for a man so fat, so instead of touching the earth with his hands, he touched it only with his eyes.

He rode south, beyond the Turtle property, until he was on a rise of ground above the Canadian, and he paused to look down at the river, which seemed to lie motionless, its surface a mirror reflecting the gray sky, like a trickle of lead or maybe old quicksilver that marked the border between Choctaw and Creek Nations.

To the west, through the bare branches of sycamore and sassafras trees, he could see in the distance the Redstripe farm buildings. A little chill went down his back, and not from the cold wind. Like many people in this place, he was afraid of Candy Redstripe. And of that Comanche kept on Redstripe farm to run those ragged little ponies.

Langston Turtle reined the horse around and started back toward his own place. Soon he had passed across the tilled fields of the Redstripe farm and was back in the thick patches of timber and the old fields gone fallow now and almost lost in tangles of sumac and black locust and persimmon. On his own land now, but the little chills did not stop running up his back. Because he was afraid of Candy Redstripe, even at a distance.

Ꮓ Ꮓ Ꮓ It was a lovely place. Even though the blue-gray color of dawn before the sun came made it appear cold. Deep valley with hills rising sharp in all directions. And the cinder-smell smoke of the locomotive lingering in the still air for a long time, seeming to have the same tint as the bare branches of the hardwoods that stood in closed ranks up each slope. There were even roosters crowing. There was even a dog barking on some far ridge. And goats bleating in the hillside pasture east of town. And from all directions, cowbells clinking with absolutely no sound of urgency but rather a sort of gentle metallic replacement for the stars that had just gone.

No sooner had he stepped down from the southbound passenger train than he wondered why he had always made his way and his home in large cities.

Renting a hack was not difficult in Weedy Rough, even early in the morning, because it was a mountain resort town. Rustic cottage hotels and even a golf course were scattered all along the ridges, all centered on the tiny village through which the Frisco railroad passed and then, within three hundred yards of the depot, disappeared into the tunnel completed in 1884 and thence south to Fort Smith and Paris, Texas, and other wonderful places.

It was not unusual to see young men in city clothes here. What with all those Texas and Louisiana vacationers who came each

year, although November was a little late for such things. But as
the people in Weedy Rough always said, you can't tell what one
of these crazy rich sons of bitches is going to do. Or when one
might show up even on Christmas Eve asking questions about
friends wintering in the hills.

So the young man, dark and charming as he asked directions
while paying for the hack and the old sorrel who pulled it, had
no problem knowing immediately his destination. The long hog-
back ridge looked down into the valley of the town and the railroad track from the west and was therefore known as West
Mountain. And all he needed to know about the road that tra-
versed that ridge was the large house midway along it now called
the Moon place. Which nobody seemed to know much about, except that there was always a bunch of hard-looking men hanging
about there and a little girl who was thoroughly hated by local
little girls because she rode a Shetland pony to school each day
and left it standing in a grove of post oak until school was out
and then rode it home, and both ways with her daddy riding just
behind her on a big horse. And neither one of them saying much
to anybody. Coming or going.

So as he whipped his old sorrel up the winding road he re-
hearsed what needed saying. It didn't take much thought, because
he had done this kind of thing many times. And soon he forgot
the problem of the moment and thought only of trying to control the horse, and congratulating himself that he'd brought
leather gloves, because it was cold.

Inside his coat pocket were all the things he needed, plus his
own initiative, of course. There was the letter identifying him as
Mapon Sample, representative of the Union Fidelity Investment
Company of Des Moines, Iowa, and a thick sheaf of papers folded
into an envelope on the front of which was written, in India ink,
the words "Last Will and Testament of Temperance Tilly."

It made no impression on his sense of morality that there was
no such thing as the Union Fidelity Investment Company, nor
did it bother him that all the pages of foolscap inside the envelope
labeled "Last Will and Testament of Temperance Tilly" were
completely blank.

The Moon place was impressive. As Moses Masada drove
his old horse hack into the wide yard before the two-story shiplap
structure, he could see what appeared to be an apple orchard

immediately adjacent to the yard on the north. Or perhaps it was a peach orchard. Although Moses Masada was an expert on many things, orchards were not one of them.

There were a number of well-tended outbuildings and white-painted wood-slat pens behind the house, and behind that, to the west, the line of a thick stand of oak and hickory timber along ground that fell off sharply into ravines that he knew pointed in the direction of Indian Territory, only twenty miles away.

As he drew to a halt at the front of the large porch, a small girl whom he judged to be about six or seven years old rode round the corner of the building on a Shetland pony with a honey-colored mane. She was dressed in high-quality woolen coat and bonnet with fox-fur trim, beneath which a number of golden-blond curls had escaped and shone in the early-morning sunlight. Her eyes were a clear chocolate brown, and when she drew rein close to the hack and smiled, Mr. Mapon Sample could see a row of tiny white teeth, obviously well scrubbed on a periodic basis.

"Hello," the child said. "Who are you?"

"My name is Mapon," Moses Masada said. "Goodness, that's a fine pony."

"He's Sparrow. That's his name. My mama bought him for me," she said, still smiling, and Moses Masada was touched by the open innocence.

And then coming from behind the house was a man, a rather waspish man with furtive eyes, bundled somewhat outrageously against the chill November with a woolen skullcap and bulky overcoat. The horse he rode was an obvious nag who had seen his better years long ago.

"Come on now, Cassie," the man said. "Have to get to school on time."

Moses Masada could not help but note that the saddle on the Shetland pony was polished leather and along the pommel and fenders were figures of birds done in what looked suspiciously like silver.

"Good-bye, Mr. Mapon," the child said, still smiling, and turned her pony away toward the road. It was impressive that such a tad could remember his name and that she could so completely control the little horse. A lineage of strong blood, Moses Masada thought, being a man who believed in such things.

While all this was happening, Masada was aware that a stout

woman had appeared on the porch, gingham-clad, a rolled back-of-the-head bun of gray hair, and half apron within whose folds she protected her hands from the cold.

"Can I help you, mister?" she asked.

Moses Masada was about to reply when a man on foot came from around the house, a man with the leathery and stubbled face of a farmer and wearing bib overalls. And asked the same question that had been asked by the woman, who Masada assumed was his wife.

Alighting from his hack, Moses Masada stated his case, along with presenting his credentials, all to the effect that certain questions needed answering in regard to the last will and testament of one Temperance Tilly, whose untimely demise had been reported only within the last week in Des Moines, Iowa.

"Well, I'm Noah Pringle, and that's my woman up there, and I might be of some help," he said. "We never knowed Miss Temperance but we have her daughter Miss Jewel for a long time."

Before the end of this speech, Mr. Pringle became very nervous, and Moses Masada supposed it was because a man with a sugarloaf domed hat, a rough woolen poncho, and the hardest black face Masada had ever seen came onto the porch and stood beside Mrs. Pringle. And further, before Moses Masada could reply, the woman turned abruptly and disappeared back into the house.

"Well," said Noah Pringle, "leave us talk a spell."

And he walked toward the apple orchard. Or peach orchard. Or whatever it was. Mr. Pringle seemed to make a studied effort to keep his back turned to the house.

"You say Miss Jewel's mama had a will?" he finally asked.

"Of course."

"Well, I never knew her. But maybe I could help. I know about them probates. I had this brother in Morrilton died and . . ."

"Yes," Moses Masada cut in. "Then you understand."

"I reckon," said Mr. Pringle. "Anyway, me and my woman, Miss Jewel hired us to make a home here for her little girl so she could go to school someplace away from Fort Smith. We ain't really family. But we feel like it."

"I understand," said Moses Masada. Looking back toward the house, he saw that now there were two men on the porch. In what appeared to be animated conversation. And from this distance,

Masada figured that the new man was white, even though the one in the poncho was obviously an Indian.

"Who was the man riding with the child to school?"

"Oh, that was Miss Jewel's husband. Clifford Bacon."

"The child's father."

"No, sir, he ain't. Do we have to get into these kinds of things?"

"Of course not. Then you've known Jewel Moon a long time?"

"Yes, sir. A long time. But we never knowed her mama."

Mr. Pringle looked back toward the house, toward the porch, where the two men were still standing, heads close together. He did it covertly, over a shoulder.

"Mr. Sample, I know its a mite cold standing out here in the wind talkin' about all this," said Noah Pringle. "But we got these two visitors and I'd as leave talk away from them men."

"Some privacy. I understand completely," said Moses Masada. "Are these gentlemen friends of yours?"

Noah Pringle spat and his lips at the corners turned down suddenly, bitter, sour, and Moses Masada suspected that those lips did not usually show such scorn.

"Ever sinct we been up here runnin' this place for Miss Jewel, these men who's friends of her mother come along, tired and dusty and with horses lathered, and just bunk in, like they owned the place. I guess they come up here because it's quiet and peaceful, but we never knowed what they did before they come. It makes me and my woman nervous."

"Have they ever harmed you, Mr. Pringle?"

"No, and they don't even go down into town. But they ain't the kind of people you'd want around a little girl like Miss Jewel's Cassie. And now, with Miss Jewel's mother dead, it looks like they gonna keep comin' up here, like them two. And I'd as leave talk away from them men."

"They're not family, then," said Moses Masada and touched his breast where the blank will rested.

"No, no, no. Of course, me and my woman ain't, either."

"Well, almost, nearly so, with keeping the little girl and all. I see those two gentlemen on the porch keep watching us."

"They always watchin'. My woman, Essie, she says it's about to drive her crazy."

"Strange. What are their names, Mr. Pringle?"

Noah Pringle glanced back over his shoulder toward the house, as though to make sure the two were still there on the porch, heads close together.

"White man's name is Sherman Boggs. He's a businessman in the Territory, got a legal paper from some Kansas court," said Mr. Noah Pringle. "The other one, he claims him and Miss Jewel's mama taken up together after her last husband run off to California. I know all that must break Miss Jewel's heart, such carryin' on. He calls hisself Goshen Crowfoot."

ℵ ℵ ℵ Moses Masada felt a little twitch of sympathy for Noah Pringle. He had seemed a perfectly honest and straightforward man and now was forced to bear imposition on the life of himself and his wife from those two men from the Indian Territory. Whom he obviously disliked and of whom he was afraid, two men who created an atmosphere of danger just by being there, always watching. Perhaps always whispering together. Moses Masada, in just the short hour he'd been on the Moon place, had felt their presence even though neither Sherman Boggs nor Goshen Crowfoot had said a word to him. They had never been close enough to say anything, yet their presence felt like a charge of electricity in blue-black hail clouds. It had been rather pitiful that Noah Pringle had made such an effort to talk well away from those two men.

But now, in the caboose of a southbound freight, Moses Masada put all of that behind him as he made mental notes of what he now knew of the first victim of this double murder Oscar Schiller had initially outlined for him. Moses Masada took pride in making notes only in his head, not on paper, where someone else might see the writing.

He was in the caboose through the foresight of Oscar Schiller. Rather than wait for the next passenger train through Weedy Rough, Moses Masada had used his most ingratiating manner with the depot ticket agent, and a few of Oscar Schiller's railroad passes, to board the first freight train going south after his interview with Noah Pringle on West Mountain. He did not show his Kansas City police badge, not because he was beneath such things but because he wanted no one in Weedy Rough to know that he had any connection with the law. And so he mounted the last car in a freight train that would bring him to Fort Smith in mid-afternoon and sat on one of the rough wooden benches and peered through a soot-streaked window. And thought about all he had learned.

That was with half of his mind. With the other half, he digested the view, once the train had passed through the Weedy Rough tunnel. It was a view of wild splendor even though all the leaves were gone from the hardwoods. It was heavy-timbered country, with sharp slopes and clear-running streams. Until the train finally came into the broad valley of the Arkansas River, some forty miles south of Weedy Rough, it was as wild and pristine as any land Moses Masada had ever seen.

And as Moses Masada watched the passing landscape, gray yet brilliant under a bright sun, he reviewed Oscar Schiller's original letter, his talk with Lucas Tilly, his short time with Noah Pringle, who kept claiming that he knew very little about Miss Jewel's mama yet revealed in his conversation that he knew more than he himself realized. As Moses Masada, being a good police officer, had found was almost always the case; it was just a matter of asking the right questions.

So, he thought. Temperance Tilly. Husbands, lovers, friends, enemies, interchangable as the parts on old Sam Colt's revolvers. Maybe Temperance Tilly recognizing, as old Sam Colt had, the advantages of such an arrangement. Civil War. Fawley. White man. Sired that only child, Jewel, him shot dead. Moon. A white man, too, giving name to a bastard child, but more, giving name to her as well for all the rest of her time because she liked the sound of it. Temperance Moon. Him dead of too much booze.

Hogan Birdsong, a Cherokee maybe, forgotten after he went to the rope, forgotten perhaps before that. Tom Turtle, Creek, important because he gave her those acres in the Nations, which she immediately named Fawley Farm in honor of that first lover. What a fantastic affront to a new husband! Maybe that was why he didn't stay home much, even having given her the land, and once too often going from home to rob a bank, maybe because she wanted him to, and butchered in the street. Shot dead.

Then Styles Jupiter, maybe in her bed before the then current husband was gone, but anyway, he stayed too close, at least to her apparent interest, and finally stole one of her horses and ran, who knew where, and she so glad to be rid of him that she didn't send any of her friends to bring back the horse.

In the chronology of passions, after her last husband, Styles Jupiter, neither Lucas Tilly nor Noah Pringle were too coherent.

There were names tossed off. Like Toby and Langston and Crowfoot. But not much substance. As though Temperance Moon was still legally married, which she was, as though somehow any depredation she might commit after her husband ran off was excused and she could lie in bed with anybody she damn well pleased. Which, of course, she had always done anyway.

And a white man Oscar Schiller had identified in his letter. A certain Sherman Boggs, in the Territory legally on a permit to buy timber for the railroads but who never bought as much as a single stave, according to the Fort Smith marshal, but who was a dealer in whiskey.

And a calm, fat Creek Indian, so Oscar Schiller had said, who with the death of Temperance Moon had come into the property of his family because he was sole survivor of that same old Tom Turtle who had given the farm to Temperance Moon in the first place before he got his ass shot off in Harrison, Arkansas.

Christ, thought Moses Masada, what a wonderful witches' brew.

And he knew the next thing he had to do. Visit this place of business where he could see the daughter of Temperance Tilly Moon. And from Oscar Schiller's letter he knew it was a place called the Commerce Railroad Hotel.

By now he could see through the caboose window that the land was rolling away gently along the valley of the Arkansas River. When the train crossed the bridge at Van Buren, he looked west and could see the low fringe of scrub timber, leafless and gray in the November sun, and knew he was looking into the Indian Territory. It gave him a strange thrill, a soft chill up the spine. He didn't know why.

ℵ ℵ ℵ The same late-afternoon sun that shone on the Frisco freight train where Moses Masada had his first glimpse of the Indian Territory was shining as well on Oscar Schiller as he hurried along Garrison Avenue to his favorite café.

It was a small, unpretentious place between 4th and 5th streets, whitewashed brick front with two tall, narrow windows on either side of a single pine-panel door. Above the door was a sign: "Cantoni's." On one of the windows was a message handwritten in white water-based show-card paint, which meant that each time it rained, the message had to be redone. "Coldest Beer West of

Nashville." On the other window, in the same impermanent medium, "World's Best Baked Beans."

As a matter of fact, both of these rather grandiose claims were close to the truth. The beer was served in half-quart steins buried in shaved ice until placed under the tap. The beans were served in three-cup crocks, in which they were baked as well, with a lot of blackstrap molasses, bacon, and home-brewed tomato sauce.

The place was owned and operated by one Maria Cantoni, widow of Enrico Cantoni, who had been the only known United States Deputy Marshal of Italian extraction in the history of Judge Isaac Parker's court. And who had been killed in a pistol fight at Kosoma, Choctaw Nation, in 1881. Only one of more than fifty of Parker's deputies who had come to a violent end in the Indian Nations.

With the money Enrico Cantoni had saved, plus what a lot of people figured was a considerable donation from Judge Parker himself, Maria had opened this little place, making a living with what she knew best. Feeding people.

Naturally, everybody on Parker's court came there. First from sentiment. But then for the beer and beans. Almost as popular as the beer and beans was the large and lively proprietress, who with almost no encouragement at all would explain her success in a rich contralto voice.

"The beer? Just the usual stuff from Max Bamberger's brewery over on South 4th Street. Only I make it colder. The beans? You start with a peck of dried navies, soak overnight with a five-pound chunk of salt pork and some of my own spices. After that, it's all a secret."

Everybody agreed it was a damned good secret.

So on that late-November day, Oscar Schiller went to Cantoni's. The long, narrow room, with tables along one side, a counter with stools along the other. Since electricity had come, there were two rotary ceiling fans that gently pushed air down to the black-and-white-tile mosaic floor. On the walls were framed lithographs of various steam locomotives pulling brilliantly lighted trains through unknown mountains. And unframed newspaper steel engravings of floods on the river. And *Police Gazette* pages with pictures of prizefighters, each wearing an elaborate championship belt and flannel tights.

Prizefighting was against the law in Arkansas. Except maybe

sometimes on the floor of the state legislature. And a few of the deputy marshals who came to Cantoni's said the reason there was such a law had nothing to do with the brutality of two men trying to knock each other's brains out in the roped square. Rather it had to do with the affront to public decency, having grown men appear in public, in full daylight, wearing nothing but large mustaches and long underwear. Such jokes were usually made after consumption of a number of steins of the coldest beer west of Nashville. And the person who laughed loudest after their telling, although she had heard them a hundred times before, was Maria Cantoni.

Oscar Schiller went to the rearmost table. It being late afternoon but before the supper bean eaters, the place was empty except for Ed behind the counter. Oscar Schiller had hardly settled himself when Maria Cantoni appeared, smelling of garlic, bacon grease, and tomato sauce.

"Well, Oscar," she said, "you still protectin' all them scissors out at Hake's factory?"

"No single pair of scissors has been stolen since I been on the job," he said, and she laughed as only a fat woman named Maria can laugh.

"How many was stole before you went on the job?"

"None," Oscar Schiller said, and Marie Cantoni laughed even louder and slapped him on the shoulder, a thing very few people would think of doing. It was not from disrespect nor because of the fact that Marie Cantoni outweighed Oscar Schiller by perhaps one hundred pounds, but because they were friends.

"Beans on the house, but you pay for the beer," she said.

"No beans now, Maria. I'm on the way over to Max Bamberger's house for kraut and bratwurst," Oscar Schiller said.

"Well, if you insist on poisonin' your gut with all that spoiled cabbage, more's the pity," she shouted, and then spun and swished back through the swinging doors into her den of gurgling pots and kettles. And Oscar Schiller could still hear laughter from the kitchen.

Perhaps fifteen minutes later, as Oscar Schiller finished with the first stein of beer, the man for whom he waited came in from Garrison Avenue. A man who was the archetypical popular image of a federal marshal. Large, sweeping mustache, big hat, khaki pants and jacket, boots, and from beneath the right hem of the jacket, the ivory butt grips of a Colt single-action .45. On the breast of the jacket, the left breast, was a five-pointed metal star larger than a prairie sunflower blossom.

This man had come in response to a note Oscar Schiller had sent to Judge Parker's marshal's office with a dime tip for the newsboy who delivered it, something to be expected in view of the fact that everybody in town knew Oscar Schiller was a man who sent little notes everywhere.

"Howdy, Oscar." The big man sat, easing himself into a chair opposite Oscar Schiller with a loud grunt. "God damned dinky little chairs."

"Hello, Nason," Oscar Schiller said. "Beer?"

"Sure," said Nason Breedlove. "But I ain't got much time. Testifyin' in a little while on a Sapulpa case."

Oscar Schiller raised his hand, and Ed, behind the counter, drew forth a frosted stein and held it under the tap.

"What was it you wanted to jaw about?" asked Nason Breedlove.

"Temperance Moon. Just between you and me."

"All right," Nason said, but nothing more until after Ed had brought the two steins and returned to his post and Nason Breedlove had blown the foam head off his beer and all over the table.

"You want some beans?" Oscar Schiller asked.

"No. I et twice already today. So Temperance Moon, huh?"

"I'd be much obliged."

"Anytime," Nason Breedlove said, taking a long drink and sighing mightily and looking at the white pressed-metal ceiling around the two fans, collecting his thoughts. "Temperance Moon.

"All right. But you know, Oscar, the world's goin' to hell. You heard about that fight in New Orleans in September?"

"John L. Sullivan, knocked out in about twenty-five rounds, or whatever?"

"Yeah. Never thought I'd see it. A little dandy like that God damned Corbett."

"John L.'s getting old, Nason."

"Ain't we all?" He finished his beer and Oscar Schiller raised his hand, and Ed, who was watching, brought two more steins. Once more, only after Ed was back safely behind the counter did Nason Breedlove speak.

"Yeah, Temperance. Eufaula bein' my district, sorta miss the old bitch. Made things interesting, you know what I'm sayin'?"

"Yes. I know what you're saying."

"Saturday. Saturday, September 10, hot as the devil. Kid come in, scared as hell, him and his mama had found the body. Taken us by late day to get there, me and the Creek Light Horse, Moma July, you know him?"

"Yes. Good police officer."

"Yeah, well, there she was. Mud in the road all trampled around, no tracks to do any good. And right in the ditch was the shotgun. Best shotgun you ever seen, Oscar. Hell, you know about it, that Belgian Mr. Courson had for years."

"I never saw it."

"Beautiful piece of work. Ten-gauge, too, and that made it special because them Belgians don't usually make 'em that big. Engraving along the barrels. A double, hammerless. Walnut stock. Beautiful piece of work. We all knowed who it belonged to, so we rode over to Mr. Courson's place and arrested him."

They waited for Ed to bring more beer.

"Clarence Courson been in the Nations over ten years. All legal. Married to a Creek woman. Cattle raiser. And him and his family had went into Eufaula early in that week to sell off some of his spring calves. Like always. Took the wife and kids. Like always. Buy 'em some peppermint ice cream and some boots for the winter. When he come home, his gun had been stole. He reported it to the Creek police the day or maybe two days before Temperance Moon was killed. We arrested him anyway."

"Naturally. You arrest anybody else?"

"I never. But the Creek Light Horse went over to Fawley Farm and arrested everybody in sight. You know how them sonsabitches are?"

"Of course."

"So the whole bunch of us come in here to Fort Smith. Commissioner Bains listened to all of it. The Fawley Farm bunch, they wasn't but three. Langston Turtle and that woman he's been living with at the farm for a long time, she's Goshen Crowfoot's sister, and Goshen Crowfoot, too. That was all they was at Fawley Farm when the Light Horse went.

"So when the commissioner taken the testimony, them three from Fawley Farm said that on the morning Temperance was shot, Toby Jupiter was over there showin' off this good shotgun he had. And it was Mr. Courson's shotgun, and them three said they was fixin' to come in the next day to Eufaula and tell the

Light Horse about it but right then they was fixin' her a birthday cake for when she come home.''

"Come home from where?"

"Lurley place."

"Jeff Lurley, who's in the pen at Moundsville, West Virginia, convicted of armed robbery? In Parker's court?"

"The same. He used to hang out at Fawley Farm all the time. And when he got his ass caught for tryin' to rob that mail car at Oologah, Cherokee Nation, on the Arkansas Valley Railroad, Temperance Moon hired a man to defend him."

"Who lost the case."

"That's right. Parker given him twenty years. And Oscar, they lived on this little ole hardscrabble farm in the Canadian breaks and they had half a dozen kids and them kids woulda starved to death if Temperance didn't go over there ever' Saturday mornin', with a couple sacks of grub. And that's where she'd went on the day she was killed, and comin' home, Toby was waitin' for her.''

"Toby."

"Who else? Hell, everybody knew him and her fought like crows and owls. And all the while, Langston Turtle and them other two makin' a birthday party for her, when she got home. Cake was chocolate."

"Just those three at Fawley Farm that day?"

"That's right. Sherman Boggs, that son of a bitch, they said he was off over here in Arkansas on business. And you know what business. Buyin' up whiskey to carry back and sell in the Territory. So the commissioner listened and done what he had to. Let Mr. Courson go and issued a bench warrant on Toby Jupiter.

"Hell, we got back to Eufaula and found out about the time we got there, that was Tuesday, I guess, that somebody'd found Toby Jupiter's body in that corncrib. Hadn't been dead too long. But long enough to make it messy, you know what I'm sayin'?"

They'd forgotten any more beer. Too involved in the details of their trade.

"Toby," Oscar Schiller said. "I'm interested in this Toby."

"Always hangin' around Temperance Moon's place," said Nason Breedlove. "His older brother, that was Styles Jupiter. Hell, Styles was into Temperance Moon's bed even before her then present husband Tom Turtle was deceased, as they say. Maybe ole Tom was away from Fawley Farm too much to suit Temperance.

And maybe ole Styles was there too much. I expect she was raisin' hell with ole Styles to get off his butt and steal a horse here and there, and I expect she harped at him so much he got a bellyful of it and finally stole a horse. One of her horses, so they say, and taken out for California or Colorado or somewheres.

"So Toby, ole Styles's little brother, was still around. I hear they didn't like one another much and when Toby'd get drunk in Eufaula he was always callin' her 'that hog-fed bitch' and so one day he got drunk, I expect, and stole that Belgian shotgun of Mr. Courson's and shot her with it."

"Well, Langston Turtle gained by it. He got the family land back, didn't he?"

"Aw, hell, Oscar, Langston Turtle never turned a hand to violence. Langston Turtle, he's just a big, fat hog, and was happy with what he had, and why not? Langston Turtle was little brother to the man that made the farm Temperance Moon's, and she was good to him. He never had no cause to shoot her."

"Well, he profited."

"Luck of the draw, Oscar, luck of the draw. Langston Turtle ain't no violent man."

"All right," Oscar Schiller said. "But who killed Toby Jupiter?"

"For Christ's sake, Oscar, that crazy bastard?" Nason Breedlove said. "Only friend he had in the Nations was Mr. Courson. I could name you fifteen people who'd like to stuck a blade in him, if they'd had the nerve."

"But if Courson was such a friend, why would Toby steal his shotgun?"

"Toby was crazy. That beautiful gun. Hell, he could a sold it in Muskogee and went on a two-week drunk in the best whorehouse they got. Temptation, Oscar. Temptation. The root of all evil."

"Yeah."

"I gotta get the hell outa here," said Nason Breedlove. "Thanks for the beer, Oscar. Lemme know I can be of any more help."

As the great lumbering man passed the front of the café he waved at Ed behind the counter.

"See ya, Ed," he shouted. "You still a worthless son of a bitch, you know it?"

At the back table, for a few moments before going to his German friend's for kraut and wurst, Oscar Schiller sat thinking, polishing his eyeglasses with one of Maria Cantoni's paper napkins that she always kept neatly folded in an empty beer stein on each table. And he thought about an expensive Belgian shotgun, left lying near a body.

Is anyone that crazy? Especially when the thing is worth so much money?

Oscar Schiller paid Ed at the crank-handle cash register on the counter near the door and then went out into the late-afternoon golden glare of sunlight along the Avenue. As he paid, Oscar Schiller had said nothing, no banter, no jokes with Ed, whom he had known for as long as Maria Cantoni owned this place. Unlike his large friend Nason Breedlove, Oscar Schiller did not make banter, nor jokes. And Ed understood that. And out on the sidewalk, Oscar Schiller paused a moment to think. Smelling the horse droppings.

And what he thought was that Toby Jupiter had not killed Temperance Moon.

֍ ֍ ֍ Max Bamberger was a typical south German brewmaster. Built along the lines of his beer kegs, quiet, methodical, good citizen, everything about him as solid as those oak casks, as dependable. He stayed out of trouble, and part of that was hard work and another part was Max Bamberger's devotion to, almost worship of, his bachelorhood. He lived in a two-room stone house adjoining his brewery on South 4th Street, in the alley behind, and the place was austere and smelled like the brewery. Like yeast. Like cooking hops. And in November, like fermenting cabbage, because he always had then a couple of five-gallon crocks of brewing sauerkraut in one corner of his kitchen, the crocks covered with cheesecloth, which did absolutely nothing to prevent the gland-constricting smell from permeating the place. He loved the odor of the beer and the kraut. He loved the sweaty rock walls of his kitchen. He loved the few friends he had made in this river town since his arrival on a barge almost thirty years ago with not much else in his pockets than wonderful recipes and forty dollars.

Max Bamberger and Oscar Schiller had been friends for a long time. Both bachelors. Both dedicated craftsmen. Both German. This late-autumn evening was no different from any other when these two met for dinner in Max Bamberger's kitchen. It happened about twice a month. Sometimes more often. Because they enjoyed each other's company. Most especially the gossip they could exchange, because they represented two entirely different segments of the community and neither of them ever finished one of those brewery suppers without having learned something.

The bill of fare that evening was as it always had been. The kraut, of course, heated in a skillet with a little bacon grease and sugar. The handmade bratwurst of lean pork, boiled in beer and then browned in a cast-iron pan above hickory flames. A gigantic loaf of grainy bread in which the beads of rye were as obvious as black ants on a West Texas sandhill. And the beer.

Oscar Schiller ate far too much. As he always did here, and knowing that it would raise hell with his constipation and when once he was returned to Clement Hake's basement room would require a double-barreled dose of Brown's Indian Root Tonic Elixir. But it didn't matter.

When they'd finished, each pushed back from the table and sighed. And Oscar Schiller produced what he always had. Two cigars. Fat as one of Judge Parker's hanging ropes, longer than the barrel on Oscar Schiller's pistol. Rolled in Havana, Cuba. Or some such place. Purchased at Paley's Tobacconist, where on the sidewalk in front was a six-foot carved wooden Indian. And from which there always issued into the street an aroma of rum and maple. Cigars. Each costing the astonishing price of a quarter. And with a band of gold and red and imprinted thereon a bumblebee, in black ink. And it was the fashion in that time and place among cigar smokers never, never to remove the band. But only as the gray, hot ash came close to slip it up closer to the mouth. So they smoked.

The room now smelled of more than beer and kraut. It smelled of the blue cigar smoke. All of which seemed to blend well together. As did their conversation.

How many were in last Sunday's congregation at the Lutheran church, and how many new faces. The terrible traffic on Garrison Avenue where on Saturday afternoon every known wheeled vehicle was being pulled about by mules or horses and not nearly enough city street sweepers with their shovels and brooms and buckets to get up the shit. The wretched state of the city's water system, all coming as it did from wells or the Poteau River so that Max Bamberger had to carry spring water in by wagon from the hills north of Van Buren to make his beer. And all those other things that good citizens discuss.

By the time they had been required to move the cigar bands a little closer to their mouths, Oscar Schiller said, "Max, you've got a lot of friends among the Jews. Haven't you?"

"Of course. So many of them from the old country. But now, others. From Spain. And from Russia. The ones from Russia have a hard time. The language is so different."

"They are a good people."

"Yes. But they never eat my bratwurst."

They both laughed. Oscar Schiller perhaps laughed more here than in any other place.

Now Oscar Schiller placed his cigar on the edge of the table, took a small bottle and a stick match from an inside jacket pocket, and went through his usual performance when requiring a small taste of cocaine. Max Bamberger, who had known of this habit for years and had no objection to it, watched with mild amusement.

Seeming much satisfied with the effect of the drug, Oscar Schiller reclaimed his cigar and returned to the Jewish friends of Max Bamberger.

"They are a wise people," said Oscar Schiller.

"As wise as they must be."

"In making money."

"Of course, in that most especially, Oscar, for centuries, because it has always been so."

"Yes," said Oscar Schiller, puffing his cigar. Moving the band a little closer toward the end. "Max, tell me. Jews are very pious people."

"Of course," Max said. "Aren't we all. To our own gods. They to theirs. Very strongly."

"But no matter how pious, they might invest in a house of ill fame."

Max Bamberger threw his hands up and laughed, a great, uninhibited laugh which came seldom to him. Then slapped his hands on his own rough table.

"House of ill fame?" he said. "Oscar, you hound dog. You sly hound dog, you know it's true. My old and dear friend, Abram Jacobson. You knew."

"No, no, Abram Jacobson, the pawnbroker?"

"And owner of the best jewelry store in this town. And owner of rent houses on the south side. Oscar, don't try to make me believe you, a police officer, don't know such things."

"Well, I just wondered what you thought about it. I mean, the whore business."

"Aw," said Max Bamberger and threw his hands up and did not laugh this time, but became very serious. "Oscar. Ten years ago. No. Eight. Abe comes to me and we talk about it and I told him, do what your ledger book says, remember, this is a new country. So he did."

"Bought into the Row?"

"No, no, no, no, no," Max Bamberger said, waving his hands. "Oscar, you never in all our years told me how crazy you are. Into the Row? No, no, no. Into only the best of it."

"The Commerce Hotel?"

"Of course!"

"How do you know it's the best, you old stag?"

They laughed, and Max Bamberger slapped the table again.

"Only what I hear, Oscar, only what I hear. But listen. Abe has made a few dollars there."

"He built it all, then. I never knew."

Max Bamberger exploded with a burst of German, beer-sprayed laughter. And pounded his hands on the table.

"You *Kind*," he said, laughing. "No, no, no. Abe only a little. Somebody else as well."

"Who?"

"Oscar, I don't know," said Max Bamberger, lifting his hands and shrugging elaborately. "Who is other money? Where is other money?"

"It would be interesting to know," said Oscar Schiller.

"Whoever it is, Oscar, he is no longer my friend's partner," Max Bamberger said. "Only a week ago, he sold his share to Abram Jacobson. For a lot of money."

"Likely an attack of conscience."

"Likely. All these years afraid someone will discover he is an absentee pimp, and him each day acting the good citizen."

"How do you know he's a good citizen?"

"A guess, Oscar. Only a guess. It is mostly the good citizens who have the money, isn't it, the ones who sit in the front pews at church."

"Well," said Oscar Schiller, "apparently your friend Abram Jacobson has had no such attack."

"No, no, no, Oscar," said Max Bamberger. "Abram Jacobson is a good businessman and he considers it the marketing of a commodity which is in demand and will always be, no matter who sits in the front pew of the churches."

They went to other topics. Casually. The upcoming inauguration of Grover Cleveland for his second term in the presidency. The new poll tax expected to be made law in the state within the next session of the legislature. The honor of having the governor of Arkansas, named Fishback, from right here in Fort Smith.

Then, as Max Bamberger was discussing the repudiation of state bonds that had been issued for establishing a real estate bank that had failed, Oscar Schiller became acutely aware of some sound from the alley outside the window. Perhaps not even a sound, but something that touched his instinct as a longtime peace officer, sending an electric charge along his spine. And then from the window behind Max Bamberger's back, a glint of light, a reflection.

Oscar Schiller dived forward, sweeping the kerosene lamp off the table and in the same movement enclosing Max Bamberger in his arms and carrying the startled and gasping brewmaster to the floor as the shots came, and liquid fire from the lamp spilling across the table, and the sound of shattering glass, and the flash of yellow-white light from the window.

"What, what, what?" Max Bamberger was screaming as Oscar Schiller scrambled like a crab along the floor to the wall and then reached for the peg where the holster harness and pistol hung, yanked the big Colt free of the leather, leaped to the door, and burst into the alley, gun up and cocked. And there was nothing there. He ran to the street and almost into a flood of people, men and women, just out from the Grand Opera House, where had been playing *Our American Cousin*, a terrible comedy but very popular since 1865, when it had run that night in Washington City's Ford Theatre. Carriages and bonnets and somewhere the sound of children shooting off firecrackers in anticipation of the coming Christmas season, and dogs barking, and urchins selling late editions of the *Fort Smith Elevator*, and pushcart vendors hawking their hot tamales to the theater crowd, and in sight along this street two Fort Smith policemen in their beehive helmets.

When Oscar Schiller came back into Max Bamberger's kitchen, there was light, because Max had started another lamp, but there was a new smell, a burning-cloth smell.

"Oh, God, Oscar," Max Bamberger shouted. "Snuffed out the fire with your duster. I'm so sorry, I'm so sorry."

"Stop yelling, Max, it's all right," said Oscar Schiller and was aware of yet a more pronounced smell of kraut and then saw that a bullet coming through the window had struck one of the brewing pots and now there was fermenting cabbage oozing out across the floor like a gray flood.

"My kraut," Max Bamberger shouted, the tears beginning to run down his cheeks. "They shot my kraut, they shot my kraut!"

Oscar Schiller was already on his knees, on the floor, both hands feeling through the liquid mess, because only the front side of this crock had been broken, which meant there was a bullet somewhere in the cabbage shreds, and he found it. Hands dripping, but lifting it out, a gray slug, and then rising and going to Max Bamberger's sink and turning on the faucet and washing all residue away and slipping the bullet into a pants pocket as though afraid his friend might see it before it was hidden.

"My kraut, look what they did to my kraut," Max Bamberger cried. "Why they want to shoot my kraut?"

"Oh, for Christ's sake, Max, they weren't after your God damned kraut," Oscar Schiller said with exasperation. "They were after me."

፼ ፼ ፼   Oscar Schiller rushed along the sidewalks of the city toward the basement of the Sebastian County courthouse, having patted his friend Max Bamberger on the shoulder only once before running out. Max Bamberger still weeping and staring at his kraut-covered kitchen floor. On South 7th Street, Oscar Schiller went down the short steps under the sign that indicated "County Coroner." And burst into the door.

Dr. Lyland Kroun, in a blood-and-excrement-smeared white smock, looked up from his metal examining table, his eyes as wide and blue as Oscar Schiller's and his eyeglasses equally thick.

"Jesus Christ, you don't knock, do you?" he said.

"In a hurry, Doc," said Oscar Schiller, and looked carefully to see that they were alone.

The place smelled of old blood, ammonia, and formaldehyde. Everything was metal and white, the shelves along the walls, the medicine cabinets, the high-pressure kerosene lamp hanging at the center of the room, and under it the table shaped like a shallow watering trough with a hole at one end. On the floor beneath the hole was a large bucket, and it was mostly full of human entrails.

On the table, face up, was a gray-blue cadaver, body opened from breastbone to pelvis and all the gaping cavity now empty.

"Who's that?" Oscar Schiller asked.

"How the hell do I know?" Dr. Kroun said. "White male, about fifty years old. They drug him out of the Poteau River a few hours ago and now there's two young deputy sheriffs upstairs waiting for me to tell them how long he's been dead and how he came to this unfortunate end. What's that you got, a bullet?"

"Yes," said Oscar Schiller, placing the slug in Dr. Kroun's wet hand. "I think it's a .41 but I need to be sure."

"I'd say you're right," Dr. Kroun said, moving to one of the tables along the wall where there were beakers and bottles and shining metal instruments. He took up a pair of delicate calipers. "Little flat on the nose. Whose belly you take this out of, Oscar?"

"Nobody's. Took it out of a crock of kraut."

Dr. Kroun's eyebrows lifted for a moment, but it was the only surprise he showed. In his line of work, there were no real surprises left.

"This official work, or recreation?" he asked.

"I don't work for Parker anymore."

"A long story goes with it, I expect."

"That's right," Oscar Schiller said, and nothing more, so Dr. Kroun applied the calipers to the bullet.

"Base measures point four one inches."

"Christ, there must be seven hundred .41 caliber pistols in this town."

"Yes, of all makes and fashions," the doctor said and measured the length. "A little hard to tell, with that nose flattened somewhat. But I'd say this slug was no longer than ten millimeters before it hit that kraut. Little less than half an inch. I'd say a derringer is your best bet."

"What I figured," said Oscar Schiller. He took the bullet from Dr. Kroun's still greasy hand and from an inside jacket pocket produced the last of the Havana-wrapped cigars with fancy band. "Have a smoke, Doc. It might cut the fresh-gut smell in this place."

"By God, Oscar, I wish all my customers were as generous as this. Got a match?"

"It just happens that I do."

5 Langston Turtle sat in what had been Temperance Moon's bedroom at Fawley Farm. Her presence was as real as the cold air; no fire had been set in the small cast-iron stove at one corner. There were her beads, hanging from one curved arm of the dresser's mirror support. Her soft leather split skirt, because in recent years she had sometimes taken to riding astride instead of sidesaddle. But still in one corner, two fine sidesaddles as well, one with a pistol holster laced into the pommel. A number of hats, each with its own distinctive flow of ostrich plumes. A row of highly polished boots, dainty and with pointed toes. A riding crop, a bag of sachet powder on the door of a wall closet, and on a shelf a number of bottles containing perfume and talcum powder.

And a rack for rifles and shotguns, set in the wall immediately beside the large bed.

Langston Turtle was cleaning one of Temperance Moon's rifles, a Savage .303 lever-action, a weapon that had never been fired, a gun she called a sporting piece, and one she had brought from Fort Smith on her last visit there about two weeks before she died.

The rifle didn't need cleaning. Nor did any of the other weapons in Temperance Moon's rack, because she had always taken great care with them. But over the past few days, Langston Turtle had been cleaning them all, furiously, attacking them with oil and cloth. Because it gave him something to do with his hands while his mind was racing.

And he hated this particular gun, this Savage with the long, slender lines. Because it represented that last trip to Fort Smith, the purpose of which was to borrow money to open a dance hall in Eufaula. The kind of dance hall where Temperance Moon had first learned the excitement of the Indian Territory just after the war, in Cherokee Nation, at Catoosa, a place about which she had constantly talked in her last days, like an old soldier talking about his youthful battles.

From the first, he had hated the whole idea. Temperance Moon operating a dance hall, in Eufaula or anywhere else, threatened his life. His easy life. There on the farm of his sister-in-law, with a good woman of his own. No worry about meat for the supper table. No concern about making money in the white man's world. A little fun now and again planning for the theft of a few horses someplace in Choctaw Nation. But that kind of fun always with the approval of Temperance Moon.

Since the time of his brother's marriage to her, and maybe even more after Tom Turtle's death, she had treated him like a prince, a prince sitting near the queen, who because he was a prince had no worries about an empty belly or a cold and lonely bed. She gave him money, too. Most of the men who came to spend various times at Fawley Farm teased him about being the fat favorite of the queen, but none of them abused him. They recognized there was a warm and personal feeling between this hard-lipped woman and this lazy Creek brother-in-law. Why, a few times she had even welcomed him into her bed, after Tom Turtle was dead and before the Crowfoots came, Goshen and his widowed sister Winona.

Then, like the gears on a white man's threshing machine meshing, Goshen had become Temperance Moon's man and his sister had become Langston Turtle's woman. Which made the bond between fat prince and hard-eyed queen even more binding.

The very idea of that dance hall and Temperance Moon becoming concerned with things other than Fawley Farm and its rough and easy life had started a little minnow of uncertainty in Langston Turtle's brain, and the minnow had grown into an Arkansas River alligator gar that ate everything in sight. It was then that Langston Turtle began for the first time to realize that he was nothing but a squatter on land that had been his own people's since the Removals.

So the Savage rifle that he cleaned represented something he sensed had been set in motion which would destroy Fawley Farm as he had known it. Would destroy the full belly. Maybe even destroy the woman he had in his bed each night, she of soft crooning Creek voice and tender hands, who because she had been incapable of bearing children to receive her love had overflowed Langston Turtle with that love, making him the child of all her girlhood fantasies of motherhood.

Somehow, some way, a business enterprise in Eufaula would shatter all of that, so he thought, and viciously he rubbed the deep-steel-blued barrel of the rifle and ground his teeth and thought that maybe even a dance hall for Temperance would have been better than what now was. Fawley Farm empty, except for him and Winona. The Creek Light Horse Police always nosing about now. Fawley Farm, no longer a place of men laughing, playing cards, drinking whiskey, lying with the women they brought with them or found there on arrival. And planning little robberies. And sitting along the east walls of the house in summer, smoking, and listening to the mockingbirds in the pecan groves. No longer a warm fire in winter and friends around a table, telling stories of thwarting federal police officers in that robbery of a baggage car near Kiowa, Choctaw Nation, or foxing the Indian police in the theft of two prize bulls from a farm near Mingo, Cherokee Nation, and best of all, men who had claimed to be there, in Okmulgee, the night Creek outlaws shot to death a United States Deputy Marshal from Judge Parker's court. A man, that marshal, whose mother had been a black African slave of the Creeks, a long time ago.

He could recall summers at Fawley Farm when he and his woman, just after she had come to him, had gone out with half-gallon syrup pails and collected wild huckleberries and brought them back to be eaten with a lot of sugar and thick milk from a goat somebody had stolen from the head rector of the Emahaka Academy for Boys in Seminole Nation.

Now, with everything that had happened, only he and Winona were at Fawley Farm. He expected Goshen Crowfoot soon, and Sherman Boggs, but he wasn't looking forward to it. He didn't trust them now, because of what they might say to some law enforcement man. He no longer trusted Winona. He no longer trusted himself. For a little while, he stopped drinking whiskey so his thinking would not be muddled. But that made everything worse.

He rubbed the Savage rifle furiously with the oily rag. It was true. He didn't even trust himself. And in his loneliness, now unable to confide in anybody, Langston Turtle often saw at the rear of his mind a thick rope, a loop with thirteen coils. He tried desperately to recall what everyone had said that day when the law took them into Fort Smith to appear before the commissioner just after Temperance Moon was shot. Sworn there to the truth, but many things were said that were not true. He tried to remember, so that when someone asked him again, his words would be the same.

He came to the awful realization that once a little lie is uttered, it becomes as hard as smoke to catch again. As hard to recapture as time itself. It frightened him very badly.

And the damned crows in this dreadful winter. Always making their screeching racket in the timber near the house. Crows had never bothered him before. But now they seemed to make a harsh and strident sound that was brutal as the squeaking hinges on the gallows in Fort Smith.

Nothing such as these thoughts had ever entered his head before. Before he had the responsibility of owning land. When strong men were about, laughing and drinking and whoring. When a night's sleep was undisturbed by wicked images. When Temperance Moon was still alive.

಼ ಼ ಼ When Moses Masada first looked upon Tishacomsie Redstripe, a great many things in his life came to an end. Or started. It took some time of rational introspection for him to adjust to this, but having been since his Detroit sidewalk boyhood days adept at rational soul-searching, it all came. And standing well away from himself and examining details as though they were nothing more than elements in an intricate criminal case, he did not dispute the findings. Even though much of it was very disturbing.

Moses Masada had never believed in love at first sight, as some of the novels he had read indicated was a fact of human chemistry. But when he first looked into the depthless black eyes of Tish Redstripe, he knew he had been all these years a victim of cynicism. Being more than an average student of his own heritage, he began to understand the reasons some of his ancient forebears might have placed at the head of their harems a captive Persian or Israelite or Egyptian woman who if by nothing more than the slant of her cheekbones proclaimed her royalty.

Next, he had never, even with many opportunities, entertained the idea of making a husband cuckold. But looking at Tishacomsie, husbands and all former moral barriers became insignificant.

And next, and worst of all, from the first moment, Moses Masada had liked this woman's husband. If only he had been a vicious, unclean, foul-mouthed bastard! But he wasn't.

It was an unseasonably warm day for early December in the Territory. There was bright sun from a cloudless sky, and the usual west wind lay dormant, at least for a while. Moses Masada rented a hack, with accompanying mule, from a livery barn in Eufaula just at noon and began the trek, a leisurely one, along the road that marked the north bank of the Canadian River directly past the Redstripe farm. It was the kind of late-fall day in which Moses Masada could imagine he smelled the elm leaves burning along the curbs of various cities he had known, but here in the open prairie, nobody bothered to burn leaves. Although along sheltered gullies and behind winding rock walls, there were plenty of leaves to burn, had anybody been so inclined.

En route, he observed what he already had in this country, the rich brown texture of the loam in the cultivated fields where summer's dead cornstalks had been pulled up and carted away for hogs' cold-weather silage, and winter wheat planted in its stead. On some of the fields were red-winged blackbirds finding a few seeds not covered. By now he knew that this rich farmland was the norm between the forks of the Canadian.

There was much of it not under cultivation, wooded as it had been perhaps for centuries past, and Moses Masada tried to catalogue the trees as the mule took his own gait along the river track. The cedars were easy, because they were the only pinpoints of green in a gray land, even under sunlight. But identifying the bare-branch hardwoods was much more difficult. Here there were not the heavy stands of massive oak and walnut he had seen in the Ozarks, but certainly a profusion of smaller timber. Hornbeam and persimmon. Sassafras and sweet gum. Mulberry and river birch.

He rode constantly in sight of at least one Cooper or redtail hawk. For it was the best time of year for their hunting now that the ground cover had been cleared from the fields so that mice foraging for a winter hoard of grain among last summer's barren furrows fell easy victim to the talons.

Moses Masada thought it all an appropriate facade of peace and tranquillity that hid a violence beneath. Like this whole land. Hawks and men the same, looking for mice.

For this country, where farm buildings ran much to logs with mud chinking, the Redstripe house was impressive. Rough clapboard with real glass windows, it had had a summer bath of whitewash and gleamed in the sun at the center of a scattered grove of young pecan trees, all on a rise of ground that looked down on the river perhaps a rifle shot away. The outbuildings, a barn and two small sheds, were of log, but even these had received a splash of whitewash. Only the snake-rail fences around the backside of the place were of naked wood, mostly locust with the bark peeling off now and hanging like Spanish moss on Old South live oaks.

Like other dwellings he'd seen in the Creek Nation, this one had a porch that ran the length of the front. And as the hack drew near, a man appeared there, slender and looking like a deacon of some church in his dark pants and vest and white shirt and narrow-brimmed black hat. And from one of the sheds came a small man, squat, bowlegged, who did not look like the deacon of anything, and he came up quickly to stand at one corner of the house as Moses Masada drew in the reins on the mule.

"Mr. Redstripe?" he asked.

"The same," said the man on the porch, and Moses Masada suspected a smile beginning at the corners of the wide mouth. There was no evidence of a smile on the moon-shaped, dark face of the man standing at the end of the porch by now. But seeming to sense the tension, Candy Redstripe added, "And this is my horse handler, Toad. From the area of Fort Sill."

"I've been asked to say that Oscar sent me," said Moses Masada.

"Yes," said Candy Redstripe, with no surprise showing on his face. "I knew you'd come."

It was at that moment that Tishacomsie came onto the porch to stand beside her husband. Her hair was loose, and long, not like her husband's close-cropped head. It flowed, thought Moses Masada, like the black water of all life's mystery across her shoulders. She stared at him boldly, and smiled.

"We'd heard you were as far as Eufaula," she said. "And wondered when you'd come a few miles further."

"I had supposed," said Moses Masada, now with his bowler hat in his hand, "that my identity had not been so well advertised."

"Not your identity," said Candy Redstripe. "But your hat. When we heard a man was in Eufaula with that hat, we knew it could only be the man from Oscar."

They all laughed. Easily. Except for the Comanche at the edge of the porch, and now, with the laughter, he turned and disappeared.

"Come down from your wagon." Tish said.

"This is Tishacomsie, my wife," said Candy Redstripe. "On this place what she says is law."

And so Moses Masada entered that house for the first time, struck by the beauty of both host and hostess, and most struck by the constriction in his throat when Tishacomsie looked at him and smiled. Which she did often.

And was invited for supper and to stay the night, and before bedtime he explained in great detail his mission for Oscar Schiller and what he had been doing in Creek Nation for the past week.

₪ ₪ ₪ Moses Masada had come to Fort Smith and spent the first night in the Commerce Railroad Hotel, where he was amazed at the decorum and atmosphere of gentle breeding that were the hallmark of the first floor in this most exquisite brothel. He had expected the rough kind of house typical of the old frontier where the ladies sat along one wall on a wooden bench and were selected by men pointing a finger, as though buying lard hogs in a stock pen. Moses Masada had been in Victorian parlors where the ladies flirted more brazenly than they did in Miss Jewel Moon's place.

And Miss Jewel Moon. He observed her from afar, as Lot's horse had observed something or other. Well, he thought it was Lot's horse, but it didn't matter now, his superficial knowledge of the Old Testament. What mattered now was seeing Miss Jewel Moon in her element. She wore a snow-white dress and her hair was piled high on her large head, exposing ears where there were pearls at the lobes, in the fashion of her mother, so he had been told.

The only conversation between them was when Miss Jewel informed him, after his second seltzer water at the bar, that he'd have to check his pistol, and he was amazed that anyone had detected it there beneath his left arm and even more amazed when

Miss Jewel Moon saw it and said, "Don't see many of those around here. Webley. A .45 caliber. You can pick it up when you leave, sir. Enjoy yourself."

Moses Masada had selected his lady of the evening only after long inspection, trying to find one who had been in Miss Jewel's employ for some time, because such a one might tell him things while in sweaty embrace. Actually, he chose the latest Natasha, who knew nothing except how to do her job and was herself amazed at this customer because he was one of few men she had known who were circumcised and also wanted to kiss on the mouth before getting down to the more serious business. Moses Masada was a little embarrassed about both of these things, because in the first instance his father had decided on the genital surgery for other than religious grounds and it seemed to mark his son for the rest of his life as a Jew, and the other because even in bed with a professional lover a tenderness flooded over him which made him want to give it at least an appearance of actual love.

The next morning, to Oscar Schiller's basement hovel, which was not hard to find for anyone knowing how to ask discreet questions. He discovered the former deputy marshal brooding over a .41 caliber bullet. There followed an exchange of information, the kind of thing two peace officers always did when they were working the same case. Moses Masada had some satisfaction on discovering that he knew more about Temperance Moon than did Oscar Schiller. Which irritated Oscar Schiller, who said, "I never handled any of the cases against her."

They decided that Moses Masada's last disguise, as the Iowa man named Sample with a Temperance Moon will, was best continued in Indian Territory, because Moses Masada had been seen at the Moon place in Weedy Rough by two men, Goshen Crowfoot and Sherman Boggs, whom he would likely see again.

Still, Oscar Schiller said, Moses Masada would have made a wonderful Mohawk.

But admitted that Mohawks, scarce as they might be west of Fort Smith, would likely know a great deal about riding saddle horses and this was not one of Moses Masada's great talents. So any Creek or Choctaw or other Indian in the Nations would quickly be aware of this shortcoming and suspect subterfuge. So it was best, they decided, for Moses Masada to claim to be only what he was, a city white man.

So into Creek Nation along the Arkansas Valley Railroad to

Wagoner and then change to the Missouri, Kansas, and Texas to Eufaula, bowler hat, Yankee suitcase, button shoes, and all, to impose on the people of that town and environs the fiction that here was a man in possession of knowledge about their most illustrious and infamous person, discounting those, of course, who had been hanged on the gallows at Fort Smith. Anyone with such knowledge could not help but raise the hackles of curiosity among those who thought they might profit and all the others whose self-interest was confined to little bits and pieces for the gossip mill.

United States Deputy Marshal Nason Breedlove, whose district this was and who could not resist helping his old friend Oscar Schiller in whatever endeavor, let drop a few hints that a man with an important Temperance Moon document was arriving. And so when Moses Masada did arrive, in his bowler hat and button shoes and Yankee wicker suitcase, proclaiming himself Mr. Mapon Sample of Iowa, everybody thought it was wonderful.

"Why that poor big-city son of a bitch can't even hardly sit a horse without hangin' on the horn of the saddle," they said. Which was true.

"He's such a nice man," they said. Which was not necessarily true.

So in this town of Eufaula, a town of five hundred souls, Moses Masada Mapon Sample found rooming at the KATY section foreman's house, a most imposing building, recently occupied by Mr. Curtis Danton, sent down from Fort Scott, Kansas, to take up where Mr. Robert Clark, the last section foreman, had left off, and Mr. Clark had left off the night he attempted to do carnal things to Tishacomsie Redstripe and was caught by her husband. All in the records of the United States Commissioner's court in Fort Smith.

Mr. Sample everybody called Moses Masada, and tipped their hats and talked with him. Maybe thinking that old Temperance Moon had been richer than they thought and that there might be a few pennies here and there, particularly for those citizens who had never, never appeared in Fort Smith or Okmulgee to explain how old Temperance Moon often violated the statutes of the United States of America or the Constitution of the Creek Nation.

Of course, most people of the Eufaula Creek District had never tattled on old Temperance. Because they always figured what she did was none of their business. Or maybe more important, they knew that if they did tattle they'd get their heads blown off.

Hell, Oscar Schiller said, that will business was like having aces back to back in a five-card-stud game. And it was, too.

But on that night at Candy Redstripe's, Moses Masada had to admit that although the last-will-and-testament ploy appeared to be accepted by everybody, it wasn't producing any information. Everybody seemed convinced that Toby Jupiter had killed the old bitch and Toby had been dispatched by some unknown drunken associate. And Candy and Tishacomsie Redstripe agreed, saying they'd told Oscar Schiller he was wasting Jewel Moon's money on a wild goose chase, their having assumed that the money for all this was coming right out of the Commerce Railroad Hotel on the Row in Fort Smith.

"As for Toby," Candy Redstripe said, "he ran with a crowd of men who could get into a killing fury just over the color of a man's shirt."

So that night, lying in a Redstripe bed, Moses Masada began to think that maybe all these people were right. That the finding from Commissioner Claude Bain's hearing was as close as anyone would ever come to the truth. That it was just another case of two almost casual killings in the Territory brought about by passion and whiskey. Mindless and hair-triggered. The only difference being that instead of the victims being two unimportant, shiftless hooligans, one happened to have been an infamous white woman whose name had appeared in newspapers as far removed as Little Rock and Joplin.

But he fell asleep remembering what Oscar Schiller had told him: "There's some kittens in this ball of twine. And they may be full-grown tomcats. And they may be tigers!"

₪ ₪ ₪ Moses Masada didn't know what time it was when he woke. He was wakened by the cold. There was the sound of wind howling under the porch roof like a runaway freight train through the tunnel at Weedy Rough. And the sound of the pecan branches rubbing violently together in the gale. He'd heard of these sudden changes of weather here on the lip of the High Plains, and now under a single blanket that had seemed more than adequate when he first lay to rest he was so cold that he considered rising and putting on all his clothes and then coming back under cover to try sleep once more.

He was hardly awake when he saw the orange lamplight at his

door that opened into the kitchen. It grew brighter and closer, and he slipped the Webley revolver from beneath his pillow and held it concealed under the blanket.

It was Tishacomsie. She stood for a moment in the doorway, the lamp in one hand, a folded comforter quilt in the other. She was wearing a long-sleeved flannel nightgown that covered her from throat to ankles but did nothing to hide the round contours of her body in the golden glow of the kerosene wick. Her hair hung over her shoulders and her eyes were bright, as though perhaps she had been awake a long time.

She moved into the room, bringing the light with her, all as silently as the sun's ray coming through a window at morning. She came beside the bed and stopped, and saw that Moses Masada was awake.

"It's getting cold," she said. "I brought more covers."

Moses Masada had no sense of time. It might have been only seconds that Tishacomsie stood there, it might have been minutes, she looking down into his face. Then she placed the lamp on a small bedside table and opened the folded quilt and spread it over him, and in her doing it he felt her hands along his legs and watched the fluid motions of her body under the gown.

"Thank you," he said.

Once more, before taking up the lamp, she stood beside his bed looking at him, her eyes gleaming. For perhaps half a minute. Then she was gone, the light with her, and he lay in the dark hearing the wind, shivering, but not from the wind. It was only after a long time that he realized he still gripped the pistol in a sweaty hand.

"Jesus Christ," he said aloud.

₪ ₪ ₪   In the room at the far side of the Redstripe farmhouse, the lamp now blown out, Tishacomsie slid into bed beside her husband and felt he was awake, because she knew from long experience that anytime she rose from this bed, he would waken.

"This is a dangerous time," she whispered.

He laughed softly, and his hands were on her under the flannel gown.

"All times are dangerous," he said.

"No. No. This time. He's Oscar Schiller's man," she said. "And we heard that thing, we heard that Oscar was almost killed. Shot at. In Fort Smith."

"Fort Smith is a dangerous town," he whispered, his hands exploring under the flannel nightgown.

"Listen, he is Oscar Schiller's man," she said. "It's all so dangerous."

"No," he said, now his hands and his body exploring all the way. "Just keep him close, to see what he does, that's the best."

"Candy, he's a nice man," she said. But making no move to avoid his hands or his body. "I don't want to see him hurt."

For a moment, just a moment, Candy Redstripe paused. Breathing heavily. His hands still on her body. Then spoke.

"I promise you, he will not be hurt."

"It's all so bad," she whispered.

"Yes," he said. "The things Oscar Schiller deals in are always bad. For somebody."

役 役 役 When the dawn came with blustering cold, Candy Redstripe opined it was a good time to sit by the fire and play checkers and drink the dark, bitter coffee that came from his wife's pot. But Moses Masada said he had procrastinated long enough and must now visit Fawley Farm. Suddenly, Candy Redstripe's face went rock-hard and his eyes shone with a hot light Moses Masada had never seen before.

"Not alone, you don't," he said.

"Grub first," said Tishacomsie and like her husband, she looked at him from a face from which everything soft had gone.

It was one of those breakfasts Moses Masada had come to expect in this country. Heavy as a railroad spike and equally indigestible. Fried pork and white gravy and eggs and biscuits and hominy. The Comanche Toad came to eat with them, saying nothing, glaring at Moses Masada when he thought Moses Masada was not looking, finishing quickly the meat and eggs, leaving all the rest, and going out.

"Blanket-ass savage," said Candy Redstripe after Toad had gone, yet with the tone of real affection in his voice.

"Yes," said Tishacomsie, "and knows more about horses than you and all your ancestors."

"And more than yours, too," Candy said. "He thinks all of us in the Nations are just another brand of white man."

And they all laughed. As they had the night before. This, their first laugh of the day. And it would be their last. But it was a suddenly delightful thing to Moses Masada that they had included him in what was obviously an Indian joke.

The wind had moved a great mass of gray cloud cover over the land. What had been only twenty-four hours before a brilliant terrain was now dull and colorless. Black birds in flight were whipped along in the gusts of air like cinders above a raging, heatless flame. The husks of summer's wild sunflowers and the few clinging leaves of the sumac along fence lines rattled in the wind like a regiment of disorganized snare drummers. And the only odor in the air was ill-defined and vague, no real scent at all, but putting the icy hint of coming winter into the nostrils with each breath.

In the hack beside Moses Masada was Tishacomsie, wearing a heavy woolen poncho. Riding alongside on a gray stud was Candy Redstripe bundled to the ears in coat and neck scarf. Moses Masada, having left Eufaula unprepared for the sudden change in weather, was lost in one of Candy Redstripe's overcoats, much too large for him.

Under all of Candy Redstripe's winter clothing, Moses Masada knew, there were two waist-holstered pistols. He'd seen them carefully checked that morning, and being a student of firearms noted they were large-bore weapons. A Smith & Wesson Russian Model .44, double-action. A Colt Bisley Model .45, single-action. Both short-barrel. Both obviously well cared for and with hand-carved walnut butts. As the hack bumped along the rocky trace toward Fawley Farm, Moses Masada felt as though he were an innocent merchantman being convoyed by a pair of those British battleships he'd read about in the *Kansas City Star* newspaper.

Riding through woodlands of butternut hickory and chinquapin oak, they emerged at Fawley Farm. It was a ragged clearing of dead weeds and scattered rocks and old metal wagon-wheel rims and a rusted plowshare that had not been used for many years, if ever. The house was set among a grove of sycamores. There were clusters of redbud and wild dogwood trees, little more than shrubs and looking dismally naked without their leaves.

It was a chink-log house, porch in front, dogtrot cutting it in half front to rear. In the rear of the main structure, Moses Masada could see other log buildings set off by rusted barbed wire and in these pens a number of hairy-chinned horses. A half-dozen multicolored hounds came out to greet them, barking viciously but making a great effort to stay clear of the mule and Candy Redstripe's big gray. Coming to greet them, too, was a fat Indian, at least coming as far as the covered front porch, wearing what appeared to be a knee-length smock with needlework of intricate design and screaming colors front and back.

"Candy! Tish!" he said, waving a fat arm. "I see you got Mr. Sample with you."

Which convinced Moses Masada, if he needed convincing, that news traveled fast in Creek Nation.

"Come in where it's warm," Langston Turtle said.

And once down from the hack and inside, Moses Masada was again astonished at the incongruity of this Indian Territory. For it was a well-furnished room, with a large hook rug on the floor, a three-panel china closet with many hand-painted dishes and porcelain figurines inside, and a large pendulum clock on the fireplace mantel. And as soon as he was seated, an attractive woman in what appeared to be a Sears and Roebuck print dress came with an etched-glass pitcher of grape juice, which she served in stem glasses.

Moses Masada and his host sat in the center of the room, more or less, and the Redstripes were in chairs against the wall near the door. As Langston Turtle spoke, he constantly watched the Redstripes, seldom glancing at Moses Masada, even though it was Moses Masada who initiated all the conversation.

"I have a will," he began, and it went on from there.

Of course, said Langston, he had known of such a document, his dear sister-in-law telling him everything. As Langston Turtle talked, which he was obviously prepared to do at great length, he moved his arms in animation. As the sleeves of his smock came up Moses Masada saw the tattoos along his biceps, swirls of blue and gray and a hint of red, which for Moses Masada had no meaning. Like puffs of ink smoke, perhaps, real only when seen but disappearing when touched.

Yes, a terrible tragedy, his sister-in-law cut off in prime of life. By a young man crazed with whiskey. And some imagined offense.

No, there were no children of Temperance Moon anywhere except the one in Fort Smith, and Temperance Moon each day sad because of it, she being a woman of virtue, and the daughter coming sometimes to visit here at Fawley Farm, bringing gifts, but never forgiven by her mother for the sordid nature of her calling. On the very day of her death, her friends and family here preparing a cake for her birthday. And she, Temperance Moon, on that day gone to help a woman and her children whose husband had been accused unjustly of crime.

"About that," said Moses Masada. "What can you tell me about Temperance Moon being convicted of a felony in the court at Fort Smith?"

"There were those who wanted to bring her down," said Langston Turtle, and he launched into a tirade about the Christian learnings of Temperance Moon, to which he himself subscribed, and about how no one of such purity could ever stoop to something like stealing a horse.

It was becoming very thick, Moses Masada thought, so shortly after Langston Turtle did his piece on Temperance Moon's resemblance to the biblical Ruth he excused himself, and they went out into the cold and quickly away.

"Jesus!" Moses Masada said. "This man is a cretin."

"Whatever that is," said Tishacomsie. "Watch him carefully."

"Yes." And he was taken with the woman, Winona, who throughout all of the talking had moved about the room, silently watching the Redstripes, as did her husband or man or whatever Langston Turtle was, and filling the glasses with grape juice time after time until Moses Masada thought that perhaps his teeth would turn purple. He drank it every time, so as not to give offense, yet noted that neither Candy nor Tishacomsie had taken a single sip, but sat with their eyes on the face of the fat Creek with the tattoos on his arms.

Jesus!

When they had moved out into the dogtrot and onto the porch and to their hack and horse, Langston Turtle followed, inviting them back. All Moses Masada could think of was that his best cases came when it was either sweltering hot and sweat ran into his eyes or else when it was so cold his toes felt like the droplets of ice hanging from the Detroit windowsills in January when he'd been a child.

"Such a facade," he said, as they went away from Fawley Farm.

"What does that word mean?" asked Tishacomsie.

"It means something is hidden, somewhere."

She said nothing, but Moses Masada noted that she exchanged a quick glance with her husband riding beside them.

Going back toward the Canadian River, Moses Masada broke the silence only once.

"Did I see someone in the other side of that house?" he asked.

"Yes," said Candy Redstripe.

"You saw it, too? Do you know who it was?"

"Yes. Goshen Crowfoot."

It took a moment, and then Moses Masada recalled the name from that hill farm in Weedy Rough, that Moon place.

"I've seen him before. Oscar Schiller and I thought we'd probably see him again. Goshen Crowfoot!"

"Yes. And now he's seen you again."

"The other one," said Tishacomsie, "was his younger brother, Claiburn."

"The other one? I sensed only one."

"There were two," said Candy Redstripe.

It did nothing for Moses Masada's peace of mind to know that all his previous big-city police experience and his highly developed intuition might not work so well in the Indian Territory. It didn't help that he'd felt no threat of danger in all this, yet the people who had insisted on accompanying him to Fawley Farm had armed themselves like Mexican bandits.

Well, he thought, brutally aware that there had been no laughter among them for a long time, and he had come to regard these two as laughing people, it was uncomfortable here now and time to go back to Eufaula and think about all he knew or didn't know and perhaps talk again to United States Deputy Marshal Nason Breedlove.

卍 卍 卍 The Eufaula to which Moses Masada retreated, if indeed it was a retreat, was a typical Indian Territory town which owed its existence to the railroad. At least owed the Missouri, Kansas, and Texas its assured growth. There had been a number of Creek towns at the confluence of the various branches of the Canadian, but the railroad's coming to Eufaula meant all the others would dry up and blow away in the wind.

Moses Masada knew the beginnings. Oscar Schiller had told him, and Oscar Schiller knew, having been a member of the Isaac

Charles Parker court for many years and having been lectured on various occasions about the problems of the Indian Territory and its origin by that same Isaac Charles Parker, who had to deal with it every day and knew all its colors.

The system devised during Andy Jackson's administration had been called Removal. It meant taking southeastern tribes away from land wanted by the white man and moving these tribes west into what was then called Arkansas Territory, a place everybody figured no white man in his right mind would ever want to claim.

So by various routes, the Muskogee Indians had trekked to this new land. Many of them settled in the valley of the Canadian and became known as Creeks. Their cousins were all around them. The Choctaw and Chickasaw and Seminole. The Cherokee had come as well, but they were not cousins. They were Iroquoian. But their problems were the same. Such as many of the people dying on the march to the new land. And once in the new land discovering that a lot of other red folk were already there and some of them adamantly opposed to any new settlers. Red folk like the Osage, for example.

In fact, old Fort Smith had originally been established so the soldiers of the United States of America could keep Osages and the Five Civilized Tribes from cutting each other's throats.

Civilized tribes. That's how the Cherokee and Creek and Choctaw and Chickasaw and Seminole were characterized. Because they built stone schools. They wore broadcloth. They tilled fields with metal plowshares. They drove spring wagons. They owned black slaves. All just like the white man. Hence, Civilized Tribes.

Of course, not many white men believed they were civilized at all.

Anyway, the Creek domain within the fingers of the Canadian was a rich land. Those fingers were the main branch, North Fork, and Deep Fork. All coming together and flowing into the Arkansas River some fifty miles west of the fort at Belle Point. A fort called Smith. Above the mouth of the Poteau and even then, in the 1830s, becoming a white man's town where produce might be marketed.

The Creeks were farmers. So in the rich, black soil of the Canadian floodplain, they began to grow squash and corn and watermelons and cotton and raise hogs and chickens and milk cows. At first, there were a lot of hard times. And many children starved. At first, there were raids on their settlements by the High Plains wild tribes, the Kiowa and Comanche. But like most farmers, this was a tough bunch. And they survived.

The social and political and religious life of the Creeks had centered around the towns in the old country, which is what they called former homes in Georgia and Alabama and elsewhere. They lived in towns and went to the fields each day. Now they lived on the land, like white-man farmers, but the towns were still the center of their lives.

In the old country, the Creeks had always held an annual green corn dance in the spring. In the new land, they still did. It was analogous to the sun dance of the High Plains wild tribes in that it focused on social and religious revival. During its ceremonies, all the past year's crimes were forgiven, washed away. Except for murder. A long time before they knew that the white man would not forgive murder, as evidenced by the lack of any statute of limitation on it, the Creeks held that killing except in self-defense could not be forgiven or forgotten. When the white man spoke of them as a Civilized Tribe, Oscar Schiller had told Moses Masada, they never mentioned this aspect of the Creek way.

The Creek people voted for a constitution in 1867 that had much of the structure and many of the functions of the document used as a model, the Constitution of the United States of America. The Creek Nation established this basis of government at about the same time that nearby states of the old Confederacy, namely Texas and Arkansas, were framing new constitutions of their own as a result of the Civil War's outcome. All these instruments were drawn up under the same circumstance, each having to be approved by the victorious federal government.

So with the passage of time, the appearance and operation of Creek Nation became more and more like that of the states of the federal union. Not only because of the similarities of the keystone doctrine but because the many excellent secretaries hired by chiefs and other officials were young men schooled in one of the white man's states. A rather important requirement in view of the fact that many of those elected Creek officials were illiterate.

Their constitution established six districts, each with its own capital town. Eufaula was one of these. As in other district capitals, there was a courthouse, a district judge, and a prosecuting attorney. There was a district chief, who was responsible under the constitution for law enforcement. For this purpose he had a company of Light Horse Police and about half a dozen men, each with a captain. In Eufaula, the captain was Moma July.

There was an elective process to choose representatives from each district to the National Council in Okmulgee, the number of men to the House of Warriors based on population, and for each district one member to the House of Kings. A bicameral legislature whose statutes and laws were overseen by a supreme court, judges being selected for six-year periods by the National Council. And finally, a principal chief, selected by popular vote.

Of all the amazements encountered in Indian Territory, this was the most astonishing to Moses Masada. A people generally considered savage by white men, yet with an exact system of government. And Moses Masada knew that had he walked into a police station in Kansas City, Missouri, or anywhere else, and said as much, everyone would have laughed and he would be accused of lying about in the alley smoking a lot of hemp.

But lovely as it might seem, it didn't work. Because the Congress of the United States of America had said that none of the Indian structure of justice was applicable to a white man. So before the Civil War, and more so afterward, a lot of white men began to realize this and go to the Indian Territory because none of the Indian police or courts could arrest and punish them for wrongdoing. The only law which could touch them was in Fort Smith, the court of Judge Isaac Charles Parker.

There were ways a white man could be in the Indian Territory legally. He could marry an Indian. Or he could have a document in hand, issued by some bureaucrat of the United States, some of whom would sign a name to such an instrument for five dollars. So even many of those whites in the Nations legally were there to savage the people.

It was bad enough at first. When the railroads came, it got a lot worse.

As in all places, in all times, the corruption of the young began. So a few Creek young men forgot the green corn dance and began thinking only in terms of money and whiskey. And the federal court in Fort Smith was all the Creeks had to fight the whites bringing the corruption. And for that fight sent their deputy marshals, who often had districts larger than the state of Rhode Island.

The good people went on, building their schools and courthouses and railroad depots and cotton sheds, and were proud of their children, who were learning the English language and white man's numbers and how to cut their hair. And Moses Masada appreciated the old stories of his father about a people being subjugated by the Persians or Romans and told they were autonomous. Except when it came to life and death and the pursuit of peaceful happiness. Then everything was in the hands of the conqueror. Regardless of good intentions up and down the line, Moses Masada understood with an impact never known before the ruthless subtlety of gentle victory without a war.

In the Eufaula courthouse, he found a document that made him smile, then cry. Only two years before, the government of the United States of America had ordered a census, which the Creeks conducted. And for their nation, they found these figures: Creeks, nine thousand two hundred ninety. Negroes, four thousand six hundred twenty-one. Cherokees, four hundred sixty. Seminoles, seventy-two. White men, three thousand two hundred eighty-nine. Those were the legal ones, of course. Nobody knew how many illegal ones there were.

Oh. And three Chinese!

₪ ₪ ₪ Since coming to Eufaula, Moses Masada had met with United States Deputy Marshal Nason Breedlove in the back storeroom of Tyler Johnson's feed store on the main and only street in town worthy of the name. It was a rough frame building, like most of the structures in the district capital devoted to private enterprise. The KATY depot and the public buildings like the school and courthouse and police station were of sandstone or rough brick, the latter produced at a local furnace and kiln operated by a Creek whose father had learned the craft in Alabama before Removal. And despite the Anglo-Saxon-sounding name, Tyler Johnson was a full-blooded Creek as well who, like so many of them, had changed his name to facilitate business with whites, because like the others who had done the same, Tyler Johnson knew the disadvantages of trying to do business with somebody who couldn't pronounce, much less spell, his real name.

Moses Masada had been painfully aware from the start that the big, blunt marshal was not overly enthusiastic about these meetings because they ate into his limited time, but nonetheless he had cooperated well enough. Nason Breedlove and the Creek police, who also knew who Moses Masada really was, trusted Tyler Johnson. He was a man they knew could keep his mouth shut. So with Moses Masada and Nason Breedlove coming together in dark of night in this back room of the feed store, unseen by citizens of the town, and Tyler Johnson ensuring that no customers or loafers or other potential gossips interrupted them, it was hoped that the relationship between them would not become public knowledge and the theme of Eufaula District gossip. That relationship had, of course, been established by Oscar Schiller in one of his little notes left for Breedlove in the marshal's office in Parker's court, where there was also no question of people being able to keep their mouth shut, and was a circumstance thus far unknown to all but a few in Creek Nation.

The feed store back room was unheated. And on the night of his return from the Redstripe farm, Moses Masada was convinced that he would turn into ice before the arrival of the big, burly federal officer. He sat on a one-hundred-pound sack of wheat-bran cattle feed and contemplated the wavering, uncertain shine of a smoky lantern on the rough pine floor that produced more stink of coal oil than it did light. He was still wearing the overcoat of Candy Redstripe, over one of his own, but this did nothing to protect his toes, fingers, or nose. By the time Marshal Nason Breedlove came through the back door, his breath blowing great clouds of white mist, Moses Masada was convinced that already he was half frozen to death.

There were no casual conversational bits in these meetings. Both men knew the value of getting them finished in a hurry. The longer you talked, the more chance of some son of a bitch knowing you were talking, as Nason Breedlove put it.

"So Candy? Tish?" Nason Breedlove asked, settling his great bulk on a sack of cracked corn. "What about them?"

"Unusual people," said Moses Masada. "I sensed a lot of secrets between them."

"Oh, yeah," Nason Breedlove said and he laughed and pulled his woolen neck scarf down from his chin so Moses Masada could see his great mouth beneath the great mustache. "I can see you ain't ever been married. You think secrets between a man and his woman is so damned unusual."

"Not the secrets, perhaps, but the unusual people. I like them," Moses Masada said.

"Sure, don't we all. You see Mr. Courson since we talked last?"

"Yes. He showed me the shotgun. A nice weapon. Nothing there, just another shotgun. He said Toby Jupiter was an overgrown kid, but addicted to drink. All he wanted, his greatest ambition, was to work awhile at Mr. Courson's farm, take his dollar and a half, and spend it at some bootleg place. And the fishing. He said Toby loved to fish more than anyone he'd ever known. An overgrown kid, fishing."

"Yeah, but Toby knew where Courson kept the gun."

"Yes."

"Well, I told you all of that before. You get to Fawley Farm?"

"Yes. The Redstripes went with me."

"I'm glad of that."

"Langston Turtle is a liar. I don't know what else he might be."

"Is that all you got out of it?" asked Nason Breedlove.

"Nothing solid. But this man made Temperance Moon a woman unlike the Temperance Moon I know from all I've found. And said he knew about the will. And there is no will. So how do you judge that?"

"Well, Langston Turtle can spread the bullshit pretty thick, if it's in his own interest. That's what we got here. He always has. So it may not mean anything."

"I'm getting nothing anywhere," said Moses Masada. "I'm about ready to go back to Fort Smith and tell Oscar it's a bust. Toby Jupiter killed Temperance Moon and somebody unknown killed him, and who the hell cares?"

"Don't do that yet," said Nason Breedlove. "When Oscar Schillar gets a bug, it's usually one that's gonna sting. I got to feelin' the same way he does. Him gettin' shot at over in Fort Smith. Why? Don't go yet. Somebody'll get drunk and say something. They always does."

Nason Breedlove was up then, off his bag of feed, pulling the neck scarf close against his neck.

"Oh, one other thing," said Moses Masada. "At Fawley Farm. The Redstripes claimed they saw two people."

Nason Breedlove now, for the first time, showed some real interest. And stopped adjusting his neck scarf.

"Who?"

"They said the Crowfoots."

Nason Breedlove's eyebrows lifted and his eyes were suddenly larger than they had been in all of this discussion.

"Crowfoots?"

"Yes."

"Son of a bitch! They're back in the Nations! Goshen and Claiburn?"

"They said. The Redstripes."

Nason Breedlove made a great sigh, his breath exploding white in the frigid air. Then adjusted the scarf around his neck.

"I didn't know that," he said. "Watch your back, Masada. You told me Goshen seen you in Arkansas. He ain't as stupid as Langston Turtle. I wouldn't wanta face Oscar Schiller if you got your ass shot off in my district."

"Thanks for your concern, Marshal," said Moses Masada.

"Anytime, anytime," Nason Breedlove said and laughed and slapped Moses Masada on one shoulder. "Well, watch your back, and keep your pecker dry."

And he was gone. Moses Masada expected, when he saw Nason Breedlove move, that because of the marshal's lumbering, awkward appearance there would be considerable accompanying noise. But there wasn't. The only sound of Nason Breedlove's departure was his voice, faint but sure, once he was into the dark alley behind the feed store where the west wind was coming like a knife.

"Gawd *damn*, it's cold!"

6 As a United States Deputy Marshal, Oscar Schiller had become accustomed to meetings with various citizens who supposed they might provide information useful to him for pending cases. But he never had had such a conference with anyone of the stature of attorney Wilford Mason Caveness, one of Fort Smith's most brillant and respected lawyers. He had such a conference now.

Caveness had his offices on the second floor of the National Bank of Arkansas building just off 8th Street on Garrison. The windows overlooked the Avenue, where, on this sunny morning, certain merchants could be seen putting up Christmas trees on the sidewalk before their businesses, decorated with red-and-green bunting and cotton puff angels and such. It was a typical law office with wall shelves for massive books which looked mostly unused and the smell of sealing wax and indelible ink. Wilford Mason Caveness, whom his friends called W.M. but whom everybody else addressed as sir, presided over this enclave of legality from behind a massive walnut desk. On the desk were stacks of briefs and assorted papers and two oranges.

According to many citizens of the town, this desk was the largest in all of western Arkansas, and had a history as well. It had belonged to W. M. Caveness's wife's father, who had been the first county judge in Fort Smith and who was a member of the state legislature for years, beginning back in 1851.

It was a quiet office, with little noise from outside except the occasional clang of bells from one of the horse-drawn streetcars moving down the center of Garrison Avenue. From the outer office, there was the infrequent ring of the telephone, which always startled Oscar Schiller. Telephones had been installed in Fort Smith a decade earlier, but he had never become accustomed to the things, nor to their loud jangling when an operator at the central office switchboard plugged in a line and twisted the crank.

W. M. Caveness looked younger than Oscar Schiller knew he was, even though his dark hair was beginning to turn white. He had an intense, somewhat baleful stare, which he used to great effect when cross-examining hostile witnesses in the courtroom. He now fixed this same stare on Oscar Schiller, who sat before the great and famous desk, on the edge of a chair, holding his palmetto hat between his knees with both hands.

"I appreciate your responding to my invitation," said W. M. Caveness. "I believe I have information useful to you."

"I appreciate it, sir."

"I don't believe that I have ever defended anyone whom you arrested during your tenure with the federal court."

"No, sir. I don't believe so," said Oscar Schiller.

"It's of no significance," W. M. Caveness said, leaning back in his chair, which was as massive as the desk, and lacing his fingers together before his necktie. Watching the attorney's hands, Oscar Schiller was reminded of the children's poem that accompanied the manipulation of the hands and half expected W. M. Caveness to recite it: "Here is the church, here is the steeple, open the door, and there are the people."

But W. M. Caveness did not recite the poem.

"I have, at various times, represented Max Bamberger," he said. "I understand he is a special friend of yours."

"Yes. He is."

"During the past week, I had occasion to visit the taproom at his brewery," W. M. Caveness said. "It was a social visit. In no manner could it be said to have involved a client-attorney relationship. And in the course of our talk, he mentioned the escapade of someone shooting through his window."

"The night someone killed one of Max Bamberger's crocks of kraut," said Oscar Schiller.

"Exactly," said the lawyer, smiling and nodding. "Now, on reflection, I have determined that Max Bamberger being the gentle soul he is, no one would want to shoot him. Nor do I subscribe to the idea that anyone so dislikes sauerkraut that he would shoot *that*. So the obvious target had to be you. For what reason, I have no notion, nor do I want to have."

"All right, sir," said Oscar Schiller. "Can I take it that you and I now have a client-attorney privilege?"

"Absolutely."

"Then I can say that I expect the assault was because I have begun an investigation into serious crime."

"I suspected as much," said W. M. Caveness. "Very well. On the night in question, Max said you showed a rather inordinate interest in the business operation of the Commerce Railroad Hotel. Max made no connection between this and the shots fired, nor do I, necessarily, but when dealing with people of a certain stripe, all bases must be touched, as the people on our baseball teams say."

"Yes, sir."

"And, of course, the Commerce Railroad Hotel is owned and operated by the daughter of one Temperance Moon, recently deceased in Creek Nation, by violent means."

"Yes, sir."

"Before I came to this city to practice law, I was a schoolteacher in Missouri," said W. M. Caveness. "At one time, I had a young lady, almost of my own age, who was a student. Her name was Temperance Tilly."

Oscar Schiller blinked rapidly.

"I didn't know that."

"Who, of course, became known as Temperance Moon. The same Temperance Moon recently murdered in the Indian Territory. I suppose you know that on many occasions when Temperance Moon was brought into our federal court on various allegations of wrongdoing, I defended her."

"Yes, sir, and usually successfully so."

"Be that as it may," said W. M. Caveness. "In view of my having decided that your safety is at stake, I will now divulge information for you which might be called client privilege except that the client is dead and the safety of the living is more important to me."

"I appreciate it," said Oscar Schiller.

"Were you aware that Temperance Moon was in this city about six weeks before she was killed?"

"No," said Oscar Schiller. "And I reckon the newspapers were not aware of it either, because anytime she came close to Fort Smith they made a big play of it on their pages."

"Exactly. Well, she spent three, maybe four days staying with her daughter, at the Commerce Railroad Hotel. She moved about the city, when she moved, in a taxi hack and not on that big gray horse she loved so well. Perhaps not incognito exactly, but near to it."

W. M. Caveness reached for one of the oranges on his desk and began to peel it, watching the rind come off under his long fingers. He did it very quickly and then opened the sections of the fruit and put one into his mouth.

"Would you care for some orange slices?" he asked.

"No, sir. Much obliged."

"Well," said W. M. Caveness, wiping the juice from his lips with a monogrammed handkerchief taken out of the top drawer of the oak desk. "Temperance Moon came to see me. She wanted to know if there was any legal bar to her opening a recreational hall in Eufaula, Creek Nation."

"A house of prostitution, Counselor?"

"She said not. Of course, I have no illusion, had no illusions, about her character. She said it was for dancing and that she would install some of these new nickelodeon game machines and serve nonalcoholic beverages."

He put another orange slice into his mouth.

"You know," he said, "they are making this candy now, shaped like a slice from an orange, and they sell them in the Woolworth store. But they don't taste like real oranges, do they?"

"No, sir." Oscar Schiller had never tasted any such candy.

"All right," said W. M. Caveness. "Having become over the years conversant with Creek law, I told her there was no reason why she could not do as she wanted in this regard. She was not under indictment in a Creek court. She had never been convicted as a felon in a Creek court. All of which was impossible, really, because although she was a legal member of the Creek Nation, having married a Creek man, she was white, and so was not subject to the jurisdiction of the Creek courts.

"Then quite gratuitously, she explained to me that she was monetarily embarrassed because she had spent so much money defending various friends who found themselves in trouble with the law but that her daughter would not advance her the money."

"Jewel Moon. Commerce Railroad Hotel," said Oscar Schiller. "The same."

Oscar Schiller leaned back in his chair and tapped the palmetto hat against his knees, and W. M. Caveness watched him, eating another orange slice as he did so.

"The next question has to be," said Oscar Schiller, "how much money are we talking about here?"

"Considerable," said W. M. Caveness. "I had the impression that Temperance Moon was fixing to build from the ground up. And she mentioned five thousand dollars twice in our conversation."

Behind his thick glasses, Oscar Schiller's eyes had begun to glint as they usually only did after a few sips of cocaine coffee.

"Another question, Counselor?"

"Of course."

"Did Jewel Moon make the loan to her mother?"

"I don't know. I do know that the next day, one of my law clerks saw Temperance Moon in City Bank. As for myself, I never saw Temperance Moon again."

Abruptly, Wilford Mason Caveness leaned forward and lifted one of the brief folders from the top of his desk and placed a pair of steel-rimmed glasses on his nose. It was a clear signal that this discussion was finished, and Oscar Schiller was an expert at reading signals. He rose and made a slight bow toward the great desk and the man behind it.

"Thank you, Counselor."

"Not at all, not at all," said W. M. Caveness, already opening the brief folder and no longer looking at Oscar Schiller. "Drop in anytime."

ℵ ℵ ℵ It was almost Christmas. So Oscar Schiller knew the Commerce Railroad Hotel ladies and Miss Jewel Moon would be busy with a particular group of clients who always had their fling to celebrate the happiness of Yuletide. On the Row, this group was called the Home Papas. Because it consisted largely of family men, men who on Christmas Day and a week in either direction of Christmas Day would be intimately involved with wives and children and grandparents and Aunt Maudes visiting from Dardanelle or some such place. Involved in putting up cedar trees, getting the old Santa Claus suit out of mothballs, buying and wrapping gifts, contracting with farmers or meat markets for live turkeys, and all the other things family men did from about mid-December until the Great Day and then for a week afterward tried to recover from it. So before all this frenzy began, a fling at Miss Jewel's.

The bordellos were geared to the Papas in that time, just before these men became involved in home hearths, and all the ladies knew Christmas itself would be less taxing because then would come only the bachelors who had no place else to go. Instead of acting as wild and unruly schoolboys just out for the summer, they were usually somber and tearful, remembering Christmastimes in the past when they had been part of gatherings that did not include ladies of the evening and their strong perfume, but rather mamas and papas of their own and the smell of sage dressing in a house overrun by laughing children.

"It's a brutal business, Nasturtium," Miss Jewel Moon always said to her little black maid.

"Yes ma'am. Drink your cocoa, Miss Jewel."

But the rush of seasonal Home Papa business was to be ignored, because Oscar Schiller had to talk with Miss Jewel Moon. He had never liked to postpone an interrogation he knew was essential, and most particularly not this one, now that he was convinced somebody was shooting at him.

There was one advantage. Perhaps this time, they could talk at some decent hour and not at the dawn. The Home Papas usually accomplished their business at the Commerce Railroad Hotel at an early hour so they could get home, unlike bachelors, who sometimes stayed the night. After all, making an alibi of business or political or lodge meetings that lasted into the wee hours was always a shaky proposition with ladies of the Victorian era, who often were upset when spouses failed to arrive in time to help tuck babes under the covers.

So it didn't surprise Oscar Schiller when he had a quick response to the little note that he sent to Miss Jewel Moon through the postal service. The very next night, Nasturtium was dispatched to the backyard of the Hakes to lie in wait under an old redbud tree until Oscar Schiller appeared, which was about midnight, after having completed a domino game with a number of old friend federal marshals in the back room of the Odd Fellows Hall.

As he came into the dark yard, the little black maid stepped out from her hiding and whispered, "Mr. Marshal!"

"Jesus Christ, girl," Oscar Schiller gasped, his nickel-plated pistol half drawn. "You're hard as hell to see in the dark, you know that?"

So well before dawn he found himself secreted with the madam of the Commerce Railroad Hotel in the combination office and pantry just behind the first-floor kitchen and with an outside door on the river side of the building. Which meant the dark side. There was the sharp odor of frying bacon from the next room, and Oscar Schiller knew Clarence the cook was making breakfast for the ladies, whose work was finished for the evening. Even better evidence of the close of business was the fact that when Miss Jewel Moon came into the combination office pantry, she was carrying a water glass full of iced sloe gin, and Oscar Schiller knew she never drank high spirits when there were customers in the house.

"My God," Miss Jewel Moon said, easing herself into the chair behind a very tiny desk. "My feet are killing me!"

Sprawled, with her legs out toward one of the canned-goods-and-condiment shelves, she pushed off her shoes, one foot with the other, and Oscar Schiller saw her wiggling her toes in the white stockings. She was wearing a Battenberg lace dress, which probably had cost forty dollars, and Oscar Schiller couldn't help thinking that she looked like an exhausted bride with a few strands of hair, in little ringlets, escaping from their pins to dance about along her forehead.

"You want some coffee, Oscar?"

"No. Just talk."

"That's what your note said. All right. Talk."

Here, as in the entry hall and other strategic places, there was a four-ounce shot glass full of Miss Jewel Moon's special black cigarillos. She lit one now with a foul-smelling sulfur match and lit one for Oscar Schiller as well.

"About the shooting," he said.

"Yeah, I heard somebody tried to dust you. Glad they missed."

"It could have been old enemies," said Oscar Schiller. "But maybe not. Maybe something to do with what I'm doing for you. About your mother. Who all knows about it and how much can you trust them?"

Jewel Moon's broad face could cloud up in a hurry, and it did so now, and her brown eyes turned sharp to Oscar Schiller's face.

"Nobody in this house knows anything about it," she snapped. "My personal business is my personal business."

"You don't need to bite me," he said. "We gotta be honest and true with one another here. That's all. If somebody out there is trying to send me up the flue, at least you owe me everything you can give. It might help. It might not. But a man can't take chances on missing a connection."

Jewel Moon sighed, and the dark look was gone as suddenly as it had come. She puffed her black cigar and stared up at the ceiling and wiggled her toes and took a long drink of sloe gin.

"I'm sorry, Oscar. It's all a little touchy. And this has been a God damned hectic night. The entire Benevolent Brotherhood of Silver Otters, or whatever they call themselves, had a big wing-ding here tonight, and if there's anything that unsettles a person it's a bunch of middle-aged horny men who are drunk enough to think they're still the Lord's own personal gift to womanhood. But listen, my people don't know nothing about any of this. You hear?"

"All right," he said. "I'll take that. You don't happen to have any of my baking-soda powder around, do you?"

She laughed. "No, Oscar, you come on me too sudden this time for me to find any."

"It doesn't signify. So on with business." Oscar Schiller took a long pull on his cigarillo before he went into the real subject of this talk. "Jewel, I found out your mother was wanting to open some kind of place in Creek Nation."

She looked at him with the beginning of resentment in the drawn-down corners of her mouth, but then it was gone and she drank from the glass of pink liquid.

"You dig into it, don't you?"

"I understand she needed money for it. Did you give it to her?"

"No," Jewel Moon said vehemently. "Personal reasons."

"Jewel, now come on."

Jewel Moon did a lot of toe wiggling and a lot of puffing and a lot of sipping before she answered. But she obviously was not angry. She was only making a decision about how to phrase her answer, so Oscar Schiller supposed.

"I figured," Jewel Moon finally said, "that I didn't want to get myself tied into something in Creek Nation that might be trouble. Just to be frank as hell, I didn't want Mother to do it."

"Good enough," said Oscar Schiller. "So where did she go for the money? To First City Bank? One of your silent partners?"

Now when she looked at him, there was no belligerence but only a kind of admiration.

"You are good, you know it?"

"Hell, Jewel, the first time we talked you practically told me who he was."

"All right," Jewel Moon said. "You know so damned much already, I'll tell you the rest. Warson wouldn't give her any loan. Mother was mad as a snake. But what's any of this got to do with things in Creek Nation?"

"I don't know," Oscar Schiller said. "Maybe nothing. But listen, about that same time, Warson sold his interest in this place, didn't he?"

Jewel Moon laughed, suddenly, harshly.

"Yeah, Oscar, you are good. Better than I ever figured."

"Sold out to the other silent partner, Abram Jacobson?"

She laughed again, her head back.

"My God, Oscar!"

"So why would he do that? This place is good money. I never knew a banker who didn't like good money."

Jewel Moon turned to slide her legs under the small desk and she pounded the desk with a fist, four, five times, making it thump.

"What has this got to do with a dirty killing in the Nations?" she shouted.

"Now, come on, Jewel."

She sighed and sat back, as though defeated, or maybe, Oscar Schiller thought, only regrouping her forces.

"All right," she said. "Maybe you ain't as smart as all that. So I'll tell you."

She spread her hands on the table and looked at the rings on her fingers, as though suspecting some of the settings had dropped out during her night of frustration with the Silver Otters. In addition to the wedding band, which Oscar Schiller thought likely meant less to her than any of the others, there were seven rings. Gold with diamond or ruby or emerald stones, or very good imitations thereof.

"The political bug has bit Mr. Warson, my recent partner," she said.

Oscar Schiller tried to connect such a thing with any information that might be useful to him, but couldn't. He recalled that Mrs. Hake, during her visits to his bedchamber, had mentioned the same phenomenon.

"State legislature now, United States Senate later," she said. "And who knows what else?"

"We're getting far afield," he said.

"Oh, for God's sake," she said, exasperated. "You're the one come in here telling me we got to talk it all out. I don't know what the hell it means. But I know what power means. Do you?"

"Power?"

"Yes. Power. You said he likely enjoys money that the girls and me make, and you're right. But all of a sudden, he likes power more. And where he wants to go, Warson thinks it might be a hindrance if the good citizens and other legislators in this state found out he was part owner of a whorehouse, a man leading ladies from virtue, what them newspapers from the east call white slavery. Now do you see why he sold out, Oscar?"

"I'm not sure," said Oscar Schiller. "From what I've seen, our state legislators and most of the good citizens around here wouldn't give a damn if a man owned a whorehouse."

"Yeah, but Warson figured he couldn't take that chance. Warson has always been two things. Nervous and bullheaded. So because he's nervous, he wants to hedge all bets, and once he decides that, he'll do everything necessary to get it done. He don't want to get into a political fracas where the Lily White Purity and Temperance League may jump up and bite him in the ass for being such a bad man. And once he'd decided that, he not only was going to sell out his deal here, but he sure as hell wasn't going to turn right around and invest in something my mother was starting over in the Nations."

Oscar Schiller studied the labels on the canned goods in the shelves along one wall. From the next room, he could hear some of the ladies chattering and laughing as they picked up their morning eggs from the cook. Jewel Moon was looking at him again. And she finished the last of the sloe gin in the water glass.

"Oscar? You still here?"

"Yeah. I was trying to connect," he said, and rose and pulled on his hat. "But I can't. Not yet. Well, thanks for your time, Jewel. Go get your breakfast."

At the door, he paused, hand on the porcelain knob. Then looked back at her.

"Jewel, you have your guests check weapons, don't you?"

"Always."

"Ever see a .41 caliber derringer?"

"God, yes. All the time. Half the men in this town got one, I reckon."

He opened the door. The air outside had lost most of its cold bite.

"Oscar?"

"Yeah?"

"Merry Christmas."

₪ ₪ ₪ It was after dawn and Oscar Schiller was still lying awake in his basement bed, hearing the Hakes upstairs. The Scissors King preparing to go to his factory in north Fort Smith, the children romping around the house, happy that school was out for the Christmas vacation.

His ears were very sensitive, picking up all kinds of subtle sounds. He heard the bread wagon pass and the milk wagon. Then the sorghum wagon, an ox-drawn vehicle that was a permanent part of Fort Smith traffic, a farmer driving his animals, a small boy in the wagon seat and behind him in the wagon bed two large wooden barrels, and the farmer calling as he went along the street, "Molasses. Molasses. Good sorghum molasses."

And between sleep and waking, Oscar Schiller waited for the next street vendor, who now because it was winter would not be the ice man or the vegetable-cart man but maybe the tamale man, about whom there were lurid stories concerning his seduction of defenseless young damsels at the Frisco passenger depot and who supposedly made his meat filling for the tamales with cats he killed in the alleys of the city. No matter about the cats. Oscar Schiller knew those grease-dripping tamales wrapped in corn husks and hawked by perhaps half a dozen vendors in Fort Smith were the best tamales short of San Antonio. Maybe even better than there. Oscar Schiller wasn't sure anymore about Texas tamales, because it had been so long since he had tasted one, he having avoided the Lone Star since 1868, when certain county sheriffs had been anxious to talk with him about some horses he'd sold in Longview without certain proof of ownership.

So, he thought, Jewel Moon says her people don't know about our peek into the demise of Temperance. So who else does? My own people, he thought, police people, and all trusted because they understand the benefit of secrecy.

He was almost dead asleep again when he started up, throwing off his cover. There were two of his people who did know and were not peace officers. The Redstripes!

He was almost out of bed, his first impulse to send a telegraph warning to Moses Masada, but he killed the thought even as it was born. Because maybe he was wrong. Nothing bad had happened to the Kansas City man to now. Maybe a sentence had slipped through the fence somewhere else. Even Nason Breedlove, even Jewel Moon herself, even Moses Masada. He knew conspiracy was hard to conceal, and the more people involved, the harder. Inadvertently. Innocently.

So Moses Masada would have to play it out. It might be dangerous, but that was the nature of the work.

"Anyway," Oscar Schiller said, "to all, a Merry Christmas!"

忍 忍 忍 Yuletide was celebrated that year as in all others, both at Fort Smith and across the river in Indian Territory. Most of the Nations tribes had taken to Christianity even while retaining many of their old religious customs. Whether they did this from true conversion to the faith or simply to accommodate the white man's view of civilization, nobody knew. Least of all many of the Indians themselves.

At any rate, the season marked high attendance in mission churches, and in those the tribes had organized themselves. There was a lot of singing. The smell of young pigs roasting over an open hickory fire was not unknown. But mostly, it was a day of rest. In that year, Christmas fell on a Sunday, which was a little disappointing, because like the white men, the tribes had taken up the habit of making Sunday a day of rest, too, so they felt cheated out of one day of avoiding labor without being called slovenly savages.

There were certain small communities that were made up entirely of black people. These enclaves came into being when all the tribal slaves were freed and continued to exist. But except for the generally darker complexion of the celebrants, there was little difference in the observance of Christmas there and in Indian places.

At Fawley Farm, Langston Turtle had finally begun to drink, reckoning that nothing could get worse than it already was, and the day turned out to be a pleasant surprise. He and all three of the Crowfoots got roaring drunk and sang old songs and told old stories about the good days past and managed to avoid getting sick and throwing up before midafternoon. It was good to be near people who, at least for a little while, put aside the disposition of wet scorpions.

Moses Masada was a houseguest, again, of the Redstripes. Tishacomsie baked a tart gooseberry pie for the Christmas dinner, and it was there at the table amid the bones of the roasted chicken and the empty elderberry wine bottles that Moses Masada gave his gifts. A fine neck scarf of Scottish wool for Candy, a delicate Portuguese lace shawl for Tish.

A close, warm relationship had developed among them over the past weeks. The Creek and the Delaware told Moses Masada much of their tribal heritage. He in turn told them of such things as crossing the sea in a great ship, and even with their intelligent imaginations they could not come to terms with so much water. These times were often spent sitting before the fireplace, eating popcorn, which one of their tenants grew.

Often when Candy was in the outbuildings seeing to the horses, Tish and Moses Masada alone in the house, she had in the casual course of things touched his hand or his arm and once even his neck. And always, even when Candy was there with them, she looked at him with a warmth in her eyes that touched him more surely than her hands could do.

Once, Candy Redstripe revealed his intention of taking some ponies to a horse race in Denison, Texas, in January and asked Moses Masada to come along. He said he would, and disappointment showed plainly on his face when Tish said it would give her a chance to finish the work on two quilts she was making.

On Christmas afternoon, with Moses Masada and Tish standing on the porch close enough for their bodies to touch as she pointed across the Canadian and spoke of things in Choctaw Nation, Moses Masada thought it the best Christmas he had ever had.

But it was painful to realize there was some kind of mutual

animal attraction between him and this woman over which neither of them had any control. Yet if not controlled would bring a sure and deadly reaction from Candy Redstripe the moment he felt himself betrayed. So Moses Masada struggled with his passion and those dark eyes and wondered if she was even aware of his agony.

In Fort Smith, it was the usual small-town Christmas, though unseasonably warm. There were groups of young people who went around singing carols. But of course, they did not carry their serenades of joy as far west in the city as the Row. But there, particularly at Miss Jewel Moon's Commerce Railroad Hotel, the ladies each evening entertained their guests with group singing, and that year the current Natasha displayed the most beautiful contralto anyone had ever heard. It was unfortunate that the day after Christmas, this same Natasha would be in the Kansas City Southern passenger depot with a ticket to Fort Worth, with Miss Jewel Moon's compliments, farewell, and enough money in her purse to cure her syphilis.

"It's a brutal world, Nasturtium," said Miss Jewel.

"Yes, ma'am," Nasturtium said. "Who gonna be Natasha now?"

"I got a Chinese lady comin' in from Gary, Indiana," said Miss Jewel.

"I never knowed them Chinamen named folks Natasha."

"Like I said, it's a brutal world."

Oscar Schiller spent the day at the brewery with Max Bamberger, two confirmed bachelors making the best of things. As they had done before. This year, they were joined by United States Deputy Marshal Nason Breedlove, in town on official business from Creek Nation. Nason Breedlove was not a bachelor but he had no notion of the whereabouts of his wife, Lutie, who only the month before had departed Fort Smith, Arkansas, and maybe even the entire United States of America with her father, who was a land speculator and had spoken of the fortune he could make in Bolivia.

"Good God damned riddance," said Nason Breedlove. "And she took the four kids, too. You know, even when you don't particularly like your old lady, you might expect to develop some respect for her daddy. But he was always making fun of my profession. I been tempted for years to shoot his ass off, which even as a civic duty can get you into a lot of embarrassment. Especially seein' as he was my one and only daddy-in-law."

Bank vice-president and state legislator Mr. Herkimer Warson was in residence. His family was entertaining the family of the Arkansas legislature's speaker of the house. Mr. Warson and his houseguest attended half a dozen church services in various parts of town, smiling and shaking hands with everyone they could reach while their wives displayed the latest fashion in hats from Sears and Roebuck of Chicago.

Mr. Herkimer Warson's bodyguard, or whatever he was, took Christmas at home with his wife and two little girls, celebrating with a meal of sautéed crayfish taken from a tributary of the Poteau River. Everyone else in the locale called these things crawdads and seldom considered eating them unless faced with starvation and then only if there were no snakes or rats available.

To Muley LaRue these were a reminder of his home in the bayous of Louisiana, so what better time to enjoy the little crustacean wonders along with all the rest of a noisy Christmas season, to which purpose he purchased a lot of firecrackers for his daughters and the other children of the neighborhood. At the same time, Muley LaRue bought two feet of primer cord, five feet of time fuse, two blasting caps, and a couple of sticks of dynamite. These last had nothing to do with the celebration of Christmas. He explained to his wife that it was time they sank a water well in their backyard and thus become independent from the Fort Smith water supply, which came from that same Poteau River and in which there were not only crawdads but a lot of mud and from time to time dead human bodies in various states of decomposition.

And with that explanation, Muley LaRue's wife's acquiesced to having such dangerous items on the property, but only so long as they were kept in the horse shed where one might suppose curious children would not venture and find the golden blasting caps and bite them as though they were candy and thus blow off their sweet lower jaws.

Of course, Muley LaRue needed no instruction from his wife in protecting the welfare of those two little girls. They were the shining point in his life, maybe because it was only they who could make him know security without the facade of cynicism he had built around himself like the palisades of a fort. He could be tender beyond all expectation when he tucked them into their beds at night and they looked up at him with shining eyes and said,

"Goodnight, Papa." Having them grow up in this uncouth land was a bitter medicine he tasted every day.

Muley LaRue thought constantly of returning to Louisiana. But any serious consideration of such a thing brought the same conclusion. That it was not time, not yet. He had no intention of taking his family back to a place where he might be required to start all over again, so to accept returning meant the necessity of money in his pocket. A good deal of money for the purpose of it would be to impress certain parties in a certain parish, parties who had been responsible for his leaving in the first place. His wife's family.

So a few more years of saving, of squirreling away part of what Herkimer Warson paid him each month. Then, one day, he could take his family back in style and say with the quality of their clothing alone "I told you so!" Muley LaRue was a man whose primary mission in life, it seemed, was to be able to say "I told you so!"

The ancestors of Muley LaRue had arrived in bayou country during the eighteenth century. They had been a part of that group of Frenchmen moved from Nova Scotia to French territory at the mouth of the Mississippi when Canada became British, the result of a long series of conflicts between England and France starting with the War of Spanish Succession and ending with the Seven Years War. In North America, these struggles were called Queen Anne's War and King George's War and the French and Indian War. In Europe, these wars had various causes and effects but in America they were primarily to decide who was going to control the new continent.

So Muley LaRue's people had become what were known as Cajuns and they were a tough and hardy crew and possibly confused because from day to day they hardly could keep up with the sovereignty to which they owed allegiance. Toward the end of the French and Indian War, to prevent it falling into British hands at the peace conference, France ceded Louisiana Territory to the Spaniards. Then, when Napoleon came to power and decided he wanted to get France back into North America, he asked for it back. The situation being as it was, and Napoleon being how he was, Spain gave it to him. So now a mob of French officials descended on New Orleans to govern the territory in place of the Spanish.

To control the vast Mississippi basin, control of the river mouth was necessary which meant control of the Caribbean which meant taking Santo Domino which was governed by former black slaves who had staged a successful revolt. So Napoleon dispatched an army to take the island. It was destroyed by an ex-slave army and yellow fever. He sent another. It was destroyed by the same forces. So he gave up and got the best deal he could, which was selling Louisiana to the United States and consoling himself with the thought that at least it hadn't fallen into English hands.

Suddenly a lot of Frenchmen found themselves citizens of the United States. Some of them shipped home but some stayed. Among these was the Delacroix family, who continued to act as though they were the representatives of the Emperor of France and proceeded to make a fortune in the shrimp trade, although it was of course completely beneath their dignity to ever set foot on one of the smelly boats they came to own. In the fourth generation of this family there was a lovely young woman named Irene.

And there was Muley LaRue, the Cajun who had come out of the bayous when he was eighteen and with a shrewd intelligence established himself among the gentlemen of the Crescent City cotton market as a most ruthlessly efficient security agent for cotton and real estate bigwigs, who due to the nature of their work, found themselves often in the company of hostile debtors or in the position of trying to collect owed money from people who were not only hostile but sometimes hard to find. Muley LaRue adapted well, learning to wear fine clothes and drink from a stem glass with the little finger extended and generally make himself acceptable on the fringes of New Orleans high society.

At one point, accompanying the employer of the moment to Little Rock, Muley LaRue had come to the attention of Herkimer Warson, who was impressed with the young man's demeanor, gave him a business card, and invited him at any time to come to Fort Smith where a good position could be arranged for him. Muley LaRue had no intention of going to Fort Smith, but smiled, pocketed the card, and returned with his boss downriver to New Orleans.

By this time Muley LaRue had met and was seeing Irene Delacroix, to the great irritation of her family who thought of him as a bayou alligator with mud between his toes, but Irene apparently saw something in the young man that nobody else had discovered and she married him. The ceremony took place in the old Spanish cathedral on Jackson Square in the French Quarter, where Muley LaRue claimed to go and confess his sins at least once a year.

Irene's family made no bones about their feelings for their daughter's husband. They let it be known that they agreed to the union only after Irene promised to elope if they didn't. When invited on rare occasions to the Delacroix home, Muley LaRue was treated like one of the servants. One of Irene's brothers told Muley once that if it was a few decades earlier, he'd challenge Muley to a meeting with pistols under the Spanish Moss and blow his Cajun brains out.

It was an unbearable pressure and it was about to drive him mad and it was Irene who finally suggested that their only recourse was to put a lot of distance between their lives and her family. So it was Fort Smith. It did not escape Muley LaRue's quick mind that here he was, run out of his native country by people of his own blood, and given succor by an Englishman. Who but the English, he thought, would ever name anybody Herkimer?

So with the dangerous materials secured from the hands of curious children, Muley LaRue tried to relax for the Yule season, safe within the palisades of his fort with Irene and the two little girls and a roast goose with chestnut dressing, and tried to forget his bitterness with that family who was supposed to be around him now at such a joyous time but who instead had forced him off into the wilds of Arkansas.

And so Christmas of that year passed, everyone trying to imagine there had been snow on the ground and that there was really peace on earth to men of goodwill. And that all the things they wished for in the New Year would come true. And through it all, the business of a thriving community went on, and the trains came each day, and in the railyards were collected and dispatched the cars with lumber, and made furniture and cotton and cases of canned tomatoes and coils of hemp rope and crossties and wagon wheels and leather harness and bags of bone fertilizer. And many times, cars sat on sidings, arriving from one direction, assigned to go another. And the cars waiting their turn in the yards. And some of them tank cars, filled with highly flammable materials. All waiting in the yards to be transported to final destination. All waiting. Just a little way from the line of Fort Smith's houses of joy.

7 Maybe it was a waste of good time thrashing around in the willows and pawpaws and blackjack oak along the Creek Nation bank of the Canadian River. But United States Deputy Marshal Nason Breedlove could no longer ignore Oscar Schiller's skepticism about the official theory that Toby Jupiter's murder had been nothing more than another of those mindless, drunken Indian Territory whacks. Oscar Schiller hadn't said anything at Max Bamberger's on Christmas Day, but afterward he and Nason Breedlove had gone to the Hake basement and spent most of the night rehashing what they knew and what they didn't know about both Toby and Temperance Moon.

Oscar Schiller kept returning to his main theme. "There's more to this than rage killings. I can smell it. I don't know yet what it is, but there's more to it."

And this: "Somebody in it knows I'm looking. That's why they took a shot at me. And Nason, they shot to miss. I know damned well. I was so close to that window it would have took a blind beggar to miss, and whoever it was missed twice."

"Why?" Nason Breedlove asked.

"I don't know. Unless they figured to scare me off. And if I'm right, does that sound like some drunk Indian Territory killer? Hell no! Somebody like that would have cut me off at the neck."

And Nason Breedlove had finally conceded that Oscar Schiller was right. Oscar Schiller's instincts in such things were too well known to dismiss. So now, instead of just half-ass support for the

Kansas City police officer in the I.T., Nason Breedlove was diving in headfirst. Now it would be one of Parker's badges in the hunt, all stops out.

So there he was, in the waning hours of the old year, on the Canadian, looking for something. He didn't know what. But when they'd found Toby Jupiter, Nason Breedlove had been so involved in other cases and so overworked, which was always the case with Parker's deputies, that he hadn't taken a close look at anything. Now, he would. He figured it was a lost cause. But at least the warming trend that had come before Christmas was holding, so a light jacket and leather chaps over heavy cord pants were enough to keep him warm.

He was riding a huge bay mare that despite her size and strength was getting a little irritated at Nason Breedlove's weight after a full day of poking into thickets of sassafras and dead cattails and wild blackberry bush. As the day had gone down, not even the best of his blue language could make much impression on her and she had increasingly fought the bit.

With him was the captain of the Eufaula District Light Horse Police, Moma July, a dark brown, almost black little Creek, smaller than most Creek men. He never went abroad in spring, summer, fall, or winter without wearing an old Union Army overcoat with three bullet holes in it. Nor without carrying a snubnosed ten-gauge Winchester shotgun. He spoke perfect English and about five other languages, although nobody had ever accused him to his face of having attended a day of school in his life.

Moma July was so dark-skinned that Nason Breedlove suspected he had a grandfather somewhere who had mated with one of the African slaves the Creeks brought with them from east of the Mississippi River at Removal. None of which made any difference to Nason Breedlove. What made a difference was that Moma July was one of the best police officers Nason Breedlove had ever seen, whether black, white, red, brown, or any hue in between.

This had been a dull day but the cloud cover was not thick enough to hide the bronze disk of sun. As it moved closer to the sea of black, leafless branches along the western horizon, Nason Breedlove reined in the bay mare and looked at the river. In this half-light, it was like a trail of dull silver, motionless, without any appearance of depth. A ribbon of light beneath the gray sky.

"Moma," Nason Breedlove said, "my butt's like it was glued to this saddle. Let's head home for beefsteak."

"All right," said the Creek. "But we been doin' good."

What they'd been doing was starting at the old corncrib where Toby Jupiter's body had been found. And now they knew beyond doubt that he'd been killed there, not someplace else and dragged into the crib. Now, over three months later, under the protection of the sheet-metal roof, the black stain on the earth marked the spot. Moma July dug into the sandy soil with a pocketknife and the blood color ran deep. Not the kind of thing where most of the blood had drained out someplace else, but all of it right there.

Nason Breedlove recalled the coroner's finding. Shot in the back, three times, so close the muzzle blast had burned a hole in Toby Jupiter's heavy jacket, shirt, and flannel underwear. They'd dug out those slugs, not a one having passed completely through the body, so a low-velocity weapon, probably a Colt .45 pistol. And the three shots so closely spaced that Toby Jupiter was likely shot while lying down asleep. Had he been standing, after the first shot he would have fallen, and the others would have been scattered. Unless the assailant had waited until Toby hit the ground and then taken pains to shoot him twice more close to the same spot. Unlikely. Those kinds of shots almost always went into the head. A *coup de grâce*.

In the crib were a couple of leafy beds, or what could have been beds. No sort of permanent camp. An overnight stay, maybe to shelter in the rain until time to check trotlines in the morning, a place to stay dry and get drunk. There was an empty whiskey bottle.

"There was some rain early in September," said Nason Breedlove.

"Yes," Moma July said. "The night before Temperance Moon was killed. Remember all the mud in that road when her body was found?"

"Yeah. Yeah. And it rained the next two nights. I remember. When we taken all that Fawley Farm bunch into Fort Smith."

There was a pathway from the crib to the bank of the river, beaten down from a long time ago through the dog fennel. They followed it to the water's edge but found nothing at first. Then a trotline, tied to a willow. A good line, not twine string. When they pulled it in, there was a fish head at the end, the rest of the fish gone, either rotted or eaten by turtles. In the fish's skeletal mouth was a fishhook, a steel hook, not a homemade one like most of the Creeks used, but a steel hook that could be had from a mail-order house or in a hardware store in Muskogee or Fort Smith.

They found half a dozen trotlines. All with the good line, all with the steel hooks. They found only one with cotton string and a homemade hook. Moma July was putting all of this into a small burlap bag he had tied to his saddle horn.

"Them hooks?" Nason Breedlove asked.

"Not Toby," said Moma July. "I never heard of him using store-bought truck when he fished."

They began combing the willows well back from the riverbank, working downstream. Where one might expect fishermen to establish a permanent camp. At first, there was nothing. Then about a half mile downstream from the corncrib, they found it in a stand of new black locusts. There was an arrangement of rocks to form a fireplace, and in that a depth of ashes that indicated fires for a number of days had been made, and Moma July estimated that the age of the ashes fit well into the framework of early September.

They found a few fishhooks, lost in the leaves. Steel fishhooks. There were lengths of the fishing line, mail-order line, which had been used for some camp purpose. There was a coffeepot with the bottom burned out. There were a number of empty whiskey bottles. And many turtle shells.

"Toby loved them turtles," Moma July said. "Catch ole turtle, whack off his head, throw him in the coals, let him cook awhile, prize off the bottom plate, eat him. Right out of his own shell. Toby loved to eat turtles like that."

"How the hell you know all this?" Nason Breedlove asked.

"Me and Toby," said Moma July, "we used to fish a lot together when I was some younger and him just a snot-nose. Before I taken up with the law and Toby taken up with the whiskey. Toby was crazy, even then."

Then they found the big prize. A small metal tackle box, hinges and clasps rusted but when opened displaying fishing gear advertised in the Sears and Roebuck catalogues.

"Ain't Toby's," said Nason Breedlove.

"No," said Moma July, and neither of them had to say what they now knew. That Toby Jupiter had been on this particular fishing trip with a white man. Who had left camp in a hurry.

And maybe not thinking too straight, what with leaving things behind. Stupid or scared. Maybe both.

Oscar Schiller is one smart son of a bitch, Nason Breedlove thought.

"Good line, steel hooks, bobbers, corks, lead sinkers," Moma July said, staring into the tackle box. "Just not the kind of things a Creek needs for fishing."

Moma July put the tackle box in the burlap bag.

"Let's get to hell in to some beefsteak," said Nason Breedlove, so they'd started the slow ride home to Eufaula, skies darkening. As they rode, Nason Breedlove said, "Moma, if you'd just killed Temperance Moon, would you go fishin'?"

"If I was as crazy as Toby Jupiter, I might," the Creek policeman said. "But even if I was that crazy, I never would have left that shotgun close to her body after I'd did it."

They took a wide detour around the Redstripe farm. Nason Breedlove knew Moses Masada was there now, as he most generally was these days, and he wasn't quite ready to talk yet with the Yankee policeman. About a mile beyond the Redstripe holdings, Moma July drew rein and sat in the growing darkness, thinking.

"You got a bite?" Nason Breedlove asked.

"That oldest Lurley boy," said Moma July. "He fishes this river a lot. I wanta talk to him."

"Nothin' like the present," said Nason Breedlove. "It ain't far out of the way. That beefsteak can wait another hour, I reckon."

卍 卍 卍 It was full dark when they rode into the scab-rock yard of the Lurley place. Two bony hounds came out to bark, but there was no threat in it. The house was a log-chink one-room affair without any windows. But they knew there was a lamp lighted inside because they could see the shine of it through cracks in the door.

"Hello the house," Nason Breedlove shouted. "Miz Lurley, it's Nason Breedlove. You there?"

The door opened and in its rectangle of light was outlined the thin body of the woman, bony as her hounds. She was wearing a cotton dress, like a smock. Below it they could see her bare feet. Above, the shine of hair docked just below the ears.

"Light down, Marshal," she called. "But I ain't got no coffee for you."

"No coffee required, Miz Lurley. Official business."

Even before they got inside, they could see the children skittering about behind the woman, many just toddlers, and all looking like foxes trying to find someplace to hide. Once in the door, all around the room were the little brown faces with wide eyes, watching them expectantly, fearfully.

The floor here was packed earth. The furniture, what there was of it, was handmade from rough lumber or fence-post locust. There was a small cast-iron cookstove at the back wall. In the center of the room was a table across which were scattered various-sized chipped bowls with the remnants of the family supper. Cornmeal mush. At the center of the table was a coal-oil lamp with a smoke-blackened globe, and still sitting at one end of the table was the eldest of the children, Samuel, about ten years old and man of this house since his daddy had gone about a year before.

Moma July, who had brought in the burlap bag with all their findings at the fish camps, spoke to the woman in Creek. She answered him in the same. Samuel, his mouth still full of the last of his mush, watched with bright eyes as he chewed and swallowed. His Adam's apple bobbed in a skinny neck.

"She says go ahead," said Moma July.

"You do it. But in English, for Christ's sake," said Nason Breedlove.

Moma July moved to the table and settled himself on one of the empty stools, putting the burlap bag on the table. His Union Army coat hung to the floor all around him.

"Samuel, you know me. We're not here to hurt you."

The boy nodded. Swallowing again. His eyes went to his mother's face, and she nodded.

Moma July reached into the burlap bag and brought out the one homemade fishhook they'd found. He laid it on the table as though he were putting down a coin for a poker bet.

"This yours?"

The boy looked at the fishhook a long time before nodding.

"I thought it might be," said Moma July.

"Made it out of baling wire," Samuel said. His voice sounded strangely falsetto in contrast to Moma July's deep bass.

Moma July took out a fistful of the steel hooks. He cast them on the table and they glinted in the lamplight.

"These yours?"

The boy shook his head.

"Them's store hooks," he said.

"All right," said Moma July. With his brown-black hands he moved the steel fishhooks about on the table, like dominoes. "Samuel, you ever fish the river with Toby Jupiter?"

The boy's eyes went quickly to his mother's face, and she, showing absolutely no emotion through all of this, nodded again.

"Sometimes."

"You ever see Toby Jupiter with this kind of hook?"

"No. Them's store hooks."

Moma July stirred the hooks on the tabletop.

"You seen them kind before, though, haven't you?"

Samuel's eyes went to his mother once more, and once more she nodded.

"That white man. Used to come a lot of times and fish with Toby. Make camp on the river. Get drunk. Fish."

"You ever with them?"

"No. That was after I fished with Toby, a long time ago."

"But you seen this white man?"

"Sure."

"Who was he?" Moma July asked.

Now the woman spoke, quickly, as though to prevent her son saying anything.

"The one useta come with Miss Temperance sometimes when Miss Temperance come to visit on Saturday," she said. "Sometimes he come with her. Here to the place."

"And Miss Temperance brought grub," the boy said. And there was a rustle of sound from some of the surrounding tiny faces. But then the woman spoke sharply in Creek and Samuel turned his head down to his empty mush bowl.

Now Moma July produced the little tackle box from his burlap bag, released the catches, and opened the lid, and the rusted hinges made a metallic squeal. The boy looked up and Moma July pushed the open box close to him.

"That's his stuff," the boy said before his mother could stop him. "I seen it lots of times."

"What man, Samuel?" asked Moma July.

The boy swallowed, painfully, and looked at his mother.

"What man, Samuel?"

"Sherman Boggs," the woman said. And the boy took a deep

breath as though glad he had not been required to pronounce the name. "Sherman Boggs," she said again.

ℵ ℵ ℵ As they left the Lurley place, Nason Breedlove put a ten-dollar gold piece into the woman's hand.

"Tomorrow," he said, "go in town and buy these young 'uns some meat and yourself some coffee."

"Did he do all right, my boy?" she asked.

"That Sam, why yes, he done fine."

"I aim to keep him out of the place where his daddy's at, if I can."

"He done fine," said Nason Breedlove.

The daddy was in a federal penitentiary serving twenty years for armed robbery. Nason Breedlove knew because he'd made the arrest and in the process had shot Samuel's daddy in the left leg.

"Thank you, Marshal," the woman said. "We can use the grub."

ℵ ℵ ℵ Muskrat Wewoka was a Seminole whose family had never been able to accommodate to so much dry land after the time old Andy Jackson and troops had caught them in the Florida Everglades and sent them off to the Indian Territory. So they took the only waters available there, which were the drainage-system streams of the Arkansas River, and thus became rivermen. At first, there were only canoes. But then flat-bottom pole boats and then barges propelled by long sweeps and finally, after the Civil War, a little sidewheel steamboat with a wood-burning boiler. One of those legendary plains river steamboats that everybody said could crawl over dry land when a spring rain had put a little damp on it.

Legend or not, by the time Muskrat Wewoka came along and took the name of the principal town in Seminole Nation mostly just for the hell of it, the river enterprise never got to touch Seminole Nation because that far west the water in most streams was so unpredictable and shallow that no boat anywhere could navigate it. So Muskrat Wewoka became a Creek Nation citizen, all right in the records of the census, and plied his trade on the three forks of the Canadian to the Arkansas just south of Webbers Falls in Cherokee Nation, thence downstream and into the state of Arkansas at Fort Smith and on to Van Buren and sometimes as far east as Clarksville.

The nature of Muskrat Wewoka's trade was the shipment of fiber bales out of the Indian Territory to the big cotton markets in Fort Smith. Or sometimes a few hogs or even a beef cow or two or twig crates of chickens. And in summer, bushel baskets filled with red-ripe tomatoes or yellow squash or ears of sweet corn, white and pearly as a five-year-old's baby teeth.

But the little steamboat couldn't carry a lot of heavy plunder like cotton and watermelons. So the trip into white man's country where Indian Territory farmers wanted to sell their produce was only a break-even proposition. Comeback was another matter. Because the little steamboat was more than big enough to carry a profitable load of bootleg whiskey.

Muskrat Wewoka wasn't a bootlegger himself. He was a middleman. A white man would contract with him to carry kegs or bottles or jugs from Arkansas. So he would load the little steamboat. Then, always minding his own business and feeding short-cut oak staves into his firebox, would churn past Belle Point and thus into Indian Nation. Past Paw Paw and Briartown in Cherokee Nation, into North Fork of the Canadian and past Eufaula, and finally come to rest on the south bank of the middle fork of the Canadian about halfway between the mouth of Deep Fork and Wetumka Mission School.

There the steamboat would nose onto a willow sandbar, a jungle. In spring and summer a jungle of green. In winter a jungle of gray branches. In fall a jungle of yellow and red leaves dying. Then the cargo would be carried back into the deep timber of walnut and oak and wild cherry to a couple of clapboard shacks with metal roofs, and there the white-man contractors or their agents would take up the containers and move them out into the Nations for the thirsty citizens. Every step of which was, of course, against the laws not only of Creek Nation but of the United States of America.

Which Muskrat Wewoka knew. But figured, what the hell! They ain't caught me yet. So long as luck rides with you, he reckoned, why go against it?

This wilderness landing, which wasn't a landing at all in the usual sense, was called Muskrat Bend. It was the northernmost quarter section of real estate known as Fawley Farm. And in fact, to use this place, Muskrat Wewoka had to pay a fee to Temperance Moon before she died. Now that she had died, he assumed he paid the new owner, Langston Turtle. But he didn't know, because he had not made landfall at the Bend even once since Temperance had been killed.

Muskrat Wewoka was not a greedy man. He made a tolerable living on the river, enough to keep him happy. There was no wife to support nor children for whom he was required to be responsible. He didn't drink whiskey himself. He was a kind of waterborne hermit.

Muskrat Wewoka had never been arrested by anyone. He knew why. The Indian police and the marshal out of Fort Smith were so busy with all kinds of things there was no earthly way they could arrest all the bootleggers in the Territory, even if they could find them. But most of all, he knew he'd never had serious troubles with the law because he'd minded his own business and been lucky. Each day, no matter that half of them were spent breaking the law, he told himself that it didn't matter so long as the luck held. A good life meant being lucky. Just lucky.

On that early January day, when it had started turning cold again and he ran the boat onto the sandbar at the Bend with a load of whiskey for a man from Arebeka, the first time he had been there since Temperance Moon had died, Muskrat Wewoka realized his luck had run out when he was met by Creek Policeman Moma July, United States Deputy Marshal Nason Breedlove, and a small man dressed in dude clothes whom the other two called Masada.

Muskrat Wewoka, standing in the trail to the shacks holding a cardboard box filled with whiskey bottles, didn't have much chance to say anything.

"Muskrat," said Moma July, holding his shotgun ready, "you're under arrest. You move, I'll kill you."

Muskrat Wewoka's eyes darted around to all these law people. He licked his lips.

"Moma," he said, "I'd sure like to set down this case of whiskey, because it's heavy as hell."

"Set it down, then."

And the white marshal said, "Better get back on that scow of yours, Muskrat, and get an overcoat. Gettin' cold again. And we goin' into Eufaula for a little talk."

Muskrat bent down with a loud grunt and put the box of whiskey on the ground, straightened, and smiled, a large smile showing teeth browned over long years of chewing tobacco.

"Well, all right," he said, looking at Nason Breedlove. "But I sure hope you aim to get me into Fort Smith and not give me to these people."

He poked a finger in the direction of Moma July.

"I sure don't cotton to get tied to a tree and whipped with a leather strop."

Moma July jabbed Muskrat Wewoka in the belly with the snout of his shotgun, and Muskrat gasped and bent down for a moment, but only for a moment.

"Hell, Muskrat," Moma July said. "We ain't gonna whip nobody like you. We gone kill you!"

Ꮓ Ꮓ Ꮓ At the Eufaula Light Horse stationhouse and jail, a log structure of two rooms just down the railroad tracks from the KATY depot, there was an interrogation. The two rooms of this building consisted of the Light Horse headquarters, which meant there was a rifle rack and table there, and a jail, which meant it had a door with a lock on it. And for both, a couple of coal-oil lamps.

It was not difficult. The information Muskrat Wewoka was suspected of having indeed he had. The questioning consisted mostly of Moma July jabbing Muskrat Wewoka in the gut with the muzzle of his shotgun while two Creek policemen stood by, obviously anxious to apply the same sort of persuasion. Nobody had to explain to Muskrat Wewoka that there might be a few Seminoles counted as citizens of Creek Nation in the census, but ever since some serious and often deadly squabbles between them over the ownership of certain slaves at the time of Removal, there had never been any love lost between Creek and Seminole.

Another big problem for Muskrat Wewoka was this little, oily, sweet-talking man in the bowler hat, coming from so many directions with his questions that Muskrat Wewoka contradicted himself now and then, and finally gave it all up. Well, not really. Why he gave it all up was the United States Deputy Marshal who asked no single question but from time to time remarked to one of the Creek policemen that it was too bad old Muskrat wasn't showing a proper spirit of cooperation, which meant that instead of hauling him off to Fort Smith he'd have to be left right here in Eufaula so the Creeks could apply their own form of justice.

Under such pressure, a law-abiding man like Muskrat Wewoka could be expected to tell anything he knew, to include the secret tattoo on his ass, because he figured they'd find it anyway, and all else he had ever done or wanted to do or expected to do. And so he did. He told them so much that there was a problem of deciding what was true and what was a babble of what Muskrat Wewoka wanted them to hear. But they got what they wanted.

Before the end of the day, Nason Breedlove was waiting beside the tracks for a northbound KATY train, to ride it to the junction at Wagoner and then change to the Arkansas Valley Railroad into Fort Smith. To pick up Oscar Schiller and go on to Van Buren, where they were sure from the words of Muskrat Wewoka they would find Sherman Boggs.

That was what it meant. Sherman Boggs.

Muskrat Wewoka didn't matter. But he didn't know that. So he went with Nason Breedlove, at least as far as Fort Smith. Where he would be secured until arraigned before the United States Commissioner on a charge of introducing intoxicating beverages into the Indian Territory. And Muskrat Wewoka was overjoyed when they put the wrist manacles and leg irons on him, because it meant he was going away from the Creeks, and was more than happy to wear all that iron to Fort Smith, wear it until the door in Judge Parker's jail closed on him.

As he was mounting the caboose, Muskrat Wewoka looked at Moma July, standing well back from the train. And shouted at him in the growing cold wind.

"Take that shotgun, Moma, and stick it in your nose now."

"All right, Muskrat," the Creek policeman said. "You ain't gonna be over there in Fort Smith all your life. I'll be here when you get back."

And standing at the caboose, ready to mount it, Nason Breedlove said to Moses Masada, "Keep playin' the little game."

"Shit! The game's played out," Moses Masada said. "Now, every time I'm in town, I see one of those two people who wear the sugarloaf hats, watching me. This Temperance Moon will thing was a bust. A bad idea."

"Nothin' for it now but to keep goin'. Don't show your hand."

"That Fawley Farm bunch, they know it's a fake."

"Sure. So that makes 'em stew in their juice awhile, if they's juice to stew in. Listen, Moma July's ass-deep in this thing now. You can depend on him. And don't go wanderin' around the countryside alone. You hear?"

"Yes, but I'm going to Texas shortly. For some horse races," Moses Masada said. "With Candy Redstripe. Denison, I think he said."

"Good, good," said Nason Breedlove. Then laughed and gripped one of Moses Masada's shoulders in a great hand. "Listen, boy, don't bet no money against one of Candy's crazy little ponies, you hear?"

卍 卍 卍 Moses Masada hated to see that train leave without him. Everything had gone flat in Eufaula District and now all left for him was to fume over the dead end to which he'd come in the case.

At this time of year, when railroad work crews spent a lot of hours out on the line checking for frost damage to rails, ties, and bridges, the section foreman was seldom in Eufaula but away supervising his people. So it was now with Mr. Curtis Danton, the present section foreman, hence few of those afternoon and evening checker games which could soak up a lot of Moses Masada's time. When he wasn't at the Redstripe farm.

Almost a week of inactivity ahead now. In a few days, he'd be going with Candy Redstripe to Texas to race horses. For the present, there was no one at the Redstripe farm to visit, because Candy had taken his wife to Muskogee to buy quilt material and other such things. Which left friendly faces only at the Creek Light Horse Police station and jail, and even there, the faces not so friendly. No matter what Nason Breedlove had said about Creek police support, Moses Masada always felt an ill-defined nervousness around these Creek peace officers and a large part of that was his sense that they were not very comfortable with him, either.

So that left the empty, barnlike section house.

It was a rough-lumber, two-story affair, three large rooms on the first floor, four small ones on the second. From the sparsely furnished parlor, a staircase ascended halfway up to the rooms above and then took a ninety-degree angle at a landing, hence straight into the hallway that ran the length of the house, two rooms on either side.

This section house served sometimes as a hotel for particular friends of the KATY line, being as it was occupied by only Mr. Danton, whose family was still in Fort Scott, Kansas, whence he had come and to which he hoped soon to return. It was to serve a hotel purpose in the plans for the Texas horse-racing trip.

Candy Redstripe had sent Toad and half a dozen ponies south across Choctaw Nation to Red River, then fording to Denison, where the horses could graze a few days and rest for the running. Candy Redstripe and Moses Masada would go by rail, taking a Missouri, Kansas, and Texas day coach on the regular-run southbound passenger train that came through Eufaula at five o'clock each morning. It meant that Candy Redstripe would have been required to rise a little after midnight on the appointed day in order to arrive in town when the train did, so Moses Masada had suggested that Candy Redstripe come to Eufaula the night before and spend the night with him at the section house. Both would be ready and waiting after good sleep when the little KATY road engine snaked its cars into town during the pre-dawn darkness.

But all of that was a week away. So Moses Masada faced seven days of trying to occupy himself in Eufaula, Creek Nation, which did not exactly provide the kinds of entertainment to which Moses Masada had become accustomed in Kansas City, Missouri. He felt, in fact, like a chunk of river driftwood lying dead in the water, caught in an eddy beyond reach of the flowing current.

So he lay in his upstairs bedroom at the section house with the face of Tishacomsie Redstripe spread across every page of his mind. And there interrupted in his woolgathering only when a freight train rumbled past, shaking the entire house violently and making the cup on his bedside table rattle in its saucer.

And each time a freight train passed and the house shook and his cup rattled, he paused for a moment in his consideration of love and passion and reflected on the adaptability of man. When he had first come here, each night as a train passed close beneath his window, he had started up violently from sleep because of the noise and shaking of the house. But in only a short time, he could sleep through it with nothing more than a vague sense of irritation. And it amused him to think of the night Candy Redstripe would be in a section-house bed as the freights came through, Candy, being accustomed to the solitude and silence of sleep far upstream along the Canadian where no metal columns rumbled close by with their clanging and rattling and bells and whistles, and smells of oil and cinders.

8 Langston Turtle felt like a mouse. A fat mouse caught in a mason fruit jar with hungry cats squatting all around just outside the protecting glass. Waiting for him to come out so they could eat him.

And behind the cats, another mouse, rushing frantically from one crack to another in the walls. But the cats never noticing.

The other mouse was Winona. And the two waiting cats were Goshen and Claiburn Crowfoot. And sometimes, in his mind, Langston Turtle saw the little female mouse transformed into another cat, to join her brothers beside the glass walls of his fruit jar, waiting with them, waiting to tear him apart and devour him. To eat his liver.

Since his sister-in-law's death, everything had changed. Langston Turtle had supposed it would change, but for the better, him a landowner and the lord of castle at Fawley Farm instead of the fat prince sitting at the feet of Temperance Moon. Well, it had changed. But not for the better. My God, he thought, not for the better. He had thought that once more all those old friends would come, bringing their women, bringing whiskey, everybody could get drunk and play cards and sing, a few slip off to Chocktaw Nation to steal a little pig, a shoat, to be roasted over an open pit with hickory fire beneath. The good times.

But it had never turned for the better. Always for the worse. There had been one happy day at Christmas, everybody singing and getting sick, but then the next morning the sullen faces, the suspicion. Everything more brittle than before. It had become intolerable. He was so afraid that he had trouble eating. He had trouble forcing down a sip of whiskey. He had trouble getting under covers with Winona because she was the sister of these other two. She stroked him, but he wondered if maybe it was because her fingers were looking for the soft spot where a blade could go in.

Everything frightened him. He saw danger behind every word, every move. He had been frightened when Goshen Crowfoot and Sherman Boggs went to Arkansas, but now when Goshen Crowfoot was back, he was frightened more. And the idea of Sherman Boggs somewhere talking to people terrified him. And why had Muskrat Wewoka been arrested and taken off to Fort Smith in irons? And with this new man with dude clothes right there at the caboose to see them off?

"That Iowa jake leg," Goshen Crowfoot kept saying. "With a will, he says. Too much poking his nose in. We need to kill him."

And Langston Turtle most terrified of all because the Crowfoot brothers might discover the money he had under the floor beneath his bed, bringing out only enough now and then to give the Crowfoots so they could go to Muskogee or some such place and get whores and drink good whiskey normally reserved for Missouri Pacific Railroad main-line conductors.

That money! A source of pride at first, but now a horror. At first, more money than most people in Creek Nation would ever see in a year, two years. And if Goshen Crowfoot began to wonder where these little dribbles to him came from, little dribbles for the whoring and drinking, he and his brother would get the wire pliers from the barn so they could pull off a few Langston Turtle toenails until they found the source of such treasure.

It gave him a headache. His feet were swollen. His eyes were so grainy that it was hard to see across the room.

And in this state, Langston Turtle came to the conclusion that Goshen Crowfoot was right. The man from Iowa with that Temperance Moon will was trouble, large trouble. That Iowa man established in a room at the Eufaula railroad section foreman's house. If he would just go away, maybe the troubles would go with him. This new man nosing around had meant nothing but trouble.

So maybe, Langston Turtle thought, maybe Goshen Crowfoot was right. Maybe, Langston Turtle thought with a shudder, we need to kill this Iowa man.

꒭ ꒭ ꒭ It had been Oscar Schiller's experience that when an attempt was made to apprehend an Indian Territory criminal, one of two reactions could be expected. The accused would either start shooting or else throw himself to the ground and confess his sins while offering up heartrending prayers begging forgiveness from a suddenly discovered although hitherto never mentioned savior.

"A solid bench warrant," Oscar Schiller told Nason Breedlove, "can convert more men to Christ than the best hell-and-brimstone preacher I ever saw."

"Yeah," Nason Breedlove said. "When a man faces the prospect of a Parker rope around his neck, I reckon he's bound to take every option he's got."

United States Commissioner Claude Bains had issued the warrant for Nason Breedlove to serve on Sherman Boggs. It was for traffic in illegal spirits in the Indian Nations. Which could be a very solid jolt, especially, as in the case of Sherman Boggs, if it involved violating a legal permit to be in the Territory in the first place. Say up to ten years in the federal penitentiary at Detroit, which was a very inhospitable place according to all who had gone there and survived to get out.

The apprehension part of it was so easy neither Oscar Schiller nor Nason Breedlove could believe it. But Muskrat Wewoka's information was rock-solid, and following it, they found Sherman Boggs holing up in a shed behind the main Van Buren warehouses of one Simon Gracy, wholesaler in such commodities as barbed wire, cattle feed, bolt cloth, cotton batting, canned goods, and whiskey.

Mr. Gracy was more than helpful, once he understood the nature of the operation. Because he was smart enough to understand that had he not been, United States Deputy Marshal Nason Breedlove could go back across the river to Fort Smith and hence to the commissioner's court and get another warrant for Mr. Gracy himself on the charge of accessory before the fact of shipping hard spirits into the Indian Territory.

So Mr. Gracy made an elaborate show of amazement that Sherman Boggs, a business associate for years and a man to whom he had just recently rented sleeping space in one of his sheds, had ever done anything against the laws of the United States of America, and then led them directly to where Sherman Boggs was reclining on two bales of cotton covered with blankets, reading an old copy of the *Police Gazette*.

It was not an impressive hideout. Later, Nason Breedlove would say that ole Sherman would have done better in some Ozark mountain limestone cave. There was a small oil stove, fighting a losing battle against the cold and making the place smell of burnt coal oil, a few empty wooden cases, an old chipped enamel chamber pot, about half full and adding its own odor, and a few dirty shirts thrown into one corner.

"Sherman," Nason Breedlove said, "you live like a hog!"

As Nason Breedlove snapped handcuffs on Sherman Boggs's hands, Boggs did neither of the things Oscar Schiller had thought he would do. He had not started shooting, and in fact, when they searched through the place, there was no firearm there at all. And he did not begin praying. But Oscar Schiller could smell fear, and Sherman Boggs's pale, almost yellow eyes darted about within their deep folds of flesh and there was a thin shine of sweat on his forehead, although the shed was not warm. Oscar Schiller had never observed this man at close quarters and he was not a man one would suspect being capable of cold-blooded murder. Rather plump, close-cropped brown hair, thick lips parted to allow a softly rasping breath in and out.

Watching Sherman Boggs, Oscar Schiller had the feeling that here was a man who had been waiting, and now that the wait was over Sherman Boggs was glad that he wouldn't have to wait any longer. Sitting on his cotton-bale bed, hands chained between his legs, Sherman Boggs looked like one of those children's doll toys, the Raggedy Ann kind of toy, overstuffed and pink-cheeked and yarn-haired and bloodless.

Nason Breedlove read the warrant. Then explained that Muskrat Wewoka was in custody and that federal and Creek authorities could assemble a dozen people from the Nations who would testify that Sherman Boggs had been dealing whiskey in Indian Territory for many years. Sherman Boggs listened with no expression on his face, no movement except the eyes that darted about as though trying to escape their folds of flesh.

When Nason Breedlove was finished, Sherman Boggs said, calmly enough, that he was ready to go into Fort Smith and be placed in Judge Parker's jail. And Nason Breedlove said they'd do that straight off and then Sherman Boggs could make bond and go back to his friends in Creek Nation and wait there until his trial. When Nason Breedlove said that, the pale eyes danced back and forth furiously and the breathing became faster, more audible.

"I won't make bail," Sherman Boggs said. His voice was like a fiddle string too tightly tuned, high and quavering. "I'll lay it out in jail."

"Well, maybe one of your Creek Nation friends can go your bond," Nason Breedlove said.

Sherman Boggs shook his head violently. "I'll lay it out."

Nason Breedlove and Oscar Schiller exchanged a glance and moved to the shed's single door and outside into the cold wind. Mr. Gracy was at the corner of his warehouse, watching.

"Go about your business," Nason Breedlove shouted and Mr. Gracy disappeared back into the barnlike structure where reposed his barbed wire and canned goods and cattle feed and whiskey. "Son of a bitch. He's the one we oughta be takin' in to Parker's jail."

"Nason," said Oscar Schiller, "you see what I do here?"

"Yeah. Old Sherman's scared out of his pants. But not of you and me. And not of a time in jail."

"Where he'd be safe from friends."

"Yeah," said Nason Breedlove, sucking at the ends of his mustache. "Son of a bitch. We seen it a hundred times. Man lookin' for jail to protect him from his friends. Shit! Oscar, let's put the big one on him, see what happens."

"Yes."

"You wanta do it?"

"No. You're wearing the badge. I'm just an innocent bystander."

Nason Breedlove laughed. "Yeah, I'd like to be so friggin' innocent. But you can spin out that tale we made up better than me."

"No. You're doing good, Nason. You're doing good."

"All right. Let's take another whack at the bastard!"

Sherman Boggs had not moved from his perch on the cottonbale bed. Only his eyes moved, except that a small twitch had developed in the fingers of his left hand. Nason Breedlove moved to him gently, placed a hand tenderly on one of Sherman Boggs's shoulders. When Nason Breedlove spoke, his voice was quiet, soft, and hearing it in this unusual timbre, Oscar Schiller had to suppress a smile.

"Sherman," Nason Breedlove said, leaning close to Sherman Boggs's face with his own, "we been lyin' to you. We don't aim to lie to you. But it's the nature of our work. I'm awful sorry. But what we come to do is arrest you for something besides runnin' whiskey. We know you been doin' that. But we come to arrest you for something else. We gonna take you across the river to Commissioner Bain's court and he's gonna bind you over to the grand jury for murder."

For the first time, the pale eyes were still, focusing on Nason Breedlove's face, and the federal marshal nodded. Then the eyes darted away again and the mouth turned down and the pink little tongue flicked out to wet the lips and the sweat had begun to grow drops large enough to run down Sherman Boggs's cheeks.

"No. No. No." Sherman Boggs whispered it. Each word. Without getting control of his eyes.

"Sherman, listen," said Nason Breedlove. "Listen now, Sherman. We found your fishin' gear. Down along the Canadian. You know. Where you left it when you run off."

"Fishing gear?" Sherman Boggs suddenly shouted, his voice rasping. "I don't know nothin' about fishin' gear!"

"Sure, sure you do," said Nason Breedlove. "Everybody seen it said it's yours. It's the gear you had when you and Toby Jupiter went out to camp for a while. In September. Remember?"

"I never."

"Sure you did, Sherman. We know that. You and Toby fished a lot together because he was crazy and none of that other bunch at Fawley ever went with him, but you did, didn't you, Sherman? Everybody in Creek Nation knows that."

"I never," Sherman Boggs whispered, his eyes darting, his tongue flicking, his hands now twitching like running spiders. "I never."

"Aw, now Sherman," whispered Nason Breedlove. "In September. Right after Toby stole that Belgian shotgun. Good shotgun, wasn't it, Sherman? Say, you know, I was wonderin' where at's that Colt .45 pistol of yours?"

"What? What Colt .45 pistol?"

"The one you had all these years?"

"I give it away!"

"You done what? Jesus, Sherman, a good pistol like that. Who to?"

"I don't remember, I don't remember."

"Well, anyway, we was wonderin' why you was up there at Jewel Moon's place in Weedy Rough there in September."

"Condolences," Sherman Boggs gasped. "For condolences. For Jewel's mother."

"You and Goshen Crowfoot?"

"What?"

"Never mind. We know who all was there. But why the hell would you go to Weedy Rough for condolences?"

"Well, you know, just condolences."

"Jewel wasn't there. She was in Fort Smith."

"We figured she might come up there."

"Shit, Sherman. We think you're a big liar," said Nason Breedlove, but still softly. Now, Sherman Boggs's entire body was twitching. His hands were shaking so badly the chains between the iron bracelets on his wrists were clinking.

Nason Breedlove glanced at Oscar Schiller, and Oscar Schiller nodded. Nason Breedlove bent close to their prisoner's face.

"Listen, Sherman, we know," he said, almost a whisper. "We know what happened. You and Toby went on that fishin' trip and he had that shotgun and he got drunk and you killed him and took that shotgun and went over and killed Temperance Moon because you was mad at her about something. That's what you done, Sherman. And you gonna hang for it!"

"I never," Sherman Boggs screamed, now yanking at his handcuffs, sweat and tears spraying around his violently contorting face. "I never done any such a thing."

"Sure you did, Sherman," Nason Breedlove said, still quietly, still with his face close to Sherman Boggs's, still with a hand on Sherman Boggs's shoulder. "You killed Toby and took that shotgun everybody knew he'd stole and you killed Temperance Moon and left the gun so we'd all think Toby done it and then you run off here to Arkansas. Didn't you, Sherman?"

"I didn't do that," Sherman Boggs said, but now his voice was a whisper, as though the last of the vehemence was burned out. As though there was resignation.

"Sherman, we got a lot of people who will say in court that you done all that," Nason Breedlove lied.

And in a last burst of fury, Sherman Boggs screamed, "Those sonsabitches, those sonsabitches."

"What sonsabitches, Sherman? Which ones?"

But after the last outburst, Sherman Boggs seemed to sag on

his bale-of-cotton bed, all strength gone, all evaporated except for the sweat and tears that ran down his face, and his head lowered, his eyes closed. And his shoulders shook under Nason Breedlove's hand.

Nason Breedlove sighed, straightened, took his hand from Sherman Boggs, and looked at Oscar Schiller. Who shrugged. They both knew Sherman Boggs had said all he would say. At least for now.

ℵ ℵ ℵ Much later that day, with bad weather kicking in from the west and a sharp, bitter little wind blowing along Garrison Avenue, Oscar Schiller and Nason Breedlove sat in Cantoni's having baked beans and beer. Sherman Boggs had been deposited in the federal jail and United States Attorney Walter Evans had been apprised of all their findings. He said that with what they had now, taking Sherman Boggs before the grand jury for murder would be fruitless but there was more than enough evidence to hold him for taking whiskey into the Nations.

"Well," Nason Breedlove said, swiping beer foam from his mustache, "that's two in a row on this one."

"Two in a row what?" asked Oscar Schiller.

"Two in a row who's happy to be safe in our jail. Ole Muskrat because the Creek courts can't get at him there. Ole Sherman because somebody else can't get at *him*. But damned if I know who."

"Remember what I said a long time ago," said Oscar Schiller. "Langston Turtle had most to gain in all this."

"Yeah, and no doubt ole Sherman was part of that pack of wolves always hangin' out at Temperance Moon's. Tell you one thing, I'd like to know where that pistol of ole Sherman's is at."

"It don't signify," said Oscar Schiller. "There's gotta be eight hundred Colt .45s in this part of the country. From what I've seen of him, it wouldn't surprise me if Boggs just forgot and left it someplace, like he did the tackle box you told me about. Scared shitless."

"Well, you know that cock-and-bull story we told ole Sherman seemed to take some effect."

"Yes. And making up what you call cock-and-bull stories is part of this work."

"You was always better at that than me, Oscar. You could always make up more shit than anybody I ever knew, and what's nice is that mostly it turns out close to the mark. Here comes Maria."

Maria Cantoni came from the kitchen, wiping her hands on a half apron. She had a flame-red ribbon in her hair that trailed down beneath the back-neck bun like a Comanche warlock, and it was a little limp with sweat. She came directly to their table, ignoring the other supper-eaters in the place.

"You boys want some more beans? Got plenty."

"Had all I can handle," said Oscar Schiller.

"Ain't my beans no good tonight?" she said.

"Good as always," he said. "But one bowl is all I can use. I only got one stomach."

She laughed and slapped Oscar Schiller's frail shoulders and then shouted to Ed behind the counter.

"Two more steins over here, Ed, on my tab."

Her hand was still on Oscar Schiller's shoulder, and now she was patting him like she might pat a lapdog. "You boys have a good one today?"

"Fair to middlin', Maria, just fair to middlin'," said Nason Breedlove. "But I'll have another bowl of them beans."

Ꮓ Ꮓ Ꮓ Afterward, in the street, both men turning up overcoat collars against the wind, Nason Breedlove said, "Oscar, I told Emory Kimes about your part in this case."

Emory Kimes was the United States Marshal for the Western District of Arkansas.

"I'd as soon you hadn't."

"Hell, you started this whole thing. Kimes and Walter Evans both don't like unsolved cases layin' around in their files. You might get your commission back out of this."

"I make more money from Jewel Moon than I ever did from the United States of America," Oscar Schiller said.

"Yeah, I know. But that ain't gonna last forever. And let's hope the United States of America will," Nason Breedlove said. "Well, I got some more business at the commissioner's office. And I think I'd better go by the Frisco depot and send a telegraph to Moma July and tell him we got ole Sherman but run into a stone wall so far."

"Have him tell my man over there," said Oscar Schiller, meaning Moses Masada.

"Yeah, and if ole Sherman decides he wants to spill some of his guts, I'll let you know. Like to have you there if he decided to make a speech, but can't do it. Havin' a civilian in the federal compound and all. Ole Kimes would raise hell, him being such a stickler for the rules."

"He's a good man."

"He thinks you are, too."

"Well, it's nice to be well thought of." Oscar Schiller almost smiled. "A man needs a little love along the way."

"Yeah," Nason Breedlove said and laughed. "And speakin' of which, say howdy to Missus Hake, you hear?"

ℵ ℵ ℵ In later years, the story would develop that it was the coldest night of the year. It wasn't, but somehow pretending it was seemed to make dramatic events even more dramatic, especially when one of those events involved a lot of people running around in the streets half naked.

As darkness came deeper the wind from the west grew colder. Railroad telegraphers knew that already there had been freezing rain in Guthrie, the capital city of the Territory of Oklahoma which had been created by act of Congress just three years earlier, a territory that extended all the way to Colorado and the high plains of Texas. A territory just west of the Five Civilized Tribes Nations and opened to white-man settlement by land run in what was once known as the Unassigned Lands, added to with ceding a panhandle strip called No Man's Land, and then enlarged again with another run in the Cheyenne and Arapaho reservation established by the Treaty of Medicine Lodge back in 1867, and already plans gone forward for more runs or lotteries or whatever else it took to take the land away from the red man and give it to the white.

None of which intruded on the consciousness of railroad key operators as they observed from afar the approaching storm. At that hour, water standing outdoors in Fort Smith was already developing a covering of sheet ice. But everything considered, it was just another normal winter night on the Arkansas.

The streetlamps had been dimmed. The police patrol had checked the doors along Garrison Avenue. The bank clock had just struck half past midnight. In the freight yards, the switch engines were all at rest near the roundhouse on the north end of the holding-tracks grid, sighing as fireboxes burned low and boilers cooled. There was no significant note taken of time or date. Until later, when the storytellers would say it was almost 1:00 A.M. on January 15, 1893. A Saturday night just turned into Sunday morning.

The city did what it always did at such an hour. It slept. Except along the Row. There, the bordellos showed lights in most of their windows. From one could be heard the tin-pan clank of a piano. Near the southernmost of the whorehouses, Squirrel Tooth Emma's, a dog had discovered the scent of a hobo trying to sleep in an empty boxcar and was barking, rather listlessly. Next in line along the tenderloin, at Henrietta's Game and Billiard Palace, there had just been a contest of fists between two section men of the Missouri Pacific line in which there was a lot of loud swearing, a lot of wild swings, but no damage to anything except tranquillity, and even that now moved back inside to Henrietta's bar for more civilized discussion of differences.

There were the usual lines of cars on the sidings east of the houses. One of these, not fifty yards from Squirrel Tooth Emma's, was a small oil tanker filled with kerosene which had come in from Pennsylvania on the Frisco and was parked now, manifested for a freight run to Little Rock on the Missouri Pacific in the next day or so. It never got there.

At precisely the moment the bank clock on Garrison Avenue struck the three-quarter-hour stroke beyond midnight, the tank car exploded. It blew up with a gigantic roar and lifted a massive ball of swirling fire into the air and splattered flaming coal oil in all directions, setting fire to any number of boxcars, setting fire to a section-gang toolshed, setting fire to a line of wheelbarrows near one of the sidings, setting fire to the dog barking at the hobo, and setting fire to Squirrel Tooth Emma's whorehouse. With the wind whipping it along, the sheet of flame leaped to Henrietta's Game and Billiard Palace. With the sudden violence of a volcano rising from sleep, fire illuminated the riverfront and the railyards and the buildings of west Fort Smith and great clouds of smoke swept close along the ground carrying the scent of oil and wood and paint burning and making a sound like some monstrous coughing animal, devouring everything before it.

People ran from the houses. Some screaming. Falling down.

Clad in petticoats or drawers or flannel underwear, one shrieking women from Squirrel Tooth Emma's with nothing covering her except high button shoes and a sheet she pulled off the bed where she had been at work when the blast came. They ran for the willows along the river. They ran for the streets of Fort Smith beyond the tracks of the railyards. They ran back and forth with no direction at all, outlined in the red, boiling glare like little black stick figures.

At the Commerce Railroad Hotel, Miss Jewel Moon, in her sergeant major mode, was getting her people out. Her hired help, her ladies, her clients. Because she could see the fire coming directly toward them, pushed before the wind as surely as a line of flaming cars would be pushed along a single track by some outrageous locomotive. Out the back door, shoving them, shouting at them, into the river willows, shouting at Clarence the cook to get an armload of blankets, shouting obscenities against all the gods of fire. Shouting encouragement to the latest Natasha, the Chinese lady, who hadn't the vaguest notion of what was happening.

The explosion rocked all of west Fort Smith and could be heard as far away as Van Buren. And immediately the night watchmen at the furniture factory and Mr. Hake's scissors factory began to blow the company steam whistles, to what purpose no one was ever quite sure. And no more sure as to why various railroad people in the yards began ringing switch-engine bells. And soon, some of the churches in the east part of town were the source of more bells ringing, as though tolling the end of time, beginning on the infamous Row.

The fire company on 6th Street came at once, of course, their horses' steel-shod hoofs striking sparks from the brick pavements, and they were ringing bells, too. And honking horns. Police officers came, many running as they held beehive helmets on their heads, others in the city's single paddy wagon. And adding to clamor from afar, ambulances from the east of town, where all the hospitals were located, running the length of Garrison Avenue with their own distinctive racket of bells, bells, bells.

Many of the scantily clad refugees from the two blazing bordellos were now in the river's willows and there watched in amazement, shivering in the cold. Others ran into the city, and one man from Monett, Missouri, was found on 5th Street, six blocks away from the fire, staggering along in a daze with nothing to hide his manhood but a black cotton stocking he held before himself. And when finally taken into a friendly home, he kept saying, "I've lost a perfectly good stocking someplace."

Within minutes, it was apparent to anyone who had reason left to think that the Row was doomed. Already, Squirrel Tooth Emma's was collapsing, sending a shower of red and yellow and orange cinders swirling into the black sky. And Henrietta's was a box of flame, the windowpanes bursting in the heat like pistol shots. The firemen there were squirting ineffective streams of water in various directions, which due to the intense heat generally turned to steam before the first drop reached a flaming wall.

Then, like a breath suddenly suspended, the wind stopped. The river willows stood straight, not bending before a flow of air. The flames along the roof and walls of Henrietta's ceased pointing like liquid red tongues toward the Commerce Railroad Hotel. But rose straight into the night sky. And then, incredibly, began to lick in the opposite direction. The wind had changed. Now was blowing as hard as it had before, but from the northwest.

Miss Jewel Moon, observing all from the willows of the river with hysterical Nasturtium clinging to her, with her robe-clad ladies all around her, and her hired help and her half-naked clients, knew what it meant. It meant that except for Squirrel Tooth Emma's and Henrietta's Palace, the Row was saved.

"Come on, honey," she said, one massive arm around the shoulders of her little black maid. "We can go home now where it's warm."

So now Fort Smith could swallow its panic and watch the fire burn down. And organize. As word of the calamity spread, almost everyone got involved. The reverends and divines of the city rose from their beds and dressed and went to add comfort to the afflicted and maybe to gloat a bit that at least two of Fort Smith's dens of iniquity lay in the same ashes as did Sodom and Gomorrah. The ladies of the Fort Smith Benevolent Society came with their cart of hot coffee, the ladies taking this opportunity to see at close hand the terrible tenderloin without threat of anyone accusing them of wicked curiosity.

Haberdashers recognized a great opportunity and rushed to the scene of disaster with hacks and wagons and wheelbarrows filled with men's clothing, which they knew would be on demand by those gentlemen in flight for their lives before the flames and with no time to catch up such things as trousers.

As the flames burned down, the first floor of the Commerce

Railroad Hotel was like a busy depot servicing a battalion of nudists. Many of those who had escaped the burning brothels of Squirrel Tooth Emma and Henrietta were welcomed. In fact, what with the great tragedy, all were welcomed. It was a place to take refuge until they could properly clothe themselves, and Miss Jewel Moon understood that, and also understood that to soothe a lot of jagged nerves, her half-clad guests would require strong drink, and so had Clarence, the cook, come from the kitchen and assist the bartender. The first thing they ran out of was ice.

In addition to refugees from the other whorehouses, there was a cross section of Fort Smith society. Policemen were there. Doctors and nurses were there, glad to report that there had been no injuries. Of course, nobody knew about the hobo sleeping in that boxcar, and if he did survive, he was likely halfway to Choctaw Nation along the rail line now, wanting to get away, because if they found him, somebody was likely to say he'd started the whole thing. So no casualties. Except the dog. The dog who had been barking at the hobo.

Squirrel Tooth Emma was there, and Henrietta, both talking to lawyers about the best action to take against the railroads. All of the ladies from the burned-out houses were there, acting snotty and Miss Jewel Moon's ladies avoiding them as though even if they said howdy they might get a good dose of clap.

They ran out of sloe gin before dawn, the favorite drink of the professional ladies. A lot of people were at the south windows, watching firemen squirt water onto the low flaming and blackening ruins of Henrietta's and Squirrel Tooth Emma's. Somebody started the player piano. About the time the pre-dawn freight went through toward Paris, Texas. About the time they ran out of sour-mash whiskey.

The city's haberdashers were selling clothes by the armful in Miss Jewel Moon's entry hall. Some mostly naked gentlemen bought as many as three pairs of trousers, none of which fit them.

They ran out of seltzer water.

A small fistfight developed in the bar, but the two gentlemen involved were quickly separated by the county judge and a cotton broker from Moline, Illinois.

They ran out of brandy.

By all accounts, once the wind changed, it became one hell of a party!

꒰ ꒰ ꒰ Oscar Schiller was one of those who came to the Commerce Railroad Hotel that night. Having heard the explosion. And in the back-room pantry and office of Miss Jewel Moon, she placed in his hand an envelope postmarked three days before, the stamp canceled in the Fort Smith post office.

Inside the envelope was a strip of newsprint, a torn-out half-page with the obituary of Temperance Moon. And across the bottom of the paper, scrawled in brown ink, the words:

"Let it rest in peace or bad things will come."

Oscar Schiller looked at it a long time without speaking. And Miss Jewel Moon, hearing her wild party beyond the door, said nothing, but her square face was set in a mask of fury.

And finally, Oscar Schiller spoke.

"I'll be damned!"

"Me, too," said Jewel Moon.

And walking back to his basement room at the Hake residence on 7th and B streets, thought with every step, do kerosene tankers just explode? Without a little help?

It was a thing to be investigated, he knew that, but events would overrun it, and he did not know that.

꒰ ꒰ ꒰ Cooperation between the Creek Light Horse Police and the Parker court had become legendary. And perhaps one of the most cooperative of all the Creek peace officers was Moma July. As captain of the Eufaula police, he found it useful to visit the Creek capital at Okmulgee and other district courthouses in order to keep his ear to the ground, as he often told Nason Breedlove. Who agreed. And these visits were essential in cases having to do with white men and hence the Parker court.

So it was that on receiving Nason Breedlove's telegraph to the effect that Sherman Boggs was in custody, Moma July went to Muskogee. Muskogee was a wonderful place for gossip because not only was it close to Fort Smith, it was the largest of all towns in Creek Nation. He went for more than the usual gossip.

Moma July kept remembering that when Toby Jupiter's body had been found, it was well known that Goshen Crowfoot was in Muskogee, where he had gone immediately after the hearing in the United States Commissioner's court dealing with the demise of Temperance Moon. To Moma July, it had begun to look suspiciously like a planned alibi trip, putting distance between Goshen Crowfoot and Eufaula District at a time when Goshen Crowfoot knew something was about to happen in Eufaula District.

It wasn't difficult for Goshen Crowfoot to establish his known presence in Muskogee, because he was often there visiting a lady. Even after Temperance Moon took him into her bed. The lady Goshen Crowfoot visited was a white woman named Wanda Porchmacher, and she lived in a soddy on the Fort Gibson side of the river in Cherokee Nation, where she raised goats and geese and gave solace to lonely soldiers and a few Muskogee civilians for a fee of two dollars. Wanda Porchmacher was married to a Cherokee who some years before had deserted her, goats, and geese, and lit out for Kansas and had never been heard from since.

Moma July knew Wanda Porchmacher because he had talked with her many times before while conducting various investigations. He was on excellent terms with the Cherokee police, and therefore when he crossed the river from Creek Nation now and then on official business without making any to-do about Cherokee permission, there was never any fuss about it unless Moma July shot somebody while on Cherokee soil. Which had happened just once, and that created only a small stir because the victim of Moma July's shotgun had been a Seminole man wanted as badly for stealing Cherokee horses as he was for stealing Creek ones. The only irritating thing was that Moma July had to pay for the man's burial.

So now, he talked to Wanda Porchmacher again, giving her the two-dollar fee, not for usual services but only for conversation. Moma July fully expected to be reimbursed from the pocketbook that he knew Moses Masada carried and that was stuffed with Oscar Schiller greenbacks. Well, Jewel Moon greenbacks.

"Sure," Wanda Porchmacher said. "I remember when Goshen was here back September last year. It was a Monday. I'd just done the washing and had it hung out when he rode in. He'd come from that Temperance Moon thing in Fort Smith, that hearing they had. Terrible thing, about Temperance Moon. A lady ain't safe no more."

"That would have been September 11," Moma July said.

"Sounds reasonable," she said. "Lemme get some coffee. Talk better with coffee."

Wanda Porchmacher was a round, fat lady, perhaps as a result of all the goat's milk and goose eggs she consumed. She had so many gold teeth that her lips seemed barely adequate to cover them when her mouth was closed, which wasn't often. They were sitting in her one-room living-working soddy, which was as ugly as all soddies were outside but rather pleasant inside, where the walls were covered with old newspapers and there was a vast array of good furniture, this being one of Wanda Porchmacher's weaknesses, to the extent that one could hardly move about the room. Featured was the largest brass bed Moma July had ever seen, and each time he looked at it he mused on the fact that people in his line of work spent a lot of time with whores but almost none of that in one of those beds.

"What did Goshen talk about?" Moma July asked.

"Oh, mostly just rambled around, mostly about that hearing in Fort Smith. He thought it was funny, that hearing. But he had a lot of whiskey with him and was about half tanked when he got here, and the drunker he got, the less fun he decided he'd had."

"Have a lot of money, did he?"

"Yeah, he did."

"How much, Wanda?"

"Hell, I don't know. But he stayed three, four days and paid right along, if you know what I mean. He'd take this wad of bills out of his pocket and throw a few on the table over yonder. Altogether, he left thirty-two dollars."

"You ever see Goshen with that much money before?"

"No, I never."

They sipped coffee from heavy china cups, the kind found in army messes. They could hear the wind outside. It was sunny, but cold. In the soddy, it was warm enough, but Moma July did not remove his Union Army overcoat.

"What do you recall of his talk, Wanda?"

"Oh, the usual shit," she said. "He kept cussing about this white man, said he couldn't trust him, said he'd likely never do what he said he would."

"About what?"

"Hell, I don't know."

"He mention the man's name?"

"Once. I remember something like Box, something like that."

"Boggs?"

"Yeah, maybe that was it. Drunker he got, the more he cussed. Hard to tell what he was talkin' about. Goshen ain't a very pretty drunk."

"He's not very pretty sober, either."

Wanda Porchmacher laughed, her teeth gleaming.

"No, he ain't. But he got off the white man and started belly-achin' about his brother-in-law, always comin' up with crazy ideas nobody could keep straight."

"You mean his brother?"

"No. No, he said brother-in-law. Said married to his sister. I never knowed Goshen's sister, but I knew he had one somewheres down in Creek Nation."

Moma July placed his empty cup on the table between them. "More?"

"No. What else do you remember, Wanda?"

"Oh, not much." She turned in her chair and yanked open the firebox door to the cast-iron kitchen stove and tossed in a few sticks of locust kindling. "Gotta get me one of these coal-oil stoves. But they stink like hell."

"Goshen say anything about Temperance Moon?" asked Moma July.

"Yeah, well he got on her, too. I knew he was Temperance Moon's boyfriend, and he acted like he was about to cry, her being killed and all. Then he said she was about to throw him out any-way, so it never come to no tears. Hell, Goshen never could love anybody anyway, I could see that. But if Temperance Moon was about ready to throw Goshen out, can't say I woulda blamed her a lot."

Moma July asked a few more questions but got nothing except that Goshen Crowfoot had stayed an extra day to sober up, then rode off to the east, saying he was going to Arkansas and try to find that white man so he could keep an eye on him.

"I figured this white man musta owed Goshen some money or something," Wanda Porchmacher said.

There was plenty for Moma July to think about on his ride in a KATY caboose back to Eufaula. As soon as he was aboard, he took out some folded pulp tablet paper and a pencil stub and made notes to himself so he wouldn't forget what Wanda Porch-macher had said. He figured Oscar Schiller's people might get excited about this, because he was a little excited himself. As excited as he ever got. And before the end of the day, there would be even more to it.

இ இ இ After the war, the Creeks had begun to administer their real estate much as was done in Texas and Arkansas. Surveys and records of ownership and transfers of deed were important because more and more there were disputes arising between citizens about who owned what, and many of these cases ended in lawsuits in the Creek courts.

During the time of the Temperance Moon affair one of the best secretaries in the office of the principal chief in Okmulgee was a young Creek named Ward Harjo. He was originally from the Canadian River area and thus had a particular interest in the Eufaula District. He had graduated from the white man's seminary for men at Cane Hill, Arkansas, and was perhaps the most knowledgeable man in Creek Nation on land tenure and all that it involved.

It was no surprise, then, that Ward Harjo should take note of a rather strange transaction reported to him by the clerk in the Eufaula courthouse, who happened to be his uncle, and after some thought should send a message to the secretary of the Eufaula District chief, one Locher Harjo, who happened to be his brother and also a graduate of Cane Hill Academy.

Locher Harjo went immediately to the district chief and pointed out that maybe the chief's constitutional responsibilities concerning law and order were involved, whereupon Locher Harjo was instructed to find the district captain of police and the two of them investigate. So when Moma July stepped down from the caboose of the afternoon southbound freight, Locher Harjo was there to meet him.

Thus Locher Harjo in his white man's suit and necktie and Moma July in his usual Union Army overcoat and wide-brimmed hat found themselves in one of the damp, cold, cavelike limestone rooms of the Eufaula courthouse, Locher Harjo with his fingers running down columns of figures in a large ledger book. And none of the numbers were anything Moma July could understand. Even though he was adequately literate in four or five languages. This looked to him like a listing of calibers for foreign pistols or some such thing. Numbers such as 35°31′N 95°21′W.

"What is it?" Moma July asked.

"You know North Fork of the Canadian? You know a place called Muskrat Bend?"

"Of course I do. I was there a couple days ago. We arrested a man there. It's a bootleg landing, everybody knows that."

"This is its legal description," said Locher Harjo, his finger on the ledger. "A part of the former holdings of one Temperance Moon. Then passed on her demise to Langston Turtle, although no challenge has been made to that in a court of law and we expect none. Family inheritance, you see?"

"All right. Everybody knows that, too."

"You see this notation?"

"Yes," said Moma July, looking at the end of Locher Harjo's finger. "What does it mean?"

"It means title to that quarter section which includes Muskrat Bend was transferred by quitclaim deed on October 10, last year. A Monday. For the sum total of one dollar and unspecified considerations."

"All right. What does that mean?"

"It means, Captain July, that the new owner of Fawley Farm deeded this quarter section more or less as a gift!"

Moma July wiped his mouth. Then his eyes.

"Gift?"

"Yes. A gift."

"Well, who'd he give it to?"

Locher Harjo's finger moved to the margin of the ledger book. Moved, then stopped. Like a spider, Moma July thought. Moved, then stopped again, and Locher Harjo was beginning to whisper to himself, saying words Moma July could not interpret. Then the finger stopped and Locher Harjo looked at Moma July and smiled.

"There it is," said Locher Harjo.

"Where?"

"Right there. Langston Turtle, when his sister-in-law was hardly cold in the ground, deeded that quarter section to a white man in Creek Nation on a legal permit to sell timber to the railroad, a man we know has been arrested in Arkansas for running whiskey, much of which probably came to this district through the Bend."

"Sherman Boggs!"

"The same."

ꑭ ꑭ ꑭ It required a lot of hard thinking. Moma July sat in the police station trying to make his mind work like a white man's would. From the next room, the jail room, a drunk Euchee Indian was chanting about meadowlarks and the spirits that reside in rocks. Outside, it was dark, the sun having departed some two hours before. Moma July was alone in the office part of the stationhouse, his men avoiding him because they knew it was best when the captain was in deep thought.

Oscar Schiller's man Moses Masada was only a short distance away, in his section-house room. And he had to be given the information now noted on the papers pressed against one another in Moma July's shirt pocket, the paper with his own notes on Wanda Porchmacher and the one with the delicate script of Locher Harjo concerning the Bend property. Was it time now for Oscar Schiller's man to dispense with this foolishness about being something other than a policeman?

Well, Moma July had pondered the question so long, without an answer, that the turning earth had provided the resolution of his problem. It was dark now, so why not continue the secret as if it were still a secret and let the white man decide for himself whether to stop play-acting and come into the open with Moses Masada's role?

He found the section house dark, as he had expected, except for the one dim light upstairs where he knew Moses Masada had his room. He opened the front door to a dark parlor and shouted.

"Mister Masada? It's me, Moma July. Gotta talk."

He was invited up by a returning shout and moved across the dark parlor without bumping into anything and up the short flight to the landing, then turning and on up into the hallway, where there was lamplight shining from an open door halfway along the building.

Moses Masada was sitting on the bed, and beside him was a book entitled *A Connecticut Yankee in King Arthur's Court*. The globe of the kerosene lamp on the bedside table was smoked at the top and added its own odor to that of the small coal-oil heater in one corner of the room. Even with the heater, Moses Masada's breath made a faint vapor of white. He was wearing a heavy woolen dressing gown.

After Moma July handed his two slips of paper to Moses Masada, he stood back against the wall beside the door, almost lost in the folds of the Union Army overcoat, the shotgun lost in the folds as well at his side. Moses Masada read both papers without changing expression. He read them both a second time, and slowly a smile began at the corners of his mouth. Without looking up, he spoke.

"So we're finally getting into something."

"Yes."

"Jesus Christ!"

"Yes."

Moses Masada read once more, and the time in the room was ticked off by the clicks of the alarm clock on his bedside table, where the lamp stood, and where lay the .45 caliber British Webley pistol.

"I need to take all of this to Fort Smith," he finally said. "Not telegraphed, but carried by hand, do you understand, Moma?"

It was the first time he had ever addressed the little Creek police officer by his first name.

"Yes, I understand," said Moma July. And he could not help but be impressed with this white man whose eyes shone with his exuberance yet who spoke quietly, calmly.

"There's a freight through here in about an hour, isn't there?" Moses Masada asked.

"Yes. But it never stops. I can flag it."

Moses Masada looked at him for the first time since taking the slips of paper into his hands.

"Good. Can you do that? But no word to anyone about why? Can you do that?"

Still the secret, then, Moma July thought.

"Yes. You can be in Fort Smith by noon tomorrow. Change at Wagoner."

"I know. Good."

"I'll stop it, and you get on the caboose on the dark side, away from the depot."

"Yes. And Moma, another thing. Candy Redstripe will likely be in tomorrow on the early southbound passenger. He's been in Muskogee with his wife."

"I know."

"Meet him, will you?" asked Moses Masada. "We were going to the races in Denison this coming weekend. He was coming in here to spend the night, the night before we were leaving, so we could catch the morning train. Tell him I'm gone to Fort Smith but tell him to come on anyway, stay here. Mr. Danton, the section foreman, will likely still be gone, but he knows our arrangement. For Candy to stay. Tell him I may be back by then but if not, I'll follow on to Texas to see his horses run."

"All right," said Moma July. "What do I tell him about you going to Fort Smith? Those?"

And Moma July pointed to the two slips of paper in Moses Masada's hand. Their eyes met and locked for about ten clicks on the alarm clock.

"No," said Moses Masada.

"Good," said Moma July. "I'll tell him you got horny for some white women and went into Fort Smith for that."

Moses Masada laughed. "It may be close to the truth."

"All right," said Moma July, turning to the door. "I'll flag the freight. Be ready. It won't stand long."

"Just tell Candy I'll be back in time for some of his races."

Moma July stood with his hand on the door, his back to Moses Masada. Then he looked back across the lifted collar of the old Union Army coat.

"Don't ever tell Candy everything you know," he said.

Moses Masada stood slowly, and there was a deep ripple of resentment across his face and Moma July knew this white man had come to enjoy the company of the Redstripes. Maybe too much.

"I know Oscar Schiller sent you here and told you to tie in with Candy," Moma July said. He shrugged. "Oscar Schiller's a good man. But this is not his place. It's my place. Don't tell Candy everything you know."

And then was gone, downstairs and out into the street and along the tracks to the police station, there to make up an official envelope for the captain of the Light Horse in Muskogee, taking some delight in trying to imagine the look on that man's face when he opened the envelope and found it empty and wondered what the hell was going on. The official envelope was necessary so that when he flagged that train to a stop the conductor and engineer wouldn't raise so much hell at being stopped since there was police business involved, and while all this was taking place, and the empty envelope was handed up to the locomotive cab, Moses Masada would be climbing onto the caboose from the dark side of the tracks.

And so long as Moses Masada was gone, just to keep the white man's secret, because he apparently still wanted to do so, Moma July would go each night, so long as necessary, to the section house and light the lamp in Moses Masada's room and go again later to blow it out so that anybody watching would think he was still there reading that book by Mr. Sam Clemens. Because this was Moma July's place. And he knew how it worked.

9 The federal jail in Fort Smith was called Hell on the Border. With good reason. It was a single-room basement dungeon where the only sanitary facilities were a few buckets and two sawed-in-half hickory barrels filled with water. Prisoners were kept there like hogs in a killing pen. Everyone, no matter the offense, was put there among the hardened murderers, rapists, degenerates, thugs. No walls between. No lights or guards at night. After a short stay in such a place, it was not surprising that men were almost happy when taken out to be hanged.

So when Judge Parker came, they built a new jail. It was an addition, on the south side, to the courthouse building. An extension to the original federal structure. It had tall, narrow windows on one side looking toward the river and on the other opening to a view of the permanent scaffold with the heavy oak beam that held the ropes. There were two-inch steel bars running the full height of these windows, which left little doubt about the nature of the building's function.

The interior of the new jail was also a single room, like the old jail, but constructed in that room was what appeared to be an iron-bar bird cage, set back from the outside brick walls and with three tiers of cells, one above the other, and with intervening metal walls and steel-plate floors and gangways. By the last decade of the century, there were light bulbs hanging from wires with yellow insulation, all in the gangways outside the cells and testimony to progress and the efficiency of the coal-powered generators of the new electric company. The garish illumination they cast seemed always appropriate to the season; in the summer hot, in the winter cold.

The exterior walls were painted in the same hue as the color of the steel bars, a dull gray. Within this great metallic box every sound echoed. The clanging of cell doors opening and closing. The rattle of leg irons dragging along the gangways as prisoners were moved from one place to another. The clatter of tin bowls in which the food was served. And the human sounds of inmates. Prayers being muttered. Obscenities shouted. Screams of defiance.

The smell in this place was of fried pork and urine and disinfectant and sweat and vomit. And fear. And despair.

Although the new jail was in many ways better than the old, it was still called Hell on the Border, perhaps for sentimental reasons, and a short stay there was enough to make a strong man weep.

Sherman Boggs was not a strong man.

He was housed on the lower tier of cells near the exterior wall where the windows opened out to the gallows. From the moment they locked him in, he could see it, during daylight hours. It was a massive structure, there on the grass of the Federal Compound, bare-limbed trees around it, looking exactly like a large city-park bandstand even to having a roof over the stage. But once its purpose was perceived, there could be no doubt that the sounds coming from it would never be those of John Philip Sousa. Sherman Boggs tried, without success, to avoid looking at it.

The trusty who swabbed the gangway outside Sherman Boggs's cell was a black man from Mena, Arkansas, waiting trial on a forgery charge. Each time he passed Sherman Boggs's cell he winked, clicked his teeth, and said, "Out yonder, ole gov'ment suspender, huh, Sherman?"

Sherman Boggs had spent hardly two hours in this place before understanding what prisoners always do in any jail. That there was a vast amount of information moving through the prison population and most of it fueled by the trusties, who had access to the free world. As in the case of the Mena black, who did his work not only in the jail but in the hallways and offices at the other end of the building. So on the afternoon this trusty paused before Sherman Boggs's cell, grinned, clicked his teeth, and said, "Hey, man, they gettin' ready to gran' jury you and before long you be out there on that big stage with a new rope rubbin' you Adam's apple,'' Sherman Boggs knew it was true.

That's when Sherman Boggs reacted as Oscar Schiller had suggested he might. He asked for a preacher and started recanting his sins, aloud, and right there in his bird-cage cell so that all the other prisoners could hear him. Many of them joined him in loud prayer. As many more hooted and hissed and spat and called him vile names. The one in the cell on the tier immediately above Sherman Boggs dumped the contents of his latrine bucket down past the bars of Sherman Boggs's cell, a latrine bucket that was supposed to be locked in place on the metal floor but on this occasion somehow was freed.

ಜ ಜ ಜ It was obvious to everyone that Sherman Boggs was defeated and distraught when he was brought in handcuffs and leg irons to an interrogation room in the courthouse section of the federal building. It was a room intentionally designed to help destroy the confidence of anyone brought there as an accused. It was bone-bare, gray walls, a single light bulb hanging from the ceiling, no windows. There was one table and a lot of hard-backed chairs. At this time of year, it was cold enough for everybody's breath to show vapor.

In this room, Sherman Boggs saw nothing but grim faces. Not hostile exactly but showing little inclination for mercy. It was, of course, a designed setting. Pity might be forthcoming if the accused showed signs of cooperation. A tin cup of hot coffee might even be provided the subject of the inquiry in such instances. But Sherman Boggs did not know these things. All he saw was the overwhelming muster of the powers against him.

There was United States Attorney Walter Evans, who would conduct the hearing; there was United States Commissioner Claude Bains; there was United States Marshal Emory Kimes; there was United States Deputy Marshal Nason Breedlove; there was a stenographer from the commissioner's court; there was a young court-appointed defense attorney whom Sherman Boggs had never seen before, and who looked just as grim as all the others; there were two jailers, with billy clubs, the ones who had brought him here.

And there was the minister he had requested, who had been

with him for an hour or so just previous to this meeting, a Baptist who had provided spiritual comfort to Sherman Boggs by repeating over and over again, "Brother, make your peace with God Almighty. Who I think you will be seeing shortly!"

"Mr. Boggs," the United States Attorney began, "this is a conference to advise you of the charges which will be made against you prior to a hearing before the United States Commissioner, the results of which will determine if you will be remanded to the grand jury, a group of your peers who have the authority to return an indictment against you for murder."

Sherman Boggs sobbed but he did not break down completely.

Quickly, efficiently, United States Attorney Evans reviewed the evidence. Fish-camp findings, expected testimony of one Samuel Lurley, expected testimony of one Wanda Porchmacher. And then in obscure language, the hint of testimony from parties having knowledge of Sherman Boggs's activities in Creek Nation. And then, revelation of the property transfer regarding Muskrat Bend in Creek Nation.

That was when Sherman Boggs broke down completely.

₪ ₪ ₪ In the basement room at the Hake residence on North 7th and B streets, Oscar Schiller was at his small bedside table going over some of the little notes he had written to himself at various times in the past. There was a small bottle of white powder before him on the table and a box of Ohio matches. There was also a match held in one corner of his mouth. Among the slips of paper he shuffled through was the tear sheet of newsprint Jewel Moon had given him the night of the whorehouse fires. Each time he looked at the brown-ink writing on it, the frown on his face deepened.

Pacing back and forth behind him was Moses Masada. He still wore his hat, and on one of his rounds of the basement room he had gone too close to an unused corner, of which there were many, and hanging cobwebs had attached themselves to the felt bowler crown. They remained there, unnoticed, like a fine white mist of fairy veils.

They had been waiting since noon. Since the material Moses Masada had brought from Creek Nation was handed over to United States Deputy Marshal Nason Breedlove, who had not left Fort Smith since arresting Sherman Boggs. Nason Breedlove had gone off along 7th Street, toward the United States Attorney's office, looking like a great Belgian horse galloping.

Now it was well past dark. And from his frequent trips to the alley privy, Moses Masada knew it was growing colder. They could hear the west wind moving the delicate branches of the redbud trees in the Hake backyard. Each time Moses Masada returned from his frequent calls of nature, he said, "Damn! It's getting colder than a witch's tit and my overcoat's in that Eufaula section house."

Earlier, Oscar Schiller had gone for food, bringing back a can of salmon and a loaf of hard Jewish bread. The can of salmon was still half full, standing open beside the small bottle of cocaine. The bread was gone, Moses Masada having nibbled pieces as the hours passed, not from hunger, but for something to do with his hands.

"Where is he, where is he?" Moses Masada kept muttering.

"Lay down and take a nap," Oscar Schiller said.

They could hear the bank clock on Garrison Avenue chiming off the quarter hours. They could hear the switch engines in the railroad yards moving boxcars, moving boxcars past the blackened rubble that had been two of the Row's bordellos. Early in the evening, they could hear the footfalls from above as the Hake family moved about, then that was still and there was only the hiss of flame from the furnace in one corner of this basement room, the hiss of natural gas burning, a constant reminder of the march of progress, just like the electric lights in the federal jail.

When Nason Breedlove came, it was almost midnight. He burst into the door, his eyes wide, his breath exploding a cloud of white vapor. In one hand he had a cardboard folder stuffed with papers. He stood in the doorway, looking from Oscar Schiller to Moses Masada, panting. Then slammed the door behind him and came to the bedside table, as though doing a hopping dance, reaching into the can of salmon.

"God, that looks good," he said. "I ain't had a bite since noon. Boys, we tore this one. Ole Sherman got religion."

Oscar Schiller and Moses Masada stared at him, wordless, waiting. Nason Breedlove shoved a handful of salmon into his mouth, threw the folder of papers on the bed, threw hat and coat on the floor.

"God, boys, where to start," he said and sat on Oscar Schiller's bed. "Hand me that can of salmon, Oscar, I'm hungry as a wolf."

Moses Masada pulled up a chair. Oscar Schiller turned his toward Nason Breedlove so they sat with heads almost together. The other two watched Nason Breedlove clean the can of salmon with his fingers.

"For Christ's sake, Nason," Moses Masada said.

Nason Breedlove dropped the empty can on the floor and held up one hand, and he was laughing.

"God, boys! God! Lemme start at the first."

Maybe it was when he realized he was going to be accused of killing Temperance Moon, Nason Breedlove said. Maybe it was because ole Evans kept making it sound like a lot of people were going to testify against him. Maybe it was that quitclaim deed. But whatever it was, Sherman Boggs collapsed.

"You were right, Oscar. It was Langston Turtle. Ole Sherman said he didn't know why. But one night when Temperance was off in Wetumka at a dance with some new man, Langston and Goshen Crowfoot and Winona had this little talk. Goshen Crowfoot couldn't have been too happy about any new man, him being the barnyard stud at Fawley like he was.

"So Langston said he had a plan. To kill Temperance."

"I knew it was there someplace," said Oscar Schiller.

Sherman Boggs said that Langston Turtle had become very apprehensive about having anyplace to live, what with his sister-in-law talking big about moving to Eufaula and starting a dance-hall arrangement. Besides, he wanted his family property back in family hands. And besides all that, Langston Turtle had said, Temperance was about ready to chuck Goshen Crowfoot for somebody else, so they needed to kill her, and he had a wonderful plan about how to do it, with nobody the worse for wear.

"Ole Langston would pay for it, see?" said Nason Breedlove.

"Pay for it?" asked Oscar Schiller. "Where'd he get money for that?"

"Evans asked the same thing. Ole Sherman said he didn't know but that Temperance was always givin' Langston a little whiskey cash, so maybe he saved up."

"All right, but just slow down a little," Oscar Schiller said. "This business of planning it, who was there?"

"Sure, it was Goshen Crowfoot and Sherman Boggs and Winona Crowfoot," said Nason Breedlove. "And they all thought it looked pretty good. So the first part was Toby Jupiter."

"Toby Jupiter," said Moses Masada. "Shot dead in that Canadian River corncrib, you said."

"That's it," Nason Breedlove said. "Ole Toby, he was the first part. And ever'body in on this thing was well oiled up with whiskey from go to stop, so things looked so God damned clever. Langston would get ole Toby to steal that Belgian scattergun and Langston would give him forty dollars for it."

"Where'd Langston get all this money?" Oscar Schiller said, but mostly to himself, and Nason Breedlove went on full speed, waving his hands.

"And hell, stealin' a little ole ten-gauge scattergun wasn't nothin' for this wild bastard."

"Sure, sure, sure," Moses Masada said, catching the enthusiasm of the big deputy. "Once Toby had the gun, he'd sell it to Langston, then Toby and Boggs would go off to Toby's favorite place. Fish camp. Lay low a week or so, swilling that tiger sweat, catching those fish . . ."

Now Nason Breedlove broke in, he and the Syrian speaking breathlessly, excitement making their eyes shine, and Oscar Schiller sitting there looking at first one then the other, a little dumbfounded.

"Right on the mark, Masada! A lot of whiskey, then," said Nason Breedlove, ignoring Oscar Schiller as though he and the Kansas City detective were singing their own chorus, "Langston and his bunch shoot Temperance and leave the gun near the body, so when they get arrested and go to the commissioner, they tell about Toby havin' the gun."

"Sure, sure, sure," said Masada, "but not telling about buying it and then to keep Toby from telling such a thing, killing him in that fish camp."

"And ole Toby thinking all he's got to worry about is explaining a shotgun being stole."

"Sure, and not realizing there was something a lot bigger to be denied. So Sherman Boggs killed him."

"Yes, and Old Sherman would get seventy-five dollars and a deed to Muskrat Bend once Tub-Butt had the property in hand," said Nason Breedlove and now began producing his documents, slapping them on the bed as he might slap playing cards down on a tabletop in a spirited game of pitch. "And here we be. Warrants. For that whole Fawley Farm bunch."

Nason Breedlove laughed suddenly.

"You know, boys, old Sherman didn't even know he'd got the payoff of that land at the Bend, that bootleg sandbar, until today, when Walter Evans told him. I think that was the final brick that broke his back."

"That deed and seventy-five dollars, that's what he got?" asked Oscar Schiller.

"That's right."

"And Goshen Crowfoot? Did he go into this thing out of the goodness of his heart?"

"He got seventy-five dollars, too, so old Sherman said, and Temperance Moon's big pearl earrings. Of course, he don't know if any of that was paid off, either. He ain't seen Langston Turtle or any of the others since that day he taken off with Toby to the Canadian River. Except he seen Goshen Crowfoot up at Jewel Moon's Weedy Rough farm after it was all over and they both run up there to catch their breath, and lay hid for a couple months."

"The hell you say," said Oscar Schiller. "Maybe Sherman Boggs run to the hills to catch his breath. Scared as he was. Goshen Crowfoot went up there to kill him, to keep him quiet. I think Sherman Boggs knew that. It's why he was so damned anxious, when we arrested him, that he stay in jail where Goshen couldn't get to him."

The other two stared for a moment at Oscar Schiller's face, and the dark look was not reassuring.

"Well, then why didn't Goshen do it?"

"He didn't figure Sherman Boggs would run so soon. And I think Goshen got a little unsettled when Masada showed up and he hesitated. And because he hesitated, and Sherman Boggs is still alive, the whole bunch will now go to Parker's rope!"

Oscar Schiller rose and took a deep breath and began to gather traveling gear. The other two watched, silent now, all the air gone out of their bubble. When it was all done and Oscar Schiller blew out his lamp, they were at the open door and Oscar Schiller spoke from the dark room.

"Let's get to business," he said. "This kind of news travels fast in the Territory. We can make that late freight to Wagoner. Be in Eufaula middle of the day. I'd sure like to know where that money came from."

As they moved across the dark yard of the Scissors King, Moses Masada thought of the day and the hour. It was Saturday night, going on Sunday. The Saturday Candy Redstripe would be coming into the Eufaula section house to spend the night and to catch the early-morning train south to Texas. The Sunday morning Moses Masada had planned a leisure journey to see the little Comanche ponies run.

10

There were buttermilk skies over the Nations. Ranks of cloud moving like waves across a beach before a gentle wind and all their edges turned to silver lace by a moon coming full above them. It had turned warm enough for mockingbirds to start singing from the pecan groves, perhaps thinking it was already spring. It was another of those crazy twists of weather in the Nations that could turn a balmy day into a sheet of ice with only one turn of the earth. Or the other way around.

In the Creek Light Horse station at Eufaula, the captain of police was rolled in a blanket on a cotton-batting pallet at a corner of the room. Not because he had to sleep there but because it was the best place he knew to sleep. There had been invitations from various widows and maidens to come help them warm their beds, which he had done from time to time, but for sleep this mud-floor room was always best.

Before sleeping, he had gone to the railroad section house and lighted the lamp in the upstairs bedroom. As he had been doing for three nights. And on this night, he lighted a lamp in the downstairs parlor so the expected guest coming later would not have to find the staircase in the dark. After the eleven-forty northbound freight passed through, which would waken him as it would everybody in town, the wheel trucks rattling and squealing and the whistle blowing for the grade crossing of Main Street at the south end of town, he would not need to go back to the section house and extinguish the lights, as he had done for three nights. Because Candy Redstripe would likely be there by then.

From the west came the expected section house guest, riding along the trace that followed the north bank of the Canadian into Eufaula. He came leisurely, allowing the gelding to set his own pace, perhaps both enjoying the dapple pattern of moonlight on the land and the warm temperature.

Once in town, he went to the livery and unsaddled the horse and walked away without bothering to waken the boy sleeping in the grain shed, because he knew that with morning the boy would recognize the horse and know whose it was and curry it and feed and water it each day until the rider returned.

Gathering up his small duffel bag, he then walked along the dark street and into the section house, across the lighted parlor, upstairs, and past the open door of a room where a second lamp was burning and into the next room, allowing his eyes to adjust to the darkness for a moment before he took off all his clothes except for long underwear and hat. Then sat on the bed and placed two large-caliber revolvers on the nightstand, lay back on the bed, pulled the blanket cover up to his chin, took off his hat, and went to sleep.

At half past eleven, a dog on the west end of town began barking. Soon it was joined by another closer to the Missouri, Kansas, and Texas Railroad passenger station. Their yammering soon died to a disinterested yip. The three horsemen thus welcomed to Eufaula paid no attention to the dogs. Nor to anything else. They rode with a kind of head-down, straightforward determination. They rode to the railroad depot and dismounted on the side away from the tracks.

The largest of them took a bottle from beneath his jacket and uncorked it and drank and passed it to the others.

"No backin' out now," he said softly.

"I know that," said the one who was short and fat, even showing fat under his ankle-length duster. "But we'll likely have to run off to Colorado."

"Better than a rope around your gullet."

They took another drink, each one. To the south, they heard a train whistle.

"God damned train," said the big one. "God damned dogs."

All wore sugarloaf-crowned hats. Two of them carried double-barreled shotguns. The fat one carried a slender sporting rifle. They moved around the depot, hearing the click of the telegraph key inside, but there was only a low light at the enclosed end of the waiting room and no operator for the Western Union and no KATY depot agent on duty at this hour of the night.

The ground had begun to shake with the approach of the northbound freight. Now with haste, they crossed the railroad tracks to the section house, where a light showed on the first floor, another in one of the rooms above. They were on the section house porch when the train came through, red ball to Missouri, roaring and rattling, and they felt the floor under their feet tremble. Then across the lighted parlor to the stairs, the two with shotguns ahead, smelling of whiskey, smelling of mindless fury, and behind them the fat one, trying to keep pace, gasping for breath, afraid not to be a part of it.

So, wakened by the train everybody called the Midnight Rattler, Moma July was up from his pallet, stretching. Yawning. Scratching his stomach. And then the explosions came. Muffled, like children's balloons bursting in the next room. And Moma July knew without having to think about it that here was gunfire and he knew as well exactly its source. And he marked it in his mind that there were no preliminary shots, but the whole fusillade coming at one instant and in another instant finished. Which experience had taught him was a very dangerous situation indeed.

With his shotgun and the lantern that always burned on a peg beside the door of the police station, Moma July ran toward the KATY section house. As always, the through freight had waked many, and now they came onto the street and the track, carrying lanterns of their own, and some with Winchester rifles, and one among these was Claudis Mopes, a Creek policeman, who carried a lantern too and followed his captain at a dead run to the section house.

Catching the excitement, dogs all over the town were barking and somewhere a baby was crying, and a cow bell, perhaps ringing before but only noted now, was making a brass clank. And the smell of coal smoke and cinders which was always there after the passage of the northbound freight would be always afterward remarked upon as most pungent and wicked.

As Moma July and Claudis Mopes approached the section house, they saw a man come onto the porch, pause as though waiting for another train, stagger to the front of the high porch, and there pitch down to sprawl in the cinders with a Savage deer rifle still in his hand. Moma July ran past him and bounded up the steps, three at a time, but Claudis Mopes stopped, bent, pulled the rifle from the unresisting hand and tossed it aside, and turned the man over, and all those men who had come running with their own lanterns gasped.

The left eye and the left ear and much of the left side of the man's head had been shot away and in the lantern shine was a gray mush, but there was enough left of the face to know that this was Langston Turtle, struggling for life and trying to talk.

"Did we get him, did we get him?"

"God love you, Langston, you son of a bitch," Claudis Mopes said and turned up the section house steps to follow his captain.

In the still-lighted parlor, Moma July saw a shotgun on the floor, still smoking, at the foot of the stairs. Halfway up to the landing, there was a bloody handprint on one wall. And at the landing, a man lying face to the wall, bent almost double, arms folded around his belly like a baby seeking warmth from the blanket and all along the floor and wall near his head a great, shining smear of thick scarlet, and even before he turned him to see his face, Moma July knew here was a man with serious head wounds.

It was Claiburn Crowfoot, and when Moma July saw his face he knew that if Claiburn Crowfoot was not now dead where he lay he would be so in only a few heartbeats.

Moma July turned up the stairs, and began to see the splintered walls where metal had struck. And began to smell the heavy sulfur. At the head of the stairs, lying face up with his head hanging over the first step and his body sprawled in the hallway, was Goshen Crowfoot. His duck jacket had come open and revealed the shirt beneath, gummy red from throat to belt buckle, and there was a bubbling froth at the corners of his mouth as Moma July bent to him.

"I'm killed," Goshen Crowfoot whispered. "Them sonsabitches! I'm killed."

Goshen Crowfoot's shotgun lay beneath his legs.

"Don't talk, Goshen," said Moma July. "We'll get ole Doc Purtry up here."

"I'm killed."

Moma July was holding his lantern high, trying to see along the hall. The smoke was hanging there like heavy gauze, some of these weapons using black powder, and Moma July tried to see. There was an orange triangle of light from the open door of the bedroom where he, Moma July, had been lighting the lamp each night. But nothing more.

"Candy?" Moma July called. "Don't shoot no more. It's me, Moma."

He went along the hall cautiously, smelling the violence, seeing along each wall the jagged scars of buckshot, and aware that behind him was Claudis Mopes with a pistol in his hand.

"Candy?"

He passed the lighted door and saw with a glance the bed had not been slept in, and then on along the smoke-swirled passageway, past the open door to a dark room, and assumed there had been Candy Redstripe's bed.

"Candy?"

And then saw him. At the end of the hall. Sitting on the floor, back to the wall. Legs straight out, wide-spread before him. Chin down resting on his chest. A spray of black hair down across his forehead.

At first glance, Moma July thought Candy Redstripe was wearing the popular red flannel underwear. Then, as he came closer, saw the red was recent dye. All across the front.

Candy Redstripe's arms were relaxed, hands lying open-palm between his thighs and in each hand a heavy revolver. Moma July came close very slowly, watching the hands, knelt down and put his lantern on the floor, and gently took one of the pistols from Candy Redstripe's hand. It was hot. Then the other, hot too. And with a quick glance, Moma July knew that all the rounds in each gun had been fired.

"Candy?" Moma July said.

He cupped a hand beneath Candy Redstripe's chin, and felt the slick, red liquid there, and lifted the face into the shine of the lantern Claudis Mopes was holding. Candy Redstripe's eyes were wide open and the pupils were like black, liquid marbles, and they did not contract in the lantern shine.

"Candy, you hear me?"

"Take me home, Tish," Candy Redstripe whispered.

After a moment, Moma July slipped his hand from beneath

Candy Redstripe's chin and touched his cheek as the chin came back to rest on the chest and said, "You lovely bastard, Candy."

Moma July rose and Claudis Mopes asked if maybe he ought to get Doc Purtry. And Moma July said no.

"Too late, everywhere," he said.

Then the little Creek police captain, with Claudis Mopes following with a lantern, walked through it all in his mind. Into the room where he knew Candy Redstripe had been sleeping. Wakened by the northbound just beneath his window. Footfalls along the stairs. Coming to the hall. Just as three armed men with long guns came, silhouetted as they arrived at the head of the stairs by the lamp in the lower room. Then everybody starting to shoot. Because there had been no preliminary shots. Just a burst. A sudden face-to-face fury. No words exchanged. Predators each ready to strike first. A hail of fire and smoke and metal and screams of defiance along this short, narrow little hallway, silent now, but forever to show the marks along its scarred walls of a moment of insanity.

"Claudis," said Moma July, "you know what this is?"

"What is it, Cap'n?"

"These sonsabitches come in here to kill our friend Mr. Masada," Moma July said. "But found theirselves a little bit different proposition, didn't they?"

"They sure in hell did."

"Well, go on downstairs and collect a few of them citizens and let's start cleanin' it up!"

11 Tishacomsie Redstripe stood at the west end of her porch, leaning against a roof post, her heavy woolen poncho around her body and across her head a shawl of fine lace, the gift of Moses Masada at Christmastime. The day matched her mood. Anything of bright sunshine and warmth would have been intolerable. Now there was a fine mist blowing along the valley of the Canadian River, a wind behind it warm now but she knew it would turn cold before dawn and leave bare-branch trees with a coating of clear-crystal ice.

Somewhere to the north of the house, jays were making a great racket, scolding one another or perhaps an owl they had found. They were always discordant voices, jays, but now more so with all the hardwood leaves gone and nothing to mute sound. It was a winter sound, and with it distant caws of crows from across the river in Choctaw Nation.

All of it was a crying sound. A sad sound. But she had cried before, and would not again, no matter the sadness. No matter the loss. No matter springs which would now never come. No matter the greening in April and the smell of new-turned earth.

She had cried. When Moma July came to tell of it, arriving at dawn with the terrible news. Now the crying was past and her heart was as heavy as the weather. Gray, like an old shroud. Moma July had told her all of it, and it was only then that she knew her husband had been alone, that Moses Masada had been in Fort Smith.

Moma July told her everything he knew of it. To include the

telegraph that came from Wagoner less than an hour after the shooting, from United States Deputy Marshal Nason Breedlove alerting the Eufaula Light Horse that there were federal warrants to be served as soon as the marshal and his party arrived. But now, nobody left upon whom to serve the warrants. Except the woman. And Tish could not help but feel sorry for the woman, Winona, who had lived among wolves for all her life and now had nothing left to her, not even the wolves.

Even the others. Tish could develop no hatred. Only a rather listless resentment. As she might with black ants who invaded her kitchen and she put a boot down hard on them, one by one. With no remembrance of their faces.

She was still there, on the porch, when Moses Masada came. She knew, without turning to see, that it was him. There was the rattle of the hack up the farm road from the river trace, then to the far end of the porch, the mule snorting and fighting the harness as mules always do.

She watched the river. She heard him come across the porch, but she did not turn. And he stopped just short of her back, just short of touching her. He was so close she could feel the heat of his body. But she did not turn to look at him.

"Tish?" he said. "I'm so sorry. I wish I could do . . ."

He stopped. He started once again.

"Tish, I wish there was something."

He touched her shoulder, lightly, with the tips of his fingers, and she shrank away from him without seeming to and he dropped his hand to his side.

"Maybe if I hadn't come," he said.

"No," she said. "It would have happened. Some other time. Some other place. There was bad blood between them."

"I feel responsible."

He lifted one hand and tried to touch her again, and she said, "Don't touch me now."

They stood for a long time, immobile, looking toward the river. The silence was like a wall between them, at the same time ephemeral as the mists along the Canadian yet solid as the oak post against which she leaned.

Finally he said, "Moma July said to tell you. He sent a telegraph to the sheriff in Denison, to get in touch with the Comanche and tell him. He should be coming home soon with the horses."

"It doesn't matter."

The wind had begun to whip a little harder around the corners of the house, blowing against them and leaving a fine, cold moisture on their faces.

"Do you want me to stay with you?"

"No," she said, quickly, emphatically. "I thank you for coming. But I want you to go back now."

"All right. But if I can help at all, Tish."

She said nothing and she could hear his shoes shifting uncertainly on the rough boards of the porch flooring. Then he was moving away, back toward the far end of the porch, where the hack and the mule stood. She let him go almost to the end of the porch before she spoke.

"Masada?"

She heard him stop, knew he had turned.

"I'm taking Candy home on the late northbound tonight. Moma July is arranging it."

"Yes, he told me."

"I'd like for you to go with me."

After a long pause, he said, "Yes. I'll be waiting."

Then she heard the hack turn away, heard the hoofbeats of the mule and the creaking of the wheels back down the slope to the river trace. Throughout it all, she had not looked at him once.

ᴎ ᴎ ᴎ Baggage cars on the Missouri, Kansas, and Texas Railroad never acquired much of a reputation for warmth in winter months, and the one Moses Masada and Tishacomsie Redstripe rode out of Eufaula with the oak box containing what was left of Candy Redstripe held true to form. He had tried to get her into a day coach, but she insisted in few words that on this last ride, she would stay beside her husband. And so they sat in straight-back chairs on either side of the coffin, neither looking at one another nor speaking once the train was underway. She had come onto this car with the help of a railroad baggage man and Moma July, still resistant to any touch from Moses Masada's hand, and the cold in the baggage car seemed to him only a reflection of her mood. And it disturbed him very much.

The mercury in everybody's glass was falling and already, in pre-dawn, they could see the shine of thickening frost on naked trees when the train stopped at all the way stations and the car doors were slid open. Checotah. Oktaha. Muskogee. Gibson Station. Wagoner. The two railroad baggage men stayed at the far end of the car, their conversation appropriately subdued in keeping with the circumstances. At all the stops, when they opened the doors, they worked quickly and efficiently to take certain items off, put others on. Crates of live chickens. Five-gallon cream cans full of milk. Bushel baskets of apples. Cardboard boxes labeled from as far south as Fort Worth, or for places as far north as Kansas City or Chicago.

There was a long wait at Wagoner, junction of the KATY and Arkansas Valley railroads, and Moses Masada got coffee from the baggage master, in tin cups, and they drank as the dawn came, still with no words between them. To the east of them now was the timbered lift of the westernmost fingers of the Ozark hills, to the west the line of tangled woodland along the Verdigris River.

Finally, out of Creek country and into the Cherokee Nation, the day grimly gray. Coming to Chouteau and Pryor Creek. Then quickly, like beads on a string, Big Cabin, Vinita, Kelso, Bluejacket. And finally Welch, just short of the Kansas state line, where they were met by a detachment of Cherokee Light Horse to unload the coffin onto a waiting spring wagon. There was a horse for Tishacomsie with a sidesaddle. Another for Moses Masada with a high pommel and horn, but he opted for riding in the wagon with the coffin, not yet having accommodated comfortably to riding a horse.

It created some embarrassment for him, but Tishacomsie, obviously seeing his distress, said loud enough for all to hear, "Good, Masada, he would have wanted you to ride with him."

It took more than an hour to reach their destination, and all along there were little gusts of wind that propelled particles of sleet into their faces. By the time they arrived at the cemetery, Moses Masada's nose was cherry-red and his toes were numb.

This was a countryside churchyard, with no town in sight. The building was of locally quarried limestone. It sat on a high rise of ground above a loop of the Neosho River, and the gravestones were in an unorganized scatter all around it. In front of the church was a wooden sign, attached to locust posts sunk in the ground:

"Delaware Mission Baptist Church."

There were a great many people there, to include the principal chief of the Cherokees, C. Johnson Harris. Testament, Moses Masada supposed, of the high esteem in which Candy Redstripe's father was held, the old man still being a member of the Cherokee Council at Tahlequah. The Cherokee policeman who had been assigned as Moses Masada's escort, primarily to keep him from underfoot, Masada suspected, presented the white man to the old Delaware, who was tall like his son, had a shock of white hair showing under the narrow-brimmed hat such as his son always wore, and had the same black, piercing eyes his son had had.

"Good day to you, sir," the senior Redstripe said, shaking Moses Masada's hand, and those were the only words exchanged between them. Moses Masada hardly knew whether to take it as formal greeting or some veiled accusation in the causes of Candy Redstripe's death.

It was perfectly obvious that all these people knew who Moses Masada was, whether from the Indian police grapevine or otherwise. In fact, when the Cherokee policeman had introduced him to the elder Redstripe the phrase was used: "This is the Kansas City peace officer."

It might have been a funeral for some farmer in Illinois. The open grave, the people standing about, the wind and sleet, the Neosho River below, the call of red-winged blackbirds as they fed in a nearby field lying furrowed with winter wheat, the line of old ladies all in men's black coats and men's hats standing well back and keening softly like a Greek chorus.

But it wasn't the same. Moses Masada didn't understand a word spoken over Candy Redstripe's last resting place. The preacher was a Wyandotte Baptist, and he spoke his service in Cherokee because the Delawares could understand it. But it was all done quickly in order to get the people home and sheltered from the weather. Even before the first spadeful of earth fell on the oak coffin, Moses Masada saw Tishacomsie move away with her father-in-law and a large group of people. Then his own Cherokee policeman was moving him to another party and they rode off, Moses Masada still in the spring wagon driven by a second Cherokee policeman.

They took him to a large farm, a farm of a well-to-do man, maybe even rich. These were all Cherokees, and once they were inside, standing in the parlor room eating roast beef and brown beans, Moses Masada supposed there must have been at least a dozen men, as many women, and any number of children and dogs of all shapes and sizes. He was surprised that they had beer, a thick brew that the Cherokees made themselves.

They treated him as a complete equal. There was no deference nor yet any sign of taking him as one below themselves. They told him about Stan Waite, the Cherokee leader who had been the last Confederate general to surrender after the Civil War. They told him about the bad times in the seventies when the border ruffians were always coming into their country from Kansas to steal cattle and horses. They wanted to see his British pistol, which they thought somewhat awkward in the hand. They found it confusing that Kansas City, with such a name, should be largely located in Missouri.

That night, with wind dying but temperatures falling, Moses Masada slept on a parlor-room pallet, before he slept hearing the strange breathing, smelling the strange smells, and knowing without having counted exactly that in this house for this night there were probably forty people sleeping. And God only knew how many dogs.

His Cherokee policeman got him to the Welsh railroad depot for the morning southbound, and there was Tishacomsie, and he saw her embrace her father-in-law before boarding the day coach. And as she joined him in the seat, she smiled, and touched his arm, and he hoped that this night, she would not send him away and he would sleep on the farm above the Canadian River.

ℵ ℵ ℵ That night it was cold. And Moses Masada thought surely colder inside the Redstripe farmhouse than outside. She spoke now in a torrent of words, about the Comanche horses that would be back soon and what she would do with them; about leasing farmland to tenants; about perhaps raising some chickens, a whole flock of brooder hens; about cotton and the markets in Fort Smith. About any number of things in which he had no interest and wanted none, and no single word about his being there, his part of her life.

He was acutely aware that she made a supper that was austere and Indian. Hominy mush and grainy cornbread and buttermilk. And half-cooked salt-pork sowbelly. And aware, too, that no sooner was the meal finished than she said he'd have enough covers in his own room, then going into hers and closing the door.

And so he found himself in the same bed where he'd always slept here, alone. From the first night. And like the first night hearing the whisper of cold wind along the jagged shingles of the porch roof just outside.

But then, just like the first night, him almost asleep, seeing the orange glow of a lamp approaching and her in the door, and her coming to his bedside and setting the lamp on the night table. But unlike the first time, her now blowing out the lamp and suddenly, hotly, under the covers with him. With no word spoken. No sound, but only her flowing over him like a sweet, hot honey, clinging and promising the comb.

In those next moments, and he had no notion of how long or short they were, he realized a heat and passion he had never known before. For himself or for any woman. Like a burst of tender yet violent fire that consumed just short of burning everything to crisp, just short of killing them in its agony.

But it was hardly accomplished when she threw off the cover, and sat naked on the side of the bed, sobbing. Moses Masada lay for a moment, thinking she was laughing, then knowing it wasn't so, and rose on one elbow and touched her naked back, and she drew away.

"Tish? What is it?" he whispered. "Get under the covers. It's cold."

"My husband," she sobbed. "My husband!"

It took another moment for him to understand the word. He tried to touch her bare back again and she drew away, rose from the bed.

"Tish, he's gone."

"Not to me. Not yet," she said, and before he really understood what was happening, she was off on bare feet across the room, toward the far end of the house. But she stopped at the door, and in the darkness and cold, he knew that she had turned.

"Go back someplace," she said. "Go back to Fort Smith. For a week, anyway. Let me have my time alone."

"Tish?"

"In the morning. Please. Go back. Before I see you again. Please. Let me have another week."

"But . . ."

She was gone, gone back to the other end of this place, and soon, Moses Masada, still half uncovered and up on an elbow, was cold, and lay down once more and pulled the thick comforter up to his chin.

"Jesus!" he said.

ℤ ℤ ℤ Walking toward the Commerce Railroad Hotel, Oscar Schiller kicked viciously at the cinders on the B Street grade crossing. And swore to himself. And watched carefully the movements of various switch engines before going across the many sidings on his way to Jewel Moon's whorehouse.

Now it was all out, published in the *Fort Smith Elevator*. The Eufaula section house massacre, they called it. In gory details. Plus the fact that federal warrants had been issued for conspiracy having to do with the property known as Fawley Farm in Creek Nation. A conspiracy which had resulted in brutal murder last September. The whole of it fantastically important, according to the *Elevator*, because it involved the unholy queen of Creek Nation, Temperance Moon. All tied together. All finished now, and another crime, many crimes, in the Nations solved by the intrepid deputy marshals of the Parker court. Everyone could sleep now, knowing it was done. Everyone could walk the streets now, knowing it was done.

Good God, Oscar Schiller thought, I didn't notice anybody losing sleep or not going on the streets for the past six months because of a Creek Nation shoot. But by God, that newspaper story this time was as accurate as any. And he knew why. Because of the source.

It came from United States Attorney Walter Evans and United States Marshal Emory Kimes, both anxious to reveal the details of another Indian Territory crime being solved, even though the rope had been cheated. At least for two of the culprits. But two more, Sherman Boggs and Winona Crowfoot, secure in the federal jail, waiting trial. The *Elevator* reported the murder warrants, which the minions of the law had been rushing to serve when the gunfight exploded in the Eufaula section house.

The massacre part was mostly speculation, except for what Oscar Schiller was sure Nason Breedlove had told some news reporter, Nason himself not being averse to what he considered favorable publicity. But he had arrived on the scene only after the fact. Even so, the copy was spectacular, in great detail, featuring word pictures of a hallway with blood-splattered and bullet-pocked walls. And four men dead. Why, exclaimed the *Elevator*, it was bigger than anything that had ever happened in Tombstone, Arizona, or Deadwood, South Dakota, or anywhere else in all Christendom. Whether it was true or not, it had the tone of civic pride. Somewhat like growing the biggest watermelon anyone had ever heard of or withstanding the most vicious hailstorm.

And the victims included a certain Mr. Candy Redstripe, so said the *Elevator*, and always ready for the lethal pun, "a man of bad stripe, a prominent horse racer in I.T. for years, and known to have associated with dubious characters of all races and involved in nefarious dealings."

Each of those victims of the Eufaula section house massacre were scum of the border and better rid of now for the good people of Creek Nation. And the woman Winona Crowfoot was "a known paramour and common-law wife to one of the men slain."

And, of course, the important part of the story. That it all had to do with a greedy man wanting property and thus charged by one of those warrants with killing Temperance Moon, a murder which was widely known and widely discussed and now, according to the federal officials, was finally brought to rest. And a second murder into the bargain. This young thug, what's-his-name, killed as a part of the conspiracy. Oh yes, Toby Jupiter. All solved now. All cases closed, thanks to the efficiency of justice as it operated from the bench of Judge Isaac Parker's court.

So one Sherman Boggs, reported the *Elevator*, in the great bird cage, charged with murder. Winona Crowfoot, in the women's section of the jail, which consisted of two cells on the attic floor above the courtroom, charged with murder. "Both on the sure road to Judge Parker's rope and the sure, dark shades of Hades, where old Lucifer himself will remind them throughout eternity of their heinous crimes."

Oscar Schiller understood that the story served a purpose for law enforcement. The successful pursuit of justice. And served the purpose of the newspaper. One hell of a wonderful bloody and sensational story. So it wasn't that everything had been published which infuriated him, nor even that in all the news accounts his own and Moses Masada's parts had not even been mentioned. The thing that infuriated him was that everybody thought the case was closed, as everybody once had before. And for him, something, in fact a lot of things, smelled very bad about this case.

For instance, when he and Nason Breedlove and the Creek Light Horse had ridden to Fawley Farm the morning after the Eufaula section house shoot to arrest Winona Crowfoot, they had found her terrified and disoriented, and it hadn't taken much pushing by Moma July to have her reveal anything she knew. Or at least it seemed so at the time. But at any rate, one of the revelations was a hole under the floor where they found a cache of money. Almost a thousand dollars in crisp, new greenbacks.

Now consider, Oscar Schiller said to himself, where would a fat, lazy Creek who had never labored a day in his life get that kind of money? From Temperance Moon? Maybe some from there, but in gold or silver or crumpled yellowback bills, and even that never in the amount of a thousand dollars. A lot more considering what Langston Turtle had spent.

So where the hell did that money come from? Winona Crowfoot wouldn't say, no matter how scared she was, and Nason Breedlove couldn't imagine, he being a fine peace officer but a little short on imagination, and Moma July had no notion. But Moma July had been perplexed, just as was Oscar Schiller. And Oscar Schiller knew from experience that when Moma July was perplexed, there were bound to be some thorns in the roses.

So with all this and much more boiling in his head, so hot it almost steamed his glasses, Oscar Schiller crossed the tracks to the Commerce Railroad Hotel, and it being well before noon, a time when Miss Jewel Moon's house would have no clients at all except maybe one or two who had passed out and were being washed in one of the third-floor bathrooms by a covey of ladies in hopes there would be a revival of life so that Clarence or Crutchfield or Homer would not have to drag a dead body off for deposit in the river, expecting to have an immediate audience.

Oscar Schiller was not disappointed. Jewel Moon came down from her third-floor bedroom in a dressing gown that flowed about her great body like the national emblem flowed about the flagstaff in the National Cemetery, red, white, and blue. They sat in the bar, Jewel Moon having her breakfast of sloe gin and kippered herring. And even before they spoke, she pushed across the table a small bottle of white powder.

"A bonus, Oscar, for a job well done," she said.

"Shit," he said. "Not done!"

"Oscar, I read the newspaper," she said. "Sit down. Have some coffee."

"Oh, you read the newspaper," he said. He sat down but he

did not take off his hat. "Well, we know who killed your mother. We know who killed Toby Jupiter. And according to the United States Attorney, we know all of this was a conspiracy to obtain property."

"That's right," she said. "So here's a bonus."

She touched the small bottle filled with white powder. Oscar Schiller seemed to grind his teeth. But he took a matchstick from some pocket in his shirt, wetted it, and jabbed it into the bottle as though he were spearing fish.

"Don't you want some coffee?" she asked.

"No," he said, sucking the match and then jabbing it again into the cocaine. Then chewing on the match. "Listen, who took a shot at me in Bamberger's brewery? Who left you that note the night of the fire? Jewel, I've been talking a lot with railroad people and I haven't found one who ever heard of a kerosene tank car blowing up on a cold night strictly on its own. So listen, who did all those things?"

"For God's sake, Oscar, those animals from the Territory were capable of doing that. Even worse," she said, and her great, blocky face was beginning to go very hard. "You forget, before I came over here, I knew those people."

"Sure, sure," Oscar Schiller said, bending toward her and spitting his words. "But can you imagine Goshen Crowfoot coming into Arkansas and shooting at me with anything less than a big-bore shotgun? Can you imagine Langston Turtle coming across the river and blowing up a tank car? Hell, he'd put the gunpowder or whatever it was right up against your back door! Providing the son of a bitch even knew how to fuse such a thing, which I doubt!"

She was frowning. She took a drink of sloe gin. On the table was a wooden bowl half filled with roasted, glazed pecan halves. She scooped up a handful and threw them into her mouth and chewed, her eyes never leaving Oscar Schiller's face.

"Are you tryin' to scare me?" she asked.

Oscar Schiller sank back in the chair, sighing, lifting his hands.

"Aw, for Christ's sake, Jewel," he said. "Listen. Whoever it was trying to scare us both wasn't in that Eufaula section house shoot. You can bet on it. All we can hope is, whoever was tryin' to scare us read the same newspaper you did and believed it like you did. That everything's all done, all finished."

"Well, it is," she said. "Isn't it?"

Oscar Schiller rose abruptly, yanking at the brim of his hat, yanking at his duster, yanking at the edge of his thoughts.

"Jewel, you said you wanted the why," he said. "You paid for that. Well, Langston Turtle getting your mother's land wasn't it. There's something else. I may be wrong. But in case I am, I'll take that bonus now so you can't take it away later."

He took the small bottle of white powder, shoved it into a pocket of his duster, and turned, swirling, his boot heels clicking on the polished floors as he went into the hall, to the stain-glassed door, and out into the railyard, leaving Miss Jewel Moon still chewing on pecan halves.

She finished her mouthful. Scooped up another from the wooden bowl. Then her large brown eyes grew larger.

"Crutchfield," she screamed.

The man behind the bar, wearing glasses, straightened, stared at her.

"Yes, ma'am?"

"Why the hell hasn't last night's stuff been cleaned off these tables?"

ℤ ℤ ℤ It was the middle of the afternoon. It had turned out cold but clear. A typical late-January day along the Arkansas valley, crisp as autumn, bright as spring. As he came into his basement room, Oscar Schiller had seen the cardinals feeding in the low cedars along the alley beside the privy. The privy. Which reminded him that he needed a jolt of Brown's Indian Root Tonic Elixir. Maybe even two jolts.

And the cardinals. They reminded of something else. A cedar tree in Virginia. Just a small cedar tree, the green turned a little brown from the past summer's sun. In Virginia. Or was it Tennessee? When James Longstreet's corps had been sent from Lee's army to lend a hand to old Braxton Bragg around Chattanooga? He couldn't remember. It was so long ago. Him a young sprout but so inured to battlefields that the sight of dead men no longer affected him one way or the other. Dead horses, that was different. Dead horses had their effect right to the end but by the time of Chickamauga, fallen men had become just another expected feature of each fire swept field.

There had been this tree. The cedar tree. Just off to the left flank of Oscar Schiller's attacking regiment. And in the flash of muzzles and the billowing smoke, there had been a pair of cardinals who didn't want to leave that tree. Fluttering up wildly, then going back into the greenish brown needles, then fluttering up again as the sounds of combat racketed across the field. As though they had a nest there, with young. But it was September, too late for cardinal nests with young. So why?

Swept along in the charge, Oscar Schiller had gone on past the cedar, never looking back to see the birds persisting in remaining there in hails of metal. Maybe at the moment, not even aware that he had seen red birds in such an incongruous setting, maybe seeing them later only in his mind, later when the noise had died and men lay panting, hands blistered on hot rifles, throats screaming for a drink of water. Maybe wondering if those red birds had been real at all, or only figments of hysterical imagination when death was pecking all around him. Just a flicker of blood-red across his confused thinking. There had been plenty of that color without imagining it.

Now, over thirty years later, those two cardinals persisted in flying across Oscar Schiller's thoughts as they had persisted in staying close by the cedar in Tennessee. Or was it Virginia? And the worst of it was that with his mania for things being set exactly in their proper place, he couldn't recall where he'd seen those birds, or else had the illusion of them. Virginia? Tennessee? Maybe even Maryland.

"For God's sake, wake up," he said aloud. "And get to business!"

He sat at his small table, making notes to himself with a stub of pencil, hearing the gentle breathing of the gas furnace flame, hearing the tamale man passing along 7th Street shouting his wares. Aware that he was hungry. And therefore perhaps glad when there was a rap on the door at the head of the stairs leading up to the Hakes' kitchen.

"Come," Oscar Schiller shouted. Quickly slipping a shirt on over his flannel underwear and suspenders.

On this day, Mrs. Hake came with a bowl of rice pudding. It was as rice pudding is supposed to be, the white grains plump, the raisins sweet, the sugar and cinnamon in correct measure. Oscar Schiller sat at his small table spooning it into his mouth and as always allowing the conversation of Mrs. Hake to be one-way and to flow over his head, unheard. Until some phrase, when Oscar Schiller stopped eating and looked at her.

"What was that last you said?"

"What last, Mr. Schiller?"

"That last, your husband talking with Mr. Warson."

"Oh, that," she said. "Oh, well, last night, another political meeting, I wish Mr. Hake would get out of this, and Mr. Warson saying to my husband how awful it is, trying for office, trying to be nice to people you don't really like, trying to make promises you can't keep, old friends being mean to you, telling lies about you, even blackmail. What is blackmail, Mr. Schiller?"

"What did Warson say about blackmail, Mrs. Hake?" Oscar Schiller was no longer interested in rice pudding.

"Well, my husband said he just mentioned it, then talked about other things, but my husband was very disturbed when he came home because he said he never thought Mr. Warson could get in a position for blackmail. Mr. Schiller, what is blackmail?"

Oscar Schiller was already up, taking coat and shoulder harness with the pistol, and duster.

"It was lovely puddin'," he said. "But I've got an appointment."

"Well, Mr. Schiller," she called from the bed, "I just wanted to talk for a little while."

But he was already gone, and had left the door standing open. Mrs. Hake shrugged, took up the half-empty bowl of rice pudding, closed the back door, and went up the steps to her kitchen.

ﾊ ﾊ ﾊ   Oscar Schiller almost never ran anyplace, not since the war when on occasion he found it expedient to move rapidly in an effort to avoid bodily harm. But now he came near to running, from the Hake residence all the way to Garrison Avenue.

He was going to the Main Hotel to see Moses Masada. Yesterday afternoon, the Kansas City detective had arrived in town, telling Oscar Schiller he planned to relax for a week, then return to Creek Nation. Oscar Schiller suspected what Moses Masada was going back for, and it was none of his business, his philosophy always having been that a man's religion and love life were nobody else's concern so long as neither of them gouged out some innocent bystander's eyes.

Moses Masada, like everybody else, was of the opinion that the Temperance Moon case was closed. And Oscar Schiller knew that it had been a great disappointment to the Syrian that he had played so little real part in its resolution. He had come out of it with perhaps more knowledge of Temperance Moon's life than anybody else could claim, with the exception of Temperance Moon's own daughter, yet had contributed nothing to the case. So now he would lie on his butt for a week, reading books and feeling sorry for himself. And in that condition, Oscar Schiller knew he would be particularly receptive to hound-dogging a lot of questions in Oscar Schiller's mind.

And better him do it than me, Oscar Schiller thought, dodging a horse-drawn streetcar in the center of Garrison Avenue as he crossed to the south side. It would take most of this afternoon to pump all the necessary information into that receptive Arab brain, with plans to visit a print shop for making up fake business cards. Because Oscar Schiller knew how Moses Masada worked. And the way he worked was a great advantage here, that plus the fact that outside the people at the federal court, few in this town knew who or what Moses Masada was or whose interests he served.

Besides, it would help to take Moses Masada's mind off that Creek beauty, and Oscar Schiller knew from bitter experience that too much thinking about beauties of any kind could be destructive to digestion. And at the thought of digestion, Mrs. Hake came to mind and her rice puddling and he said to himself, God bless her and her mindless talk. Blackmail! Why in hell hadn't I thought of it before? It's as obvious as the mole on Mrs. Hake's lovely fat neck!

As he had suspected he would, Oscar Schiller found Moses Masada lying half dressed on his bed reading a copy of Oscar Wilde's *The Picture of Dorian Gray.* And on the floor a copy of the *Chicago Inter-Ocean* newspaper featuring a lurid story about a half-dozen London prostitutes being killed and then sliced like frogs on a dissecting table.

"Oscar," Moses Masada said, "two old law dogs like us ought to go to England and find this Jack the Ripper for them."

"We got problems of our own," said Oscar Schiller, throwing his hat aside and sitting on the one chair in the room. He leaned forward, and the glint in his eyes behind the thick lenses of his spectacles caused Moses Masada to push the other Oscar aside and sit on the edge of the bed, leaning forward as well in anticipation of what he knew was coming. Opening the chase again.

"Later, I will tell you a great many things," said Oscar Schiller. "Many of which I have already told you. Some I have not.

But first, let me tell you a story. It's my story but it may be close to dead center true."

"I have always enjoyed stories," Moses Masada said. "Especially those which are close to dead center true."

Oscar Schiller closed his eyes, the better to concentrate. It was like turning off a lamp, the eyelids closing over the fire.

"Man owns a bordello," Oscar Schiller said. "Man gets political ambitions, high ambitions. Needs to get out of the whore business to protect his reputation."

"Naturally," said Moses Masada.

"Man sells his share of the whore business. So far, so good?"

"Yes. So far so good."

"Now a woman. Not directly connected to the loose-lady business the man has sold, but knows all about it. She comes to him to ask for a loan, the man with the reputation being in the business of making loans. But the man, to protect that same reputation, figures he has just got shed of one association with women who are not members of the Lily White Purity and Temperance League, and can't afford to get into another. Refuses the loan."

"Naturally. The reputation," said Moses Masada.

"Woman is a very tough woman. Woman is also very angry at being refused the loan. So woman tells man if he doesn't come across with the money she wants, she will turn the monkey loose and reveal to all and sundry his years of profit-taking in the white slave trade. Now," and Oscar Schiller opened his eyes. "You finish the story."

Moses Masada laughed.

"Easy. But question."

"Shoot."

"How important is saving that reputation to our man?"

"Very important."

"Question."

"Shoot."

"How ruthless is this man?"

"Very ruthless."

"And the woman?"

"Even more ruthless."

"Blackmail," said Moses Masada. "The time-honored, classic example of the horns of dilemma."

"Never mind the horns," said Oscar Schiller impatiently. "The story."

"Of course. Blackmail. When a man is blackmailed, he has three selections. He can say, go ahead and turn the monkey loose. But if he thinks the revelation is too severe to tolerate, he can take option two. He can pay off. But he's got to figure that once he pays off, it is not necessarily finished. The blackmailer can come back time and time again. He may be paying off for the rest of his life. And if that is also too severe, he ends with the third option."

"Which is?"

"Kill the blackmailer!"

"Aw." Oscar Schiller sighed and leaned back in his chair, his eyes closed once more. "Moses, you are good at storytelling."

"It's part of the job, isn't it?"

"Yes, but now listen," and once more Oscar Schiller was leaning forward, as though about to leap at something. "Our man with the reputation has that reputation for good reason. He doesn't go around killing people. He doesn't even carry a weapon. He probably doesn't even know how to use a weapon. So if he comes down on option three, how does he do it?"

"Just like he'd do if he wanted his apple trees pruned," said Moses Masada. "He'd hire somebody to do it."

"That's a big step."

"You said he was ruthless."

"I don't know if he's that ruthless."

"All right. Suppose he takes option two. Suppose he gives our woman the loan?"

"Not likely," said Oscar Schiller. "It would defeat his purpose in protecting that reputation, you see? It's just a loan, she'd say. No reason to conceal it. Even if there was no record of it like on a signed contract, she'd be using the money to build a dance hall. And the source of the money would naturally come out."

"So there's that association between our man with the reputation and people of lowly intent," said Moses Masada.

"Exactly."

"So in fact, once she mentions blackmail, it has gone too far for just a normal loan, which she asked for at the start."

"Exactly. Everything has suddenly changed, once she makes the threat of turning that monkey loose."

"So now, no matter what he calls it, if he gives her money, it's blackmail money to him because he is going to end with an association he can't abide. That reputation and all."

"Exactly. So it's the third choice."

"Well, let's think about that," Moses Masada said. He looked to the window, where the afternoon sunlight was slanting against the screen to make little golden patterns of brilliance. "Suppose our man decides that killing won't set well with his breakfast eggs for the rest of his life. So he gives her the money, fooling himself into thinking it is really a loan and that he's not vulnerable for her tapping him again and again. And then her friends discover she has the money and kill her for it. Our man can't say anything because if he gets involved, it's going to reveal some of the very things he's been trying to keep quiet all along. And besides, somebody else's killing her has served his purpose."

"But we know most of her friends didn't end with a wad of money," said Oscar Schiller. He had begun to peck Moses Masada's thigh with a finger. "The most we found was a thousand dollars. And one of them only got seventy-five. And we know when she went for the loan, she would ask for at least five thousand because she told her lawyer that before ever approaching our man with the reputation."

"All right," said Moses Masada, moving away from Oscar Schiller's jabbing finger, "it appears our man didn't pay blackmail or give a loan or whatever you want to call it. He went to the third option."

"And you've seen this work before."

"Of course," said Moses Masada. "Somebody like our man with good reputation threatened comes up with a lot of money, say five thousand dollars. He gives it to a party of the second part with instructions as to who needs to be dispatched. The party of the second part keeps half the money for himself. The other half, he pays to someone with appropriate instructions. That person keeps half and does the same. All down the line, all down the line, at each step someone taking his own and at each step it going lower and lower on the scale of bonebrains until finally you end up with somebody who actually pulls the trigger and willing to do it for, say, seventy-five dollars."

"All right. What do you think of our story so far?"

"It's a damned good story," Moses Masada said. "But like all such stories, with so many people between start and finish, it's hard to trace the track of the money."

"How do you do it?"

"Start at the bottom. But here, a lot of our people at the bottom are buried over there in the Eufaula graveyard."

"We've still got Winona Crowfoot and Sherman Boggs. But let's talk about starting at the top."

"Sure," said Moses Masada. "That's a good way, if you know who to start with. And in our story, maybe we do. At least, I think we're making some good guesses."

"Hell, Moses, our work is mostly guessing, until we can prove it."

"That's true. I think our guessing is fine, but how do we prove it?" Moses Masada asked.

"I don't know. Not starting with the man and his reputation. Too hard to get to. But with that party of the second part maybe. And if our guessing is close to home on the man at the top, then we got a handle on the one who does his dirty work."

"Point me."

"We've got to compromise him. We've got to scare hell out of him. Enough so that maybe he'll either jump or else be willing to tell us things we'd like to know."

"Dangerous man, this party of the second part?" Moses Masada asked.

"So they say."

"Point me, Oscar."

"We've got to put this party of the second part, if that's what he is, into this case. We probably got to put him in Creek Nation or somewhere in Indian Territory before last September when Temperance Moon was killed."

"Yes, I like this," Moses Masada said. "And you knew I would, you old law dog. But this one particularly. I'd like to really make it solid. For Temperance Moon."

"Oh?" said Oscar Schiller.

"Sure," and Moses Masada shrugged as though he didn't understand it himself. "I feel as though I've really gotten to know the old girl. Maybe like so many of those men she had all her life, like I owe her the best I can give her. Funny, isn't it? Never saw her in my life, but she's right here in this room with us."

"Moses, you Yankee peace officers are crazy as hell," Oscar Schiller said, and Moses Masada laughed.

"All right. So point me."

"Muley LaRue. That's who we're dogging. Muley LaRue!"

"Why him?" asked Moses Masada.

"Because," said Oscar Schiller and actually almost smiled, "if the man with a reputation in our story is who I think it is, Muley would be the logical one to be party of the second part."

"I like your mind, Oscar," said Moses Masada. "It's a bulldog mind."

"Be that as it may," said Oscar Schiller, taking a fistful of little notes from a shirt pocket along with some kitchen matches and a small bottle of white powder. "So, let's get to business!"

12 In the late 1880s, Fort Smith had a very important, diamond-stickpin-in-the-necktie kind of visitor. They didn't get many of those. This one was Mr. Jay Gould, railroad tycoon and other things for which he had never thus far been indicted. This famous gentleman was in town to explore the possibility of a bridge across the Arkansas River from near the end of Garrison Avenue, a bridge reaching across into Indian Territory. A venture in connection with Mr. Gould's interest in the Arkansas Valley and Missouri Pacific railroads.

There was a lot of excitement. It stirred up considerable civic pride. After all, everybody said, there was a bridge across the Arkansas at Van Buren, north of Fort Smith, which had been serving rail traffic since 1887. Now damn well time there was a bridge at Fort Smith, no matter where it led.

Time, they said, to dispense with those damned ferryboats, which were mostly wagon beds caulked against the water. And now, as was not true in earlier times, the people in the Nations were not opposed to such a bridge, their realizing that a three-hundred-yard stretch of water could not isolate them from the white man's culture. So when the bridge was completed in May 1891, a prominent part of the program of dedication was speeches by the principal chiefs of Cherokee and Choctaw Nations.

Everybody agreed it was one hell of a fine bridge. Steel girders on round concrete pilings. And a place in the center, at midstream, where a turntable could move a whole section so that high vessels might pass along the river. It was seldom used because there were not any high vessels that passed along this river.

The year after its completion, there was one of those furious Arkansas River floods. And they loaded open gondola cars with scrap iron and cotton bales and ran them out onto the bridge and left them to set, hoping the added weight on the pilings would be enough to avoid rushing water taking the whole thing away. And it was.

This was more than a railroad bridge. It was designed to be used by wagons and even pedestrian traffic. The cost for a wagon to cross was two bits. A quarter of a dollar. For a person, a nickel. And horses were considered as human. Because a man riding across paid his five pennies for himself, another nickel for the horse. There were men at each end of the bridge, taking the toll and keeping everybody clear when trains were coming.

These men had to be dependable. And the railroad made sure they were, hiring those with an established record of reliability, many of them handicapped in some way. As with the man who had all the fingers of his right hand cut off at the Fort Smith Rim and Bow Company sawmill. Or the one whose left foot had been mangled in the couplings of two freight cars when he was working a night shift in the Missouri Pacific yards. Or the one who had an eye knocked out when a steel cable snapped at the Arkansas Valley Cotton Press.

Good men. Sober men. And with stable memories.

So one of them recalled, with reference to his toll ledgers, that Muley LaRue had crossed the bridge into Indian Territory one late night in August 1892. Just after the Wagoner freight had passed. Just two weeks before Temperance Moon was killed. The toll man didn't say that, of course. The toll man didn't understand there was any connection. But did know that Muley LaRue returned two days later, after what he said was a hunt for turkey, and also in dark of night, just before the Wagoner freight.

Then there was Consolidated Mining Equipment Company. An outfit with acres of lumber and steel and mules and wagons and sheet-metal buildings located in a small hamlet south of Fort Smith called Jenny Lind, close to the area where a lot of people were drilling for natural gas and sinking shafts into the soft-coal deposits under the surface. And CMEC, as they called themselves, contracted everything to drillers and diggers, even those who had begun to explore across the line in Indian Territory.

CMEC sold to big outfits, who were taking the resources from beneath the surface of the land. But now and then, they sold a bit here and there to individuals who were associated with such institutions as a bank where they did their money business, and yes, according to a Consolidated yard supervisor, they had sold some dynamite and primer cord and caps and fuse to Muley LaRue. In December. A week before the tank car in the Row freight yard exploded. Of course, the Consolidated supervisor didn't make any connection. He was just enjoying the Havana-wrapped cigar and the conversation of the dapper young representative of a new drilling outfit.

"Ole Muley, he was gonna cut him a water well in his backyard, and needed something to get through the sandstone," the supervisor said.

Then there was Hanley's Gun Shop, just two doors from City Bank on Garrison Avenue and the best gun and ammunition mart in the city. It was the first place along the Avenue where one of the new retractable iron grillworks was installed to protect plate-glass windows looking onto the sidewalk. Here it was disclosed, after much conversation, that indeed there were a lot of people about who owned .41 caliber derringers. One of the most noticeable of these was Mr. Muley LaRue of City Bank, noticeable because he bought so much ammunition, going as he did perhaps three, four times a week to the Poteau River to collect crawdads and while there pot-shooting turtles with the two pocket Remingtons he owned. Crack shot, that Mr. LaRue, so said the owner of Hanley's, shooting turtles with a weapon designed to inflict bodily harm only across the length of a poker table.

And then there was City Bank, a progressive establishment. So progressive that all City Bank employees used fountain pens instead of quills even though this novel device that had been around since early in the eighteenth century enjoyed little popular success because it leaked so much. And McRoy Stationer, where City Bank contracted for all office supplies, maintaining an inordinate inventory of brown ink in quart bottles because, as any clerk could explain, that was the color they used down the street at the bank.

It was as easy as taking marbles from children. Especially for an experienced peace officer like Moses Masada when he did not expose his true identity, when he had a pocketful of expensive Havana cigars, when he had a gift of gab, when he knew from the start what he was looking for, and when he had a fistful of business cards printed for each occasion.

ENRICO SPAZI
TRUNK LINE & BRIDGE INSPECTOR
MISSOURI PACIFIC RAILROAD
ST. LOUIS, MISSOURI

Or:

ENRICO SPAZI
CHIEF OF EXPLORATION
KEYSTONE NATURAL GAS COMPANY
TITUSVILLE, PENNSYLVANIA

Or:

ENRICO SPAZI
SALES SUPERVISOR
REMINGTON ARMS COMPANY
HARTFORD, CONNECTICUT

And others.

None of the people to whom Moses Masada spoke had the vaguest notion that as a result of their little conversations there might be a federal government subpoena arriving one day requiring them to say under oath what they had said to the handsome young man in the bowler hat.

₪ ₪ ₪ Oscar Schiller's pale eyes glinted behind the thick lenses of his glasses even without dipping cocaine. Because in less than a week, this Syrian had placed Muley LaRue in every place and in every position Oscar Schiller had guessed he'd been in, and if there was a single thing that made Oscar Schiller happy it was fortifying his own speculative stories and guesses and assumptions. So here it was, Muley into the Nations at the right time, Muley buying explosives at the right time, Muley without doubt a .41 caliber derringer man, Muley likely to use brown ink in anything he was stupid enough to write.

Of course, it was all circumstantial. And Oscar Schiller knew a peace officer worked mostly on circumstantial until hard evidence came to hand. And all that circumstantial business was admissible in a court of law. And with just a few other hard items would make a damning case.

For Oscar Schiller, it was already damning. Money, he reckoned, had gone into Creek Nation to keep Temperance Moon silent. And Muley LaRue had been the agent.

"Moses," he said, "I'll need a little time to figure out where to put the screw on Muley's thumb. I'll have to go talk with the United States Attorney. I'll have to get some backing on this side of the river for arresting somebody, if and when it comes to that. And it will, by God, it will. That frigging Muley LaRue, he'll lead us to our man. And all of them on the same rope."

"You people down here think about that rope a lot, don't you?" asked Moses Masada.

"It's a big rope."

Well, the Syrian had done his job, and his week was up, and he was off to Indian Territory like a kid going after the cookie jar, licking his chops. What the hell, Oscar Schiller thought, he's earned a few cookies.

That night in his Hake basement bed, Oscar Schiller thought about Moses Masada and Tish Redstripe. And Oscar Schiller was jealous of Moses Masada. Not because the Syrian loved the Creek woman, but because he had the capacity to love at all.

From his early life, Oscar Schiller had had the normal urges of the glands and curiosity of mind. At least, he assumed it had been normal. And he assumed it normal to have satisfied these things at various times along the way. There had been a bordello in Richmond during the war. There had been the sister to one of the rowdy men Oscar Schiller had run with in Texas during Reconstruction getting into all kinds of trouble with constituted authority. There had been the matron in Shreveport fallen on evil times and who had to sell all the family horses. There had been a lot of these. But there had never once been anything beyond the urges and the curiosity.

Even Nason Breedlove had a wife. Did love go with that? Oscar Schiller didn't know. All he knew was that nothing he'd ever experienced could be called love. The nearest he'd come to it was with that Tonk Indian woman in San Antonio, and that had been more boyish adoration from afar than any kind of intimate affection.

Hell, he'd even been a little proud of being above tender entanglements. He'd too often seen how such situations could turn a man inside out, make him crazy, end in misery, sometimes even crime and the rope. But he thought now that there might be something of value that he was missing. Not that he could do anything about it because it wasn't the kind of thing a man could consciously turn on and off like the hot water valve on the Hake furnace.

Well, obviously the Arab knew about such things. Maybe that was what made Oscar Schiller jealous. Moses Masada knew something that Oscar Schiller didn't.

Such introspection didn't keep him awake long. Possibly two minutes at most.

זּ זּ זּ To Moses Masada, riding the trace from Eufaula to the Redstripe farm, the Canadian River had never been more beautiful. It was running almost spring-full because unseasonable warm weather had melted all the snow in the Antelope Hills far to the west and in the Glass Mountains and along the rolling country north of the Washita. And the lifting ground on either bank seemed to suck in the fresh moisture and gleam, the fallow fields and those planted to winter wheat and the stands of leafless hardwoods like gray smoke along the far ridge lines. The sun was glaring bright and a little frost with each breath was not enough to chill the spirit of the land or of Moses Masada's heart.

He was riding a saddle horse. A gentle mare, but a saddle horse nonetheless. Because he was determined that in his final days in this country he would ride astride a leather saddle like a man and not on a seat in a spring wagon like a woman. It wasn't easy, but he had seen a great many people doing it recently and he was extremely good at imitation.

As he rode up the slope to the now familiar whitewashed farmhouse, she came onto the porch to greet him, and she could hardly help noticing that he was riding a horse and her great smile came, with the teasing look in the depths of her black eyes, a thing Moses Masada had not seen since Candy Redstripe died. On her head was the Portuguese shawl he had given her at Christmas.

"Tish," he said.

"Masada," was her only response.

There were no more words then. Yet a deliberate, inexorable haste, she smiling and looking at his face, their going inside, arm in arm, across the parlor room and into the place that had always been his bedroom here, where the door had been closed and it was cold and quickly undressing and under the cover of quilts with a kind of urgency not brought on by the temperature.

"The Comanche is back," she said as he drew her near to his body.

"I don't care," he said.

She cried again, when it was finished. But only for a moment and then they lay in the warmth of the bed, hearing the crows in the woodlands behind the barns, hearing the gentle huff of air in the kitchen stove flue in the next room.

"He's still with you, then?" he finally asked.

"Only a little," she said. And then continued with something he did not understand, but would cause him to think for a long time. "He was so weak. People expected everything from him and he could never resist money. He knew money was the white man's world."

"So weak?" he said. "So strong."

"No."

But no longer any chance to speak of what he didn't want to speak of anyway, for she was up and out into the other rooms, tending a chicken she had had roasting in the oven since morning, knowing he would come this day.

"You're sure of me, are you?" he asked.

She laughed. "Yes," she said.

Comanche Toad may have been back, but Moses Masada didn't see him. Not at first. He and Tishacomsie ate each time they ate without the horse tender. After each meal, she laid a lot of food on a metal platter and placed it outside the back door, as though she were feeding a dog. It gave Moses Masada an unpleasant stiffening of hair along the back of his neck.

So on the third day, he went out to the sheds, to help with the horses, what little he knew of such things. Toad spoke no single word to him, although Moses Masada knew the Comanche could speak English, if not too well. But no word passed. The only communication, if that's what it was, a sullen glare from bloodshot eyes where the lashes and the brows above had been plucked with bone tweezers as in the fashion of the old buffalo-hunting High Plains tribesmen.

"He's only a barbarian," Tish said. "Here just for the horses. He can talk to horses, you know."

Moses Masada could not help but recall some of his old father's stories, and the values shared by whole generations of people.

"Toad doesn't like me much," said Moses Masada.

"He doesn't like anybody much," she said. "Only Candy. He worshiped Candy."

It didn't matter. Nothing mattered. Only that he was here. Yet, with each ecstasy realizing more and more that this was not his place. And more and more speaking of the beauty and glory and opportunity of northern cities, leaving out, of course, the rats and garbage.

"We'll go to Kansas City," he said.

"I'd like to visit one of your places."

"No, no, not visit," he said, holding her close. "To live. A man and his wife."

Without seeming to, she drew away. It was something she was so expert at, drawing away without seeming to.

"I couldn't live in the white man's world," she said. "The white man's world has taken everything away from me."

"It's brought you me," he said, like any man yearning for a first love to tell him how valuable he is to her, and sorry he'd said it from the moment the words were spoken.

"Yes," she said.

And he had the terrible feeling that what she meant was, Yes. As a substitute. Because there is nothing else.

№ № №   Oscar Schiller was surprised to find a second guest in the brewery kitchen when he went there for the first sampling of the sauerkraut made from last summer's cabbage. This was kraut which had survived the assailant's attack with the Remington derringer. So it was special kraut.

Max Bamberger's other guest was special as well. Mr. Abram Jacobson, prominent Fort Smith businessman, whom Oscar Schiller knew on sight but had never met. And whom Oscar Schiller knew to be the sole remaining silent partner in the enterprise of the Commerce Railroad Hotel. With that in mind, Oscar Schiller realized there was special kraut and a special guest and it would be a special supper, all arranged by his friend Max Bamberger, who Oscar Schiller suspected had begun to enjoy playing detective.

Mr. Jacobson was a small man, which seemed to be emphasized

by his black woolen suit and white starched shirt. Oscar Schiller remarked to himself that there were not many men in Fort Smith who wore starched shirts. Mr. Jacobson had dark, intense eyes, yet with a gentle melancholy that proclaimed here were eyes which had seen many of the world's troubles. He had very large, delicate hands, and expressive. Expressive because when he spoke he used them much as though he were conducting a full symphony orchestra. The tone of his accompanying voice would have fit nicely into the cello section.

Out of respect for Mr. Jacobson, Max Bamberger did not serve his usual pork bratwurst. Instead, there were fillets of catfish, crisp-fried, and they worked well with the mild kraut, the black bread, and the thick beer. The meal progressed as it always had in Max's kitchen. The only difference being that heavy wooden shutters had been installed on the two windows opening onto the alley. There was a great deal of male gossip and a great deal of laughter and a great deal of food and drink consumed. By the time they pushed back their pewter plates and lit the Havana-wrapped cigars Oscar Schiller had brought, there was an atmosphere of respect and trust among them, as there had always been between Max Bamberger and Oscar Schiller, and now a niche in that fellowship was comfortably occupied by Abram Jacobson.

"Oscar, Oscar, these fine cigars," said Max Bamberger. "How can you afford them?"

"Sometimes good fortune smiles, Max."

"I will say no more, I will say no more," Max said and laughed. Then grew suddenly sober. "Oscar, my friend Abram has something to say to you."

"Yes," said Abram Jacobson, his hands beginning to conduct the overture. "Max informs me of your interest in the affairs of a certain businesswoman of this city. I have a similar interest, for different reasons, of course, as I know you understand."

"Of course."

"I am aware that due to the nature of your calling, there are many things you know, important things, the source of which you have the honor to hold in confidence."

"Yes."

"What I have to say does not require that stricture, but I would not expect that you will go to the *Fort Smith Elevator* newspaper and tell them everything I tell you."

They all laughed.

"Of course not," said Oscar Schiller. "Mr. Jacobson."

"Please. Abram. Or as Max calls me, Abe."

"Thank you. Abe."

They laughed again.

"But you know that anything I hear I will use if it helps me place a criminal where he belongs," said Oscar Schiller.

"Naturally," said Abram Jacobson, and the hands took up the music once more. But then, without a note, stopped, and pulled the black-and-white-striped shawl around his shoulders closer to his neck.

"You're cold, I'll put more wood in the stove," said Max Bamberger.

"It's no matter. Only an old man's little chill. A reminder of the approaching grave."

"Nonsense," said Max Bamberger. "You're strong as an ox."

"Yes, an old ox. A very old ox," said Abram Jacobson. "Now, Mr. Schiller . . ."

"Oscar."

"Aw. Thank you. Oscar then." The hands were still silent as Abram Jacobson puffed his cigar, not inhaling the smoke but blowing perfect little smoke rings into the light of the lamp hanging from above the table.

"Sticking my beak into somebody else's business is done with trepidation," said Abram Jacobson and then produced the most elaborate shrug Oscar Schiller had ever seen, and smiled, and placed the cigar on the edge of the table. "No. It's not true. Poking my beak into other people's business has always been my favorite hobby."

They all laughed again. And the hands began again.

"Innocence is not bliss," he said. "Ignorance can be dangerous. So I tell you all this, Oscar. Because I suspect you not knowing it might be dangerous.

"I have a close associate. He is in the banking business. Many of my people are close to banking people when not the bankers themselves. It is historical with us. Because in so many places, they would not allow us to do anything else.

"This friend has always spoken with me of his little trials and tribulations. Of his big trials and tribulations as well. So he has done now."

The hands stopped conducting long enough for Abram Jacobson to lift the cigar once again to his lips for another small puff.

"My friend had occasion to refuse a loan to the mother of this businesswoman to whom we have referred already. You are aware of that, I'm sure, Oscar."

"Yes, I am."

"But on reflection, which I judge you are not aware of, he changed his mind and sent her the money. Not bank money, but his own. She had by then returned to her home in the Indian Territory, and you know where it is."

"Of course."

"Shortly thereafter, this woman was murdered, and my friend was sure those who had done it, as reported in the *Elevator*, did so to get that money. And he felt somehow responsible."

The hands stopped conducting and the intense eyes were on Oscar Schiller, who sat for a long while drumming his fingers on the tabletop.

"Why would your friend change his mind?" Oscar Schiller asked.

"There was a matter of embarrassment," said Abram Jacobson. "Without making the loan, my friend would have been embarrassed, so he thought. Thus decided to make the loan, because it was the lesser of two embarrassments, perhaps."

"How much money?"

"I had the sense of five thousand dollars."

"Why didn't your friend go to the law with this story?" Oscar Schiller asked.

"Aw," said Abram Jacobson, and the hands were working again. "Let me assure you first that I trust this man in what he says to me. This is a good man. And he did not go to the law because there was that embarrassment I pointed out, and besides, what purpose would it have served? The deed, the foul deed, was done."

"Well," said Oscar Schiller, "I've got to be brutal about it. He profited from that murder, because it stopped the embarrassment, didn't it?"

"Precisely," said Abram Jacobson. "That was the most terrible thing about it."

Oscar Schiller was frowning. "I don't think I follow that, Abe."

"You have heard of confession? A cleaning of the soul? When there seems to be no other way to live with one's human frailties? The Catholics made a holy sacrament of it, but we all do it in various ways."

"Well, maybe. I'm not a Catholic."

"Nor am I," said Abram Jacobson. "But Oscar, here was a man crying to be free of his conscience. Who had, regardless of what he thought were embarrassing past indiscretions, innocently set in motion a horror."

Oscar Schiller took off his glasses, laid them on the table, and rubbed his eyes with the fingers of both hands.

"I've seen it happen," he said. "Many times. Coming clean, we call it."

"I thought it best you know," said Abram Jacobson.

"Yes, it is." Oscar Schiller replaced his glasses. "All right, a loan and he sent the money. She didn't come back here for it."

"Correct."

"How did he send the money?"

"I don't know," said Abram Jacobson, and then with the expressive shrug once more and this time with a smile, "But I could guess. Couldn't you?"

"Abe, you are a born police officer," said Oscar Schiller, and they laughed once more.

"Yes. I've always made fantasies that I was a policeman."

"But Abe," asked Oscar Schiller, "isn't it possible your friend was sending money to keep her silent?"

"Just that?"

"Yes. Just that."

"Well," said Abram Jacobson, "my friend at the time of this telling and with tears close to his eyes waved about a piece of paper which he allowed me to see, once he had stopped waving it. A receipt. The sort of instrument one has when a loan is negotiated. You must understand, I have seen many of these."

"Whose name was written on it?"

"No name," said Abram Jacobson. "That's one of the reasons my friend was crying, I would suspect. It was a receipt for a loan that nobody ever signed for."

צ צ צ When he left Max Bamberger's kitchen that night, Oscar Schiller was furiously distraught. First, because Abram Jacobson had made an impression on him that few men ever had at first wash. One did not distrust this man's judgment, because here was a man who had survived a long and brutal life on the basis of his judgments and obviously made a damned good show of it.

No need for Warson to try to deceive such a man, an old and trusted associate. So Oscar Schiller knew the little story he had put together with Moses Masada had to be revised. In fact, at the time the story was composed in the Main Hotel room, Moses Masada had himself suggested there might be this angle to it.

And that was really the second part of his fury. Why couldn't this be as simple as it once was, him with a federal badge, going into the Territory and arresting the murderers and rapists and bringing them in to jail and allowing the people who wore neckties to see justice was done? He was beginning to understand the difficulty of proving conspiracy in a court of law.

And the more he thought of it, the more furious he became. Because he had been dead wrong. Why would a man like Warson or anybody else spend five thousand dollars to have somebody killed in the Indian Territory when one could get such a thing done for a hundred dollars or less?

He thought about all the possibilities he and Moses Masada had discussed. He thought about his own long service in the Indian Territory. He thought about five thousand dollars being set loose in Creek Nation and knew that such a sum of money in such a place was no longer money at all, but a force, like lightning. Sometimes beyond control. Sometimes beyond understanding.

And that amount of money had been set loose. Maybe innocently. But once crossing the river, all innocence gone. All control gone.

He walked that night directly to the Missouri Pacific Railroad depot and the telegrapher there, who was still on duty in his little wire cage and under his little green cap-shade. And Oscar Schiller printed out the words on one of the Western Union yellow forms.

"Night letter?" the man asked.

"No. Urgent."

"That'll be eighty-five cents."

"Jesus Christ, pretty expensive."

"Night letter's cheaper."

"No. Here's the money."

And so the next morning in Eufaula, Creek Nation, as United States Deputy Marshal Nason Breedlove had his breakfast of six eggs, four pork chops, a mound of grits, biscuits with white cream gravy, a glass of buttermilk, and a two-quart pot of black coffee, he took in his hand the message from Fort Smith, took it from Moma July, who monitored everything in this town, and tried to digest, along with his light breakfast, the thing that Oscar Schiller had sent:

"Inform Masada soonest he can relax and enjoy cookie jar stop the man in our story took option two stop more later stop maybe stop."

And that morning, even as Nason Breedlove was trying to make sense of a telegraph message, Oscar Schiller was sitting hat in hand in the office of the only man he knew who might understand how to unravel conspiracy. United States Attorney Walter Evans.

It was almost noon before the United States Attorney could find time to speak with the former United States Deputy Marshal. The long wait had done little to soothe Oscar Schiller's frayed nerves. And when he was finally ushered into the office of the Great Man by a law clerk who appeared to be about twelve years old, little of it registered on his mind. The desk cluttered with papers, the law books on every level surface in the room, some open, some with markers in them. An odor of chewing tobacco. An obviously overworked gentleman who peered at him over the tops of steel-rim spectacles much like those Oscar Schiller wore. The United States Attorney's opening words did little to settle Oscar Schiller's stomach.

"Oscar, I don't intend doing anything to get your commission reinstated."

"Mr. Evans, that's not why I'm here. I'm here about the Temperance Moon case."

Walter Evans leaned forward, blinking. "The what?"

"Temperance Moon case."

"Dear sweet God in heaven, aren't you ever going to understand the case is closed?" said Evans.

"Listen to me," said Oscar Schiller. "Just listen to me."

The United States Attorney sighed and sat back in his swivel chair, threw his glasses on the already cluttered desk, took a small bone-handled pocketknife and a pressed plug of tobacco from a vest pocket, cut off a chunk, positioned it in his mouth, and began to chew.

"Oscar," he said, "if I did not know what a fine peace officer you have always been, I would have you arrested for public nuisance. So I'll give you five minutes. Nothing more."

So began the torrent of words. From the beginning, as Oscar Schiller knew it. Respected member of the community profiting for years as a landlord of sin, and from there on and on and on, and the United States Attorney interrupting now and then to exclaim, "I didn't know that!"

Then the blackmail possibility and all the things Moses Masada had found concerning one Muley LaRue.

By now, the tobacco in Evans's mouth had been well worked and he turned toward the brass cuspidor at the wall behind his desk and squirted an amber stream that missed.

"You're naming some rather well-to-do citizens here," Evans said. "Without a shred of evidence not circumstantial. You know that, don't you, Oscar?"

"Just listen to my story," Oscar Schiller said.

"It's beginning to fascinate me. Go on, Oscar."

"All right, sir, but let me ask what you've got."

"That's easy," said Walter Evans, spitting again and wiping his beard with the palm of one hand. "Sherman Boggs confesses. That plus a lot of circumstantial means conviction. We'll convict Sherman Boggs of murder, Winona Crowfoot of accessory. If Sherman recants, which will destroy our case, we still know a lot of things. Langston Turtle paid Toby Jupiter to steal a gun. Used gun to implicate Toby. Paid Sherman to kill Toby to keep him silent."

"So now," said Oscar Schiller, "my idea is that Langston Turtle paid Toby, Goshen, Sherman, *before* Temperance Moon was shot!"

"How?" Walter Evans asked, his jaws working on the tobacco, and by now leaning forward across the cluttered desk.

"He had to pay them all ahead of time. He couldn't tell them everything would be fine and he'd pay them afterward. He had to have the money before Temperance Moon was shot. None of that bunch would have done it on suppose!"

Evans chewed violently. His hands began to work in and out of the papers on his desk.

"So?" he asked.

"So, no matter whether the money came from Fort Smith as loan, Temperance Moon never saw it. It went to Langston Turtle. It means somebody funneled the money to Langston and not to Temperance, and somebody along the line saw a chance to make a nice little profit for his own self, and get shed of Temperance Moon, who'd be asking where at was the money!"

"So?" said Walter Evans, chewing furiously. "You're trying

to tell me somebody just had Temperance Moon killed for a little share of the money supposed to be going to her?"

"Maybe more than just a little share," Oscar Schiller said. "Maybe a large hunk of it, because whoever did that would understand that when it got down to the end, when it got down to hiring a killer, it wouldn't take much."

"Wouldn't take much?"

"Hell, Mr. Evans. You know what it's like over there in the Territory. Life is cheaper than a ten-dollar goat. You hanged a man in '88 who murdered a citizen of Cherokee Nation for seven dollars and fifty cents! Plus a pocketknife which likely wasn't as good as the one you use to slice your chews. Same year, you executed another who murdered a Choctaw man for ten dollars and two quarts of whiskey. A contracted killing. You hanged another one in '89 for bashing an old man to death for twelve dollars. These are just a few I recall on the spur, but another one you hanged, I remember because I arrested him, for killing a traveler who was a violin player going to Fayetteville, Arkansas, to put on a show and he had his little nine-year-old boy with him, and the killer did them both one night with an ax and a shotgun and the only way we caught him was when he tried to sell that little kid's jumping-jack toy in Spavinaw. And that reminds me of—"

"All right, all right," Walter Evans shouted, throwing up his hands.

"It's all on the records," said Oscar Schiller. "Right here in this courthouse."

"All right, all right."

"And on top of that, Temperance Moon was not the most loved lady in all creation, was she?"

"All right, all right!" Walter Evans said. "But it still bothers me that you're making some serious accusations against prominent citizens of Arkansas."

"No," said Oscar Schiller. "Whoremaster, yes. But I'm not saying Warson sent money to kill Temperance Moon. He sent money, I think, whatever you call it. Loan or payoff on blackmail. Whatever he calls it. But I think he sent it in good faith. And all Temperance Moon ever got of it was a couple loads of buckshot."

Evans rubbed his beard with both hands, as though trying to dislodge sand pebbles from the thick hair, and Oscar Schiller hoped, watching him, that it was a good sign, not a bad one. And it was a good sign.

"Oscar," Evans said, "what you've told me wouldn't make a case against anybody in a court of law. All that LaRue business is very impressive, but all circumstantial. But I'm interested here. I'm going to speak with his honor about getting you reinstated so you can follow through."

"Well, Mr. Evans, I can't accept a commission now."

"Why not?"

"Because the oath says I'm not supposed to take any outside pay from anybody. And I'll still have that for a while yet."

"All right," said Evans. "You'll continue to have our cooperation."

"Like I was one of them derby-hat Pinkertons?"

"That's right. Now, thank you, Oscar, and keep me informed."

Oscar Schiller knew this conference was finished, so he rose quickly and was to the door before Walter Evans spoke again.

"Oscar? This Temperance Moon case. What is it that makes you dog onto it so hard?"

"I don't know," said Oscar Schiller. "Except that everything about that woman smells like the old days that once were but aren't anymore."

"And you liked those old, wild days, huh, Oscar?"

"They were better for my digestion than this present slop is."

And as soon as the door closed, the United States Attorney called in his senior law clerk.

"You know where Mr. W. M. Caveness maintains his law offices?"

"Yes sir."

"Get over there. Tell him I'd like to talk. In regard to one of his clients now upstairs in our women's jail."

"Winona Crowfoot?"

"Yes. Tell him now that she's decided we're not going to hang her at the next sunrise, tell him . . ." Evans looked out his window toward the river, toward the Indian Nations. "Tell him I might have a little proposition for him."

13

It was a gray, overcast day in the Territory when the migration of the goldfinches came. Much too early for such a thing, according to Tishacomsie, yet there they were along the slopes of the Redstripe farmhouse in their thousands, the males already in their yellow plumage as though they had captured a speck of light from the hidden sun. The browns and grays and golds flickering across the ground as they fed on the grass, like little flowers gone mad with animation. They came at dawn, and by noon they were gone.

Moses Masada could not overcome his own migratory urgings, to fly away north where he belonged, some yearning for cities with their concrete and glass and clatter and odors, yet knowing that if he left, he would be abandoning his present dream of almost adolescent joy with the woman. Because the more he insisted that she come with him, the more fiercely did she resist, once even to the point of flashing anger.

"No!" she said, and there was a wild fury in the light of her eyes that he had never seen before. "I will not be of the white man's world. They treat us like ignorant savages!"

"But Tish, I am a white man," he said.

"You?" she laughed. "You? Look at you! You're darker than me! You're as near to being a white man as sorghum molasses is to being clear corn syrup! You call yourself a white man because you walk on little lace shoes and because you never tasted the prairie and because you want yourself white, but if you'd been born here, they would have called you a red nigger and used you as they use us all."

And she stomped out to feed her chickens, although she had fed her chickens less than an hour before, leaving him to ponder the fact that in this little garden of rapture a few weeds might be growing.

It was more than that one outburst. Over their days together, he had been more and more aware of some deep resentment, some vicious bitterness, in her, coming out only in little comments, but all pointing to her belief that all the troubles of her people originated with the white man.

Well, he couldn't very well argue with that. But being a child of an ethnic ghetto, he knew that many of her complaints could not be laid to a simple cause. Like leopards and baboons, a lot of people just couldn't get along very well together. Oh, in this wild frontier, he'd seen respect and trust and cooperation between many kinds of people. But there was an underlying spiderweb of antagonism as well, no doubt about it, and now, in their idle moments, Tish seemed intent on educating him to the ways of Indian frontier prejudice, brought about by the white man pushing a lot of people close together. People who would just as soon not be pushed close together. Like leopards and baboons, Moses Masada thought. And no matter all the mutual friendships, there it was, like a caste system they would have been proud of in Calcutta, he thought.

At the top, whites in all the surrounding organized states like Texas and Kansas and Arkansas. They looked down their noses at anybody in the Territory, Tish said. Then the whites in the Territory legally. Then whites in the Territory illegally. Many actually working on the railroads. But many more the hyenas who not only preyed on good citizens but encouraged many of the tribesmen to do the same with their whiskey and whoring, Tish said. Then among the Civilized Tribes, some considering themselves better than their neighbors, as like the Cherokees and their new alphabet or the Creeks and Seminoles or Choctaws and Chickasaws with old enmities that went back to Removal. And all of those denigrating people who had been here before they ever came, like the Osage. And the whole of them, everybody, hating the High Plains wild tribes, most specifically the Comanches.

"If you dislike him so much," Moses Masada said of Toad, "send him away."

"I'm afraid of him," she said. And Moses Masada knew it was more than fear. It was jealousy. Because this little riding man had meant so much to Candy Redstripe.

And here another one of those weeds in Moses Masada's garden, because he knew that Candy Redtripe was in this house as surely as he had ever been. Sometimes when they were in tight embrace, she called his name. And in her final climax never called the name of Moses Masada.

"Send him away," he kept saying. Hoping to break the hold, whatever it was, and always her reply that she was afraid of Toad.

"Anybody who's not afraid of a Comanche is crazy," she said.

But the day came when she did, and called Toad into the kitchen, him standing looking at her and at Moses Masada with his bloodshot eyes and saying absolutely nothing as she told him to take two of the ponies and go home to Fort Sill and the reservation of his people there, and took from a shelf in her pantry a tin can marked "Ceylon Pekoe Tea" and from the can took two fifty-dollar bills and gave them to him. And without a word he left, and she said, "Tonight. He'll burn this house."

"No, he won't," said Moses Masada, but not sure. "He was Candy's friend."

And knew as soon as he said it a great mistake had been made, because her face contorted and she ground her teeth and went off to her own bedroom and he slept alone that night.

But lying in the cold, Moses Masada could not stop thinking like a policeman. He could not help but recall in detail that those bills Tishacomsie had handed to the Comanche were crisp and new, exactly like the ones he knew were being held as evidence in Fort Smith, the ones taken from beneath the floor at Fawley Farm and a part of the case against Winona Crowfoot in the case of Temperance Moon's murder.

And so, regardless of his passion and his adolescent joy, he began to see the weeds, and they had taken on the wicked green color of suspicion. Because he could not stop thinking like a police officer.

ℤ ℤ ℤ Two of the most distinguished men of law in western Arkansas sat facing one another in the office of the United States Attorney in Fort Smith. Walter Evans and W. M. Caveness, whose styles contrasted sharply but who had for many years shared a mutual respect.

Outside the courtroom, where he was famous for being calm and methodical, Walter Evans was a man of fits and starts. Charging off in many directions, scribbing notes, chewing tobacco with such intensity that he often forgot the cud was in his mouth and therefore ugly brown juice seeped down into his beard from time to time without his being aware of it. The hair on his head was always in disarray, as though he had just stepped indoors from an Indian Territory tornado.

W. M. Caveness, they said, was cooler than an unshot pistol barrel. Neat, trim, always with the scent of expensive bay rum on his clean-shaven cheeks. In the long coat with a fur collar that he always wore was a pocket here and there with an orange in it, which he could peel and eat without seeming to get any juice anywhere on his chin. If oranges were unavailable or not to his liking, he substituted a lemon, which he bit into and then sucked, squeezing the juice into his mouth. Watching W. M. Caveness with one of those lemons made the throat glands of ordinary citizens contract like a closing fist.

On this day, just beyond the door, in the hallway on a straight-back chair, wearing a gingham dress that fit rather loosely because she had lost ten pounds since being here, was a client of W. M. Caveness, Winona Crowfoot, the Creek-Yuchi woman charged on grand jury indictment with accessory to murder. Two counts.

It was not particularly cold. There was fire in the small coal space heater in one corner of the room, but the new electric rotary fan on the ceiling was turned on and it made a sound like somebody sweeping the streets.

"It has occurred to me," said Walter Evans, masticating his moist cud, "that perhaps now your client has lost some of the trepidation accompanying her incarceration here and has thus regained her senses enough to think straight."

"Perhaps," said W. M. Caveness, sucking his lemon. "Although there is little in your jail to recommend optimism in any regard."

"Be that as it may and should be," said the United States Attorney, "it occurs that she knows a great deal, perhaps, about a case soon in hearing. And could help herself in large bit with certain testimony under oath."

Walter Evans spat in the general direction of the brass spittoon some five feet from his desk.

"Walter, you've got to move that thing to a more modest range," said W. M. Caveness. He took a last suck on his collapsed lemon and leaned forward and placed the yellow hull on the forward edge of Walter Evans's desk.

"What did you have in mind?" he said.

"Reduction of charge."

"You can't prove the charge you've got on her now."

"Oh, yes, we can. She's already said too much. And we've got a full picture from Sherman Boggs."

"Aw," said W. M. Caveness, looking up at the ceiling, where the fan turned lazily. "Charged with accessory to murder."

"Which we can prove."

"Remains to be seen. However, this is your conference."

"Yes," said Walter Evans. "If she goes down on this, it means a great deal of time in a penitentiary. Maybe life."

"At least you're not trying to send her to the rope," Caveness said. "So what's the proposition?"

"If your client would be willing to testify for the state concerning this conspiracy, I think I could reduce the charge, and therefore the sentence."

W. M. Caveness rocked back and forth, still looking up, still watching the slowly turning blades of the fan.

"Reduced to what?"

"Obstruction of justice."

"She could go free?"

"No, no," Evans said, and squirted another stream of amber juice toward the spittoon. "You know the judge wants some time for people like this. But a year. Just a year on obstruction, spent right here, and time already spent counting on it. Not a pen in Detroit."

"Aw," said Caveness. He drew a deep breath. "You'd talk to the judge?"

"Of course. But now listen, W. M., for this thing to work, she's going to have to provide some important evidence."

"I doubt," said W. M. Caveness, taking another lemon from his coat pocket, "that will be any problem. Shall I ask her to come in now?"

ㄹ ㄹ ㄹ It was almost as though the Old Comanches had been waiting for something that eluded them up until the seventeenth century. Something that would distinguish them from neighbors and enemies. They didn't know what it was. But finally, they found it. It was the Spanish horse!

Almost from the beginning of that time when the conquistadores brought the animal that many Indians called the Great God Dog, it was apparent to observers that there was a special kind of relationship between this strange new beast and the Comanches. Among all who saw them in the buffalo days, explorers and trappers and scouts and soldiers and settlers, it was universally agreed that of all the people in North America who had been afoot for who knew how many centuries but were now astride, Comanches were better with horses than all the rest.

It was more than their ability to ride as no one else did, more than their ability to use this new mobility to become Lords of the South Plains against even people like the Apaches. It was more. Somehow, they knew from the start how to care for their herds and how to geld and breed, and by the time of the Civil War there were Comanche chiefs who owned more horses than entire tribes of other peoples.

Comanches did not consider horses gods, as they did almost every other living thing. They considered horses brothers. And there were observers who would swear that when a Comanche was mounted on his pony, it was impossible to tell where horse stopped and rider began. It was commonly supposed that a Comanche would eat anything, including snakes and lizards and even large spiders, yet they ate their horses only as a last hedge against starvation. Not surprisingly, a Comanche valued a woman in terms of how many horses it would take to buy her. And among them, it was a greater crime to steal a friend's pony than it was to run away with his wife.

In the late nineteenth century, when Toad was sent from the Redstripe farm, all the mystic of the old horse culture was still strong in his heart. He, like his father and his grandfathers, could breathe into a horse's nostrils and feel the heat of the returning breath and somehow know the capabilities of this particular horse. Some people had been known who talked to parrots, some talked to dogs, some talked to their milk cows. Comanches talked to horses.

And so when Tishacomsie told him to take two ponies, he took the best two. A piebald and a blaze-faced blue roan. Both stallions. They were not the fastest of the string nor the most handsome, but they had the best potential for breeding, which Toad had learned through conversations between them.

Then he put all he owned into a small burlap bag, the most important items of which were gifts he had received from Candy Redstripe—a compass, which Toad didn't understand at all, a mother-of-pearl and brass bracelet, and an old percussion Colt pistol for which there were no caps, powder, or balls. Then rode off toward the west, into the setting sun, following the north bank of the Canadian, because although he knew nothing of maps he did know that if he followed this river far enough, he would come close to the Kiowa-Comanche reservation at Fort Sill, Oklahoma Territory. Of course, there was no problem in going cross-country, because his horses did not require heavy white man's grain feed. Comanche horses ate grass.

But by full dark, he stopped. And after a while of caressing his horses, turned back and retraced his route to the Redstripe farm, where he saw no light, then on past that to the Missouri, Kansas, and Texas Railroad bridge near Eufaula and crossed there to the south side of the river, into Choctaw Nation, and rode along the tracks. He had ridden in races for Candy Redstripe throughout the length and breadth of this country and knew that along the steel road he followed was a town called McAlester where a man's pleasure could be found, if there was money, whether that pleasure was illegal whiskey or illicit women or both.

While in the service of Candy Redstripe, he had always been allowed these kinds of little pleasures from time to time, in some out-of-the-way place, because Candy Redstripe understood the appetites of men and made no fuss about them and even financed them in Toad's case, and this was one of the conditions that in Toad's mind placed Candy Redstripe in the position of great chief, maybe even as great as Quannah Parker, although for different reasons.

Toad knew that in the Nations there were no real language barriers. There had been such a mix of cultures over the past thirty years that it was always possible to find somebody who understood stated requirements, especially if there was a fistful of good money involved. English was a basic trade language among the Civilized Tribes. How else to do business with the white man? And in his years with Candy Redstripe, Toad had learned a lot of English. It was sometimes rough-edged, but English nonetheless. So in McAlester, obtaining what he wanted was in no way difficult. McAlester was as democratic as most towns in the Territory. If a man had a little money, he would be allowed to spend it, even if he was a Comanche.

But a long time before even a small part of the hundred dollars had been spent, Toad came into conflict with Choctaw Nation law and order. Whereupon Moma July, in Eufaula, received a telegraph message from his counterpart in the Choctaw Light Horse that the rider of the late Candy Redstripe, who was well known in the area, was making a very large nuisance of himself and that in view of his being until recently an employee of a citizen of Creek Nation, maybe Creek Nation would like to have him back. Besides, this man had two horses for which he could produce no bill of sale and a pocketful of currency.

Moma July, as skeptical from the start as Oscar Schiller about the resolution of the troubles surrounding Fawley Farm, wanted Toad or anybody else in his district who got drunk and started talking, so he was on the caboose of the next southbound KATY freight. He found Toad on the outskirts of McAlester, tied to a tree, slobbering drunk and screaming a lot of Comanche words. Surrounding the tree were a number of Choctaw policemen and a larger number of Choctaw citizens, and all of them had Winchester rifles.

Moma July had grown up on the western edge of the Seminole and Creek Nations back in the days when Comanche was the trade language of the plains. So he understood a great deal of what Toad was screaming.

"It's something about witches," said the Choctaw police captain. But Moma July knew it was a lot more than that, and as they untied Toad and put leg irons on him, leg irons Moma July had brought from Eufaula, Moma July spoke to the Comanche in his own tongue.

"You're lucky I'm here. These people were about to shoot you."

To which Toad replied, "You are an eater of hog dung."

"We got the horses downtown in the livery," the Choctaw policeman said.

"Take some of that money you said he's got and use it to feed and keep the horses until I get back to you."

"All right," the Choctaw said. "Moma, be careful. This here is a damned barbarian."

"Yeah, well even barbarians understand buckshot."

Going back to Eufaula in the baggage car of a northbound passenger, Moma July heard everything he wanted to hear, splattered in the Comanche gibberish. He knew who the witch was, and he knew about the old Comanche belief that barren women sometimes call on the supernatural to cast their evil spell on strong men. And he knew that to Toad, Candy Redstripe had been that strong man.

There was more in Toad's screaming than witches. There were white men. There were memories of Sallisaw and races when white men came from Fort Smith, not too far distant. And there was a recurring theme of what Toad's old brethren on the High Plains would have done to a fat, tattooed Creek if that individual had ever come there.

"What Creek, Toad, what Creek?" Moma July kept asking.

"Dung eater, dung eater," Toad always responded.

At Eufaula, Moma July paused only long enough to tell his subordinates where he was bound—and also to take three quart bottles of white whiskey that were being held in the Eufaula jail and had been confiscated only two days before from a bootlegger in Wetumka.

And to his people, Moma July said, "I'm going to keep ole Toad drunk all the way to Fort Smith, because he talks so good when he is just before being booze-sick."

It never entered Moma July's mind that he might take Toad into some dark corner and break his nose or his arm, as he might have done with someone else, in order to restore his memory, because he knew that with a Comanche physical violence to his person would never make him say anything he didn't want to say in the first place. But whiskey would.

So even though it was against all the laws of the Creek Council and the Congress of the United States of America, on the trip to Wagoner and then the change to the Arkansas Valley, beneath the old Union overcoat of Moma July was not only the sawed-off shotgun but three quarts of white whiskey, which he used on the Comanche as though he were priming a gooseneck well pump. Because Moma July knew that Toad had some things to say that would make the authorities in Fort Smith pause for a moment.

Of course, it did. When Oscar Schiller and United States Commissioner Claude Bains heard the things Toad had to say, there were bench warrants issued and subpoenas, all in the cause of the

United States of America versus various persons in the matter of murder in Creek Nation.

And Oscar Schiller, almost beside himself with excitement, took Moma July to Cantoni's on Garrison Avenue and bought the little Creek policeman two crocks of baked beans and half a dozen steins of beer.

"Oscar," Maria Cantoni said, "I'll feed any savage Indian in creation so long as you bring him in here and pay for it!"

"I appreciate that, Maria," Oscar Schiller said.

"Just don't make a habit of it!"

丙 丙 丙　After beans and beer, there was a short strategy meeting with United States Marshal Emory Kimes. He said that Nason Breedlove was somewhere in the Osage reservation trying to find and serve a warrant for rape against a white bootlegger who normally operated out of Okfuskee on Deep Fork of the Canadian River in Creek Nation. So unavailable for action now in the present case. A young deputy named Leviticus Tapp would be assigned to accompany Moma July back to Eufaula to serve all the papers in the name of the United States of America, and if Oscar Schiller wanted to go along it would be just fine.

Oscar Schiller thought about it. It wasn't easy to turn down such a proposition, but after a ten-minute period of plucking at his lower lip, he declined. For a lot of reasons, maybe the most important being that he could use this time to visit the Commerce Railroad Hotel and explain to Jewel Moon that his mission was complete, thus freeing him from any obligation to her and her money and cocaine. Thus freeing him for what he really wanted now, reinstatement of a commission as a United States Deputy Marshal.

All of which should have put Oscar Schiller in high spirits, but in view of what Moma July had brought from the Territory there was a lead feeling in the gut, as after one of Mrs. Hake's pecan pies, because there were terrible things afoot. Most obvious of which was Oscar Schiller's realization that he had made an unbelievable mistake in this case. Not in its direction but in its principal actors.

丙 丙 丙　It was February 16, a Thursday. The day was bright and crisp along the Canadian. A cold day, but to Moses Masada colder inside the house than out. Because the woman had begun to sense his uncertainty about who and what she was, and even for the short time he had been there, Moses Masada recognized that this woman, this Tish, from her childhood had been uncomfortable in the company of men she did not dominate.

And even from the beginning, the sweating, panting beginning, the touch of silky flesh, the darkness fluids of glands, the wilderness of explosion, he had known. Only a small bit of him had known. Because all the rest of it was overwhelming, but he had known. Even after that one time when she refused his bed, and after that every night, he'd known. It was and had always been an exercise of body and not spirit. A release of glands and not soul. God, he hated the idea, but there it was! If not me, he thought, then maybe whoever might be available! God, he hated the thought!

So, Thursday. She had traditionally ridden into Eufaula on Thursdays. To shop. To gossip with friends over mercantile counters where bolts of cloth lay. Even talking there with her family members, the women anyway, because after she had married Candy Redstripe all the men of her clan had disowned her. But, of course, could not disown her completely, because she was the princess of the whole family and no matter that the men would not speak to her, she was still Tishacomsie!

But on that Thursday, she did not go in, although it was a sunlit day of splendor and ideal for riding along the river. She did not go in. She chose that day to take a large bacon rind to clean the top of her cast-iron cookstove.

In the afternoon, Moses Masada was in the backyard splitting oak firewood into slender staves for Tishacomsie's stove. It was a task he had come to enjoy, even though the handle of the ax had been cruel to hands unaccustomed to such work. It was there, splitting wood, that he saw them.

And he knew as soon as he saw them why they were there. It was a small group of horsemen, and the only one Moses Masada recognized was Moma July. But they rode with a kind of silent determination, close together, coming off the Canadian trace and up the slope toward the Redstripe farm. And even at a distance, Moses Masada saw that most of them carried in their hands a weapon. He dropped the ax and ran into the house.

"We got visitors," he said.

"I saw 'em," she said. She threw aside the bacon rind she'd

been using to clean the stove, took up a small towel, and wiped her hands. "Stay out of it."

Walking to the front door, she took from a wall peg her woolen poncho and pulled it over her head. And then went onto the porch, and there stood feet planted well apart, the valley wind blowing her raven hair. The horsemen drew rein at the end of the porch.

"Tish," said Moma July.

"Moma."

Moma July's shotgun was not concealed beneath his old Union Army coat. He held it in his hand, easily, yet obviously, across the pommel of his saddle. Now, with his free hand, he pointed to the man next to him, a young white man.

"Tish," said Moma July, "this here is United States Deputy Marshal Leviticus Tapp."

"How do, ma'am," Leviticus Tapp said. "I got a warrant here to serve on you."

"Tish," said Moma July, "we gonna have to take you along, just to ask some things."

"Where to?"

"Fort Smith."

"Moma, why don't you just shoot me right here?"

"Tish, now come on."

"You know, Moma, I wondered how long it was gonna take before you came," Tishacomsie said. "Can I get some stuff?"

"Sure," said Moma July. "But I gotta send one of my policemen with you in there."

"I understand that."

It was only at this point that Moses Masada came onto the porch. And when he did, he was aware that with each step he took, Moma July tracked him with the shotgun, still sitting in his saddle, still without expression, still in his old Union coat. But the double eyes of his shotgun looking at Moses Masada's belly from start to finish.

"Moma," Moses Masada said.

"Masada."

"It's a bad day."

"I've seen worse," said Moma July. "This here's a federal marshal, name Tapp."

The young man nodded. As did Moses Masada.

"Always delighted to meet a federal peace officer."

"I'm glad to hear that," said Moma July, and his shotgun was still rather casually pointed in the direction of Moses Masada's belly.

One of Moma July's men brought a horse around from the barn, sidesaddle cinched on, and then Tishacomsie came out of the house with a small duffel, went down off the porch, and was helped up by two Creek policemen onto the horse. The entire group turned away from the house and moved off along the slope toward the Canadian trace to Eufaula, without any word, without any wave, almost without any sound, leaving Moses Masada on the porch watching and remembering that through this whole bloody thing Tishacomsie had not once looked at him. Had not once let her gaze touch his face. Had not in any way recognized that Moses Masada was even there!

Watching them riding down toward the Canadian trace to Eufaula, Moses Masada could not help but see that as long as they were in sight, Tishacomsie was obvious among them, for the wind played with her raven hair, unbraided now, uncaptured now by the Portuguese lace shawl he had given her for Christmas. A free-flowing black defiance among the grim riders around her.

And all of it infuriated him, quietly, volcanically infuriated him. At himself, at Tish, at Oscar Schiller for getting him here, at the whole bloody Indian Territory.

First, he went to the barn and saddled his mare and opened the gate for the remaining Comanche ponies. To fend for themselves. Second, back into the house, where he banked the fires in the two stoves and collected his gear, all then packed in his small wicker bag. So, to the pantry, where he took down the tin can marked "Ceylon Pekoe Tea" and looked inside and found more than one thousand dollars in new greenbacks, and put the can in his bag. Then awkwardly into the saddle and off to Eufaula, but slowly, because he didn't want to catch up, he didn't want to find himself on a caboose going to Fort Smith with Tishacomsie Redstripe sitting opposite him, close enough to burn him with her eyes.

And through it all, his fury and his heartbreak both fed on that front porch at the Redstripe farm, where he had first seen her and now had seen her last and she had not even acknowledged he existed.

ᛃ ᛃ ᛃ In the attic above the courtroom at the federal building in Fort Smith, there was a hallway with two cells on one side. These were not the usual steel-bar cells of the regular jail. These were the women's cells, and the walls were of chicken wire with gingham drapes that could be drawn across them. During the summer months, when temperatures and humidity along the Arkansas River Valley each touched close to one hundred, these places were so hot it was near impossible to breathe. But in February, they were the most comfortable spaces in the building.

In one of those chicken-wire cells now was Winona Crowfoot. And in another, Tishacomsie Redstripe. She had been there a number of days before Oscar Schiller came and stood on the free-world side of the wire with his hat in his hand.

"Tish," he said.

"Oscar," she said, looking at the six-pointed badge on his jacket. "I see you're the law again."

"Yes," he said. "Just this morning, I got my commission."

He could not help but notice that this woman, the most beautiful woman he had ever seen, was no longer so. Some kind of inner ugly had seeped out so that the light in her eyes was not laughing but brittle, and the fine lips were turned down at the corners. Even the hair seemed to have lost its luster.

"Thought I'd come say howdy," he said. "Can I do anything for you?"

"Yes," she said. "Keep all these white men with neckties away from me."

"Only two of those that matter," he said. "The United States Attorney and W. M. Caveness. He's a fine lawyer. Listen to him."

Oscar Schiller shifted from one foot to another, and all the while her eyes were on him as she sat immobile as a stone road marker on the edge of her cot.

"Well," he said, "can I get you anything? Popcorn? They got good popcorn right down here on Rogers Avenue."

"No."

"Hot tamales?"

"Well, maybe a few of those."

"I'll have Zelda Mores bring some up for you. She's your lady jailer here, she's a good lady."

"That big cow with the black mustache?" Tishacomsie said.

"She's all right, Tish."

"Sure, for the white man."

"Well," said Oscar Schiller, anxious for this to be over. "I just hope you don't get burned too bad on this."

Suddenly, Tishacomsie laughed, and it was no bitter laugh, but one that made her eyes light brilliantly as Oscar Schiller had seen them light before.

"For old times' sake," she said. "Oscar, the day I sent that Comanche away, I said he'd burn the house down. And now he has."

"It looks that way, Tish."

೫ ೫ ೫ Before leaving the building, Oscar Schiller paused in the corridor where two sets of double doors opened into the courtroom. The doors were open and the courtroom was empty, an unusual thing for late afternoon during the Parker tenure. Staring at the empty gallery, the empty jury box, the small tables in the pit, the high bench, he thought of all the people whose fate had been decided in that room. Acquittals and sentences to hang and everything in between. He thought of the old saw that the stones of justice grind exceedingly slow, and a wry smile touched his thin lips.

Not always, not always in this court. Sometimes those stones spun as rapidly as the drive wheels on a red-ball freight locomotive.

Tishacomsie Redstripe had hardly been in Fort Smith an hour before she was presented to the grand jury and on the basis of Toad's testimony remanded for trial on a charge of conspiracy to commit murder. In Fort Smith, under Parker, there was always a sitting grand jury, so no time need be lost impaneling one. Sometimes those stones ground rapidly indeed.

The next morning Tish had been arraigned before Judge Parker, W. M. Caveness standing beside her. On advice of counsel, she had pleaded guilty to obstruction of justice, a plea accepted by the court on recommendation of United States Attorney Walter Evans, who stipulated in return for her reduced charge that she would cooperate in another indictment. And on the basis of her expected testimony, outlined by her and Caveness, Evans had requested a document from the United States Commissioner, and now it was time for that document to be served. Oscar Schiller had asked that he be allowed to serve it.

Oscar Schiller had made many arrests during his time as a

peace officer. Sometimes arrests of depraved killers and rapists. Always, they had been cold, objective exercises of his commission. Part of his efficiency had always been his ability for detachment from all the personal, human passion of such things. But now, he felt a vicious vindictiveness, because it served in some small way to cut the sharp edges off a case in which he had made a horrible misjudgment. And that misjudgment had played a major part in the Eufaula section house killings, or at least Oscar Schiller assumed that it had. And it weighed heavy on his thinking. Every one of those four men slain was likely a good candidate for Parker's rope, but coming to that end was very different to Oscar Schiller from being cut to pieces by metal without a day in court.

The sun was setting when Oscar Schiller left the Federal Compound and crossed Rogers Avenue to the German bakery and mounted the stairs to the chambers of the United States Commissioner. He felt like hell. Seeing Tish in that jail and thinking about Moses Masada losing his cookie jar made him feel like absolute hell. He knew the Syrian would take his sweet time about showing up, and maybe he wouldn't show up at all but take a Missouri, Kansas, and Texas passenger all the way from Eufaula to Kansas City. Straight through.

It didn't help much to recall that he, Oscar Schiller, had been the one who'd gotten the Kansas City policeman into this whole business to start with, and as it turned out, to little purpose except to get him involved in a sweet-ass coupling with a Creek Indian woman now in serious trouble. All of it put Oscar Schiller's disposition on hair-trigger dangerous.

Commissioner Claude Bains was not in chambers. But sitting beside his desk, still in field clothes, was United States Deputy Marshal Nason Breedlove, his hat on the back of his head, slouched in one of those uncomfortable government-funded straight-back chairs.

"Oscar, been expectin' you," said Nason Breedlove, holding up a folded document. "Commissioner Bains said you was comin', so I said I'd give you this warrant he'd made out."

"I thought you was over on Bird Creek in Osage country looking for a whiskey man," Oscar Schiller said.

"I was," the big marshal said and grinned. "But he got drunk in his mother-in-law's house at Pawhuska and determined to take a stand."

"So where'd you bury him?"

"Naw, he wasn't much account at takin' stands. So now he's over yonder in Parker's jail with some bumps on his bean." Nason Breedlove waved the warrant again, like a Chinese fan before his face. "You want me to help you serve this?"

"If you're so inclined."

"I sure as hell am. Remember, Oscar, I'm the one opened this thang up again with them fishhooks."

"All right. One thing. Take no chances with this son of a bitch. He'll gut-shoot you with a belly gun."

"Them kind don't bother me," said Nason Breedlove. "The kind that bothers me are the ones with Winchesters who wait for you in the woods when you're coming home from church. Speakin' of which, you want me to get my rifle?"

"No. Just short guns in town. Makes it safer for surrounding citizens in case there's a shoot."

"Well, then, leave us take in after this bastard. You be the server, me, I'll be the shooter."

"Good. I'll stay out of your line of fire. If he farts, kill him."

"My kinda law, Oscar, my kinda law!"

ㄗ ㄗ ㄗ The covered shed that served as the City Bank employees' horse stable and buggy stall was on an alley halfway between Rogers Avenue and Garrison. Each evening in the winter months, George, the old black roustabout for the bank, went there to light three kerosene lanterns to hang on their wall pegs, giving some dim and uncertain light to bank personnel who were still working and had not yet come for their horses or vehicles. On this day, he had two of the lanterns in place on their pegs and held the third in his hand, globe raised and unstruck match in his other hand, when the two men, one large and one small, walked into the shed, each of them displaying on his coat a six-pointed star that George, even though he could not read or write, knew proclaimed them as United States Deputy Marshals, who George knew were the first human steps toward a process that led to the great gallows in Judge Parker's compound.

"I ain't done nothin'!" George said, the lantern and unlighted match still in his hand, suspended before his face, like dice suddenly stopped in their flight.

"I know that, George," said Oscar Schiller. "Muley LaRue gone home yet?"

"Naw, naw, Mist' Marshal, he ain't in the bank, he gone craw-dad huntin' this afternoon and he ain't back yet."

"Where, crawdad huntin'?"

"Where he always do. Along the Poteau," said George. "Listen, Mist' Marshal, I'm gone back in the bank now, you know, it's cole out here."

"You're not going anywhere, George. Get over there behind a bale of hay."

"I will. I will."

George watched, horrified, from behind his bale of hay. These two men took out pistols and checked the loads. The small one positioned himself along one wall, the other along another, each in shadows. Then everybody waited. They could hear the faint clang of streetcar bells from the street. Even less pronounced, the chimes of the Catholic church from the east end of Garrison Avenue. And newsboys on the sidewalks, hawking the *Fort Smith Elevator*.

"Maybe he ain't comin'," Nason Breedlove said from his dark corner.

"His horse is here."

"Mist' Marshal, I'm gettin' mighty cole," said George.

"Shut up, George," Oscar Schiller said.

"I will."

They knew when he was coming as soon as he turned into the alley from Rogers Avenue, because he was whistling. He whistled all along the alley and right into the middle of the shed, long coat and derby hat impeccable as always but a thick coat of mud on his boots and carrying a small burlap bag across his shoulder. Then he saw the large shadowy figure in one corner of the shed with a pistol.

"What?" Muley LaRue said.

And just had begun to back away when Oscar Schiller was there, unseen until one hand grasped the shoulder of the coat and turned Muley LaRue and then the second hand, a fist, came straight and hard into Muley LaRue's face. Muley LaRue slammed back against the wall of the shed, blood spurting from his nose and the sack falling away and opening. Crawdads went skittering all over the straw-scattered floor, backing up like little scorpions retreating.

"Don't move, you little turd," Oscar Schiller said, his hands going into the coat pockets and coming out with two snub-nosed

Remington derringers, and then holding LaRue's coat front like a table napkin, hoisting him to his feet and slamming him against the wall, the blood streaming along Muley LaRue's chin to his shirt collar, and Oscar Schiller holding him tight against the rough, pine planking of the shed. "You're under arrest."

Muley LaRue had begun to scream, "No jurisdiction, no jurisdiction," and they handcuffed him and only then did Nason Breedlove slip the big Colt back out of sight under his jacket. Together they shoved Muley LaRue out into the alley, crushing under their boots some of the still-retreating crawdads, each one popping like a small balloon when they stepped on it.

They had been gone a full twenty seconds when George called from behind his bale of hay:

"Mist' Marshal? Can I get up now?"

꼮 꼮 꼮 There was the sound of the southbound Frisco freight at just past midnight and the clock on the Avenue striking when Oscar Schiller came home. There was a light in the basement room at the Hake house, and he knew even before going in who it was.

Moses Masada sat with his hat on and his coat as well, on one of the basement chairs, and when Oscar Schiller came in, he did not look up, did not turn his gaze, but only sat. Oscar Schiller moved slowly, because he thought it was the best way to move under these circumstances. He went to his bed, and sat, facing the Syrian.

"Moses."

"Oscar."

And before Oscar Schiller could say anything else, Moses Masada handed him a long, square tin, with printing on the side identifying it as tea.

"It may be evidence," said Masada. "Open it."

And when Oscar Schiller did and saw the fresh, new greenbacks, he shrugged.

"Well, maybe not. . . ."

"Shit, Oscar," said Moses Masada. "Take it downtown."

And Oscar Schiller put the lid back on the can and sighed and rose and said, "All right, Moses. Lay down here on my bed and get some sleep. You look like you need it. And if our lovely hostess comes down from upstairs while I'm gone, eat anything she brings. Just don't shoot anybody."

14 United States Attorney Walter Evans sat at his cluttered desk, chewing tobacco, eyes sparkling behind spectacles, smiling. From a drawer in the desk he drew a pair of pince-nez glasses, which he always wore while trying a case in the court of Judge Isaac Charles Parker, especially when he knew he was going to win. He cleaned the pince-nez carefully with a cotton handkerchief, humming a little to himself. Then he sang aloud, as he often did to his grandchildren:

> *"Six little ducks, I once knew,*
> *Fat ducks, pretty ducks they were too.*
> *But the one with a feather curled up on his back,*
> *He led the others with a quack, quack, quack!"*

And now he had fat ducks quacking. As always in conspiracies, if you could just get the first one to quack all the rest would quack even louder, each hoping thereby to avoid the ax. It was his favorite theory about conspiracies. And it always worked. Quack!

Walter Evans sprayed a jet of amber juice toward his cuspidor, and it was a wonderful omen that almost everything ended in the spittoon and not against the wall or floor.

On the desk before him was a massive folder, the notes for this case arranged. Items to be produced like cartridges in a gun fired one by one at the jury, twelve good men and true, selected from a panel legally drawn from the voters and taxpayers of western Arkansas. A jury with honest toil showing on the sunburn of their faces and the calluses on their hands. Not the bow-tie, pointy-toe-shoe, bay-rum-smelling city businessmen who always found ways to avoid jury duty, but the salt of earth in the jury box.

And this day, as soon as his honor finished his lunch of oatmeal and toasted biscuits, that jury and Walter Evans would be face to face.

He smiled for any number of reasons. Maybe most because now, with this trial, there would be a beginning to the end of this God damned Temperance Moon thing. And smiling, too, because it was a trial unfolding as he thought such a trial would, even though he had resisted at first even thinking about trying it. That God damned Oscar Schiller!

He smiled because there were so many of those quack-quack people, trying to remove themselves from a one-inch, pitch-treated hemp rope. Had it not been so serious, the songs of those ducks would have been hilariously funny. And in fact, alone in his office, thinking about it, the whole thing *was* funny. Which made Walter Evans a bit ashamed of himself in view of his oath to send people to the rope anywhere along the line. But, by God, it *was* funny, all that quack, quack, quack!

Now a jail full of ducks waiting for mercy and justice. There was Sherman Boggs, whiskey man and murderer, and he would surely hang. After a fair trial, of course. Because he had quacked loudest of all but to a different purpose than the others. He had told Walter Evans that he needed to wash all mortal sins from his soul in order to stand a better chance of redemption in the next life. To which Walter Evans had responded that it was a good idea because the only appeal Sherman Boggs could expect would be from the highest of all courts and most certainly the Judge sitting at that bench took unkindly to defendants coming before Him with a bad record of unconfessed sin during life on earth.

The chorus of quacking from the others was of a more common variety. In the parlance of the legal community, they were going to turn state's evidence. Which meant they would quack about co-conspirators in order to save their own asses. This was, in Walter Evans's experience, what always happened when various members of the court could convince people that unless they unburdened themselves of secrets the last sound they heard with their ears in this life would be the trap dropping. He was very good at convincing people of such things, as were some of the deputy marshals, like Schiller and Breedlove.

God love our deputy marshals, Walter Evans thought.

Of course, no one was more aware of the fact that none of the people in this case, other than Sherman Boggs, would hang. Prison sentences, perhaps. But hang, no. But what they perceived to be the truth was to them the truth, and so be it! Like all good prosecutors, Walter Evans took every advantage he could get, no matter where found.

In his mind, Walter Evans checked them off one by one. Mr. Toad, the Comanche. Once he had finished his quacking under oath, likely to be released to go back to Fort Sill. After all, western Arkansas and the Indian Nations had enough problems without having a Comanche in residence, even if that residence was the federal jail for six months or so.

Tishacomsie Redstripe, the pretty one. And the enigmatic one, too, because Walter Evans was not sure what she might say on the witness stand and it had been only after much persuasion by her attorney, W. M. Caveness, that she had agreed to cooperate at all. There was a smoldering light of resentment or hatred or something in those deep, black eyes.

Winona Crowfoot. No problem there on the quacking, she was frightened silly, but after she said her say probably at least a year of prison time. Even with a plea of guilty to obstruct.

And now, the case at hand. Creighton Muley LaRue. No quacking there. And Ennis Merriweather had come from Little Rock to defend him. Walter Evans had known Ennis Merriweather for years and had done battle with him in the pit of various circuit courts. An entertaining challenge. More so because courthouse rumor had it that he was being paid a fee to defend LaRue by LaRue's employer, Herkimer Warson, who was one of the prosecution witnesses. More interesting still because Merriweather was a member of the Arkansas state senate and hence a legislative colleague of Herkimer Warson.

All of which delighted Walter Evans, because he enjoyed cases with unusual twists.

Even so, this Warson thing was like a small gnat in his legal salad. On his desk beside the trial folder was a copy of last night's *Fort Smith Elevator*, wherein it was reported that Herkimer Warson had resigned his vice-presidency at City Bank and was step-ping down as well from his position as state representative to the legislature, meaning the governor would be required to appoint someone to serve out the unexpired term. For health purposes, the item reported. Walter Evans knew better. And it made him feel a little guilty. In the last election, he'd even voted for Her-kimer Warson.

There was more to the guilt than Warson's sudden withdrawal from public life. There was the arm-twisting. And even though arm-twisting was a completely accepted technique for pretrial maneuvers, it always left Walter Evans somewhat uneasy with himself.

Now, Evans swiveled his chair so that he might look from his west-facing window toward the Nations. He did it often, so often that he had come to think almost that the window itself was the Indian Territory. And as he so often did, sitting there chewing slowly and gazing into the haze-shrouded country of the Five Civilized Tribes, he reviewed in his mind the steps that had led to this trial. Specifically, the arm-twisting with Herkimer Warson.

Herkimer Warson was a tall man who always seemed to be peering down his nose at the world below, contempt and impa-tience showing in pale eyes. He had a regal bearing, enhanced by an expensive wardrobe. He had often been observed in broad day-light on the streets of Fort Smith wearing gray suede spats, a swallow-tailed coat, and top hat. Citizens who routinely read the *Atlantic* or *Frank Leslie's Illustrated Newspaper* said Warson looked as though he might have stepped right out onto Garrison Avenue after an audience with Queen Victoria at Osborne House in England. People who routinely read the *Police Gazette* said he looked as though he might be a stuck-up son of a bitch.

Yet, they voted for him. He could go among the people from Towson Avenue saloons to the rich parlors of the Belle Grove district and win their confidence, his bald head shining when he doffed the top hat. A living, breathing contradiction in terms.

The United States Attorney did not normally make house calls. But on this case preparation, he had gone to Warson's City Bank office and there been ushered in like any other supplicant for a loan. But soon all such pretext vanished as Evans outlined his case and possible cause against Mr. Warson's man LaRue, having by then heard what Tishacomsie Redstripe would say on the witness stand.

Herkimer Warson was incredulous. Then furious. Then indignant. Then horrified. Then confused.

"Mr. Warson," had said Walter Evans, "I will issue a subpoena for your appearance at that hearing."

"But I have nothing to add," Warson had shouted, the red in his face extending up past his eyebrows to his bald pate.

"I think you do. And whether or not you are willing to cooperate, I will subpoena you and, if necessary, examine you as a hostile witness."

"What could I possibly add?" Warson had said, slipping now from indignation to innocence.

"A great deal. A lot of people believe you are at no fault in all this. I reserve judgment. And if you do not come willingly, I will bring you before the grand jury on suspicion of many things."

"What?" Now from innocence to pained concern. "On what charge?"

"Mr. Warson, we know a great deal about you."

"My God," had said Warson. "Do you know what it would do to me, to appear and tell you what I think you want me to tell?"

"Not so bad as going to the grand jury on a charge of murder, Mr. Warson, no matter what the grand jury finds."

"Wait. Wait. If I do what you want, I forsake a trusted employee."

"No," had said Evans. "You tell the truth."

"I can't do that."

"You see? If you do not, then I must assume, as will a grand jury, that your loyalty extends to any felony one of your employees might do."

"My God," Herkimer Warson had said and lay over his desk with his face in his hands. "How much do I have to say?"

"All of it."

And so this legislator, this bank vice-president, quacking as loud as all the others. Quacking to avoid something more terrible if left unquacked. Quack, quack, quack.

He turned away from the window, sprayed the wall near the cuspidor with a brown stream, opened the file, and read once more the document that set it all in motion.

UNITED STATES OF AMERICA,
WESTERN DISTRICT OF ARKANSAS.
IN CIRCUIT COURT. FEBRUARY TERM: 1893.

UNITED STATES		FRAUD AND
VS.	}	CONSPIRACY TO COMMIT MURDER AND
CREIGHTON LARUE		MURDER

The Grand Jurors of the United States of America, duly selected, impaneled, sworn, and charged to inquire into and for
the body of the Western District of Arkansas aforesaid, upon
their oath present:

That one Creighton LaRue, known also as Muley LaRue, did
in the month of August, 1892, through deceit and dishonest advantage use funds entrusted to him for other purposes to enter
into an agreement and contract for the death of one Temperance
Moon, a white woman and citizen of Creek Nation within the jurisdiction of the Western District of Arkansas aforesaid, result-
ing in the violent homicide of Temperance Moon and one Toby
Jupiter, an Indian and citizen of Creek Nation, all contrary to
the form of the statute in such cases made and provided, and
against the peace and dignity of the United States of America.

Robert O'Brien
Foreman of the Grand Jury

OFFICIAL
Walter C. Evans
United States District Attorney
Western District of Arkansas

彆 彆 彆 The great corridor running the full width of the federal
building, its doors opening into the court of Judge Isaac C. Parker, had benches along each wall whereon witnesses sat waiting
to be called. Once people had come in to become spectators to the
trial, like patrons of the Opera House, this hallway was cleared
by United States Deputy Marshals with their badges on vest or
coat, their stag- or ivory- or walnut-handled six-shooters in hip
holsters, and their brushed mustaches and grim lips beneath. A
group of people who would take no foolishness from mere civil-

ians, a group of people coldly polite unless somebody questioned their authority, at which time they became silently efficient enforcers. Everybody knew this. Nobody questioned their authority. There had been, in the history of this court, deranged men who did question that authority with a pistol and who had been immediately dispatched with return fire. And so the people always said, "You do not mess around with Parker's deputies unless you're asking for suicide."

So everything was in place as the doors were closed and the trial began in the courtroom, the prospective witnesses sitting silently and as somber as mourners at a Methodist bishop's funeral. Oscar Schiller and Moses Masada were there, beside one another, but they did not talk. Both were in dark moods, the Syrian thinking about what might happen to Tishacomsie Redstripe and the deputy marshal thinking about Masada thinking about Tish.

The courtroom itself was packed. Front to rear, side to side. The oak benches for spectators were full. Beyond the banister separating spectators from participants, the pit was full as well— the jury box with its twelve men good and true duly selected; the defense table where the defendant sat dapper and calm with his equally dapper and calm attorney beside him, each of them smoking a cigar; the prosecution table with Walter Evans and two clerks; the court clerk and the court reporter, at their small desks at the base of the massive bench with the high-backed, leather-cushioned chair.

It was late winter and none of the coal space heaters about the room had been charged, yet it was hot in this long room from the heat of all the people there. Expectant faces were packed from the high windows at the east end to the oak banister between spectators and pit. From this writhing mass came a murmuring, like the mewing of great cats, punctuated now and again by the rattle of popcorn sacks. Along each wall, and at the door leading into the hall, were deputy marshals, watching the crowd with an intensity reserved for peace officers who suspected anything.

At two minutes after noon, Monday, February 27, 1893, a tall man in a black gown moved to that oak bench and everyone rose. Those who had seen him before whispered about the white hair, the white beard, the deep lines on the face now after twenty years in this service, but there was no softness in the eyes, as the chief bailiff spoke the words:

"Oyez, oyez, oyez. The Honorable District Court of the United

States for the Western District of Arkansas having jurisdiction in the Indian Territory is now in session. All having business with the court step forward and you will be heard. God bless the United States and this honorable court.

"Be seated!"

෴ ෴ ෴ "Gentleman of the jury," Walter Evans began as he stood behind his prosecutor's desk immediately in front of the jury box, peering over his pince-nez. It was a position he would seldom leave throughout the course of the trial. "I normally waive opening statements but in this instance I will take a moment of your time for a short one."

Evans turned slightly and looked toward the defense table, where Merriweather and LaRue were puffing their cigars.

"Gentleman, for the benefit of those among you who have never observed court proceedings, the man there is the accused in this case. You can distinguish him because he is the one wearing leg irons."

There was a ripple of laughter through the gallery spectators, and a number of jurors smiled.

"Your honor," Ennis Merriweather said, rising to his full five foot ten of haughtiness, "I had hoped that the district attorney would not attempt to titillate us with his so-called sense of humor in a cause as serious as the one in which we are engaged here."

"I had supposed," said Evans, smiling, "that a touch in lighter mood would be appreciated by defense counsel in view of the heavy burden he carries today."

"All right, all right," said Judge Parker, a note of resignation in his strong voice as though he knew he could not control the situation as completely as he might have liked. "I am aware that you two gentleman have jousted many times in this sort of arena and expect to test the sharpness of your blades against one another at the outset. But neither I nor these gentlemen in the jury box have time for such foolishness, and I warn that contempt of court assessments are not far off if such useless, nonproductive wrangling should continue. Now please carry on, Mr. Evans."

Merriweather sat down, puffing his cigar furiously. Evans faced the jury box. As he began his opening statement, it was so quiet in the courtroom that those in the front rows could hear the scratching of the reporter's pen as he took his shorthand notes at his desk below Parker's bench. There was a strong odor of buttered popcorn. On the front row, her two little girls on either side of her, Irene LaRue sat leaning forward slightly, her eyes wide and teary in what Fort Smith people described as her French-valentine kind of face.

"Gentleman," Evans began. "In the cause that confronts you, the government will show how Creighton Muley LaRue, the defendant here, attempted to discourage by violent intimidation an investigation into the Temperance Moon murders of last September. The government will then reveal the results of that investigation, beginning with the killings in Creek Nation, the Indian Territory, and proceeding step by step to the source of a murder conspiracy, proving beyond a reasonable doubt that the aforementioned Creighton Muley LaRue initiated this cold-blooded felony with money entrusted to him for another purpose."

As Evans took his seat, the youngest of the LaRue children said, "Mamam, the man said Papa's name." A hissing whisper came from the French-valentine face: "Hush, hush!"

"Defense?" Parker asked. And Merriweather rose. In a cloud of cigar smoke. Court watchers would say that he always seemed to rise majestically from that blue-gray smoke, like a phoenix, or maybe like a red-combed rooster from a burning chicken coop.

"My friends," Merriweather said, and court watchers would say later that when Merriweather spoke he faced the jury squarely, as though aiming his navel at them in the manner of a cannon about to be fired. "Having lived for some time in the environs of this honorable court, I am sure you understand that under the law a defendant must be proved guilty beyond a reasonable doubt. Today, the government will do no such thing. The government will not. Instead, defense not only will show that the government has failed in this effort to make a scapegoat of an honest, hardworking family man of your community, but will show as well the true origin of the terrible conspiracy. Defense will show that the culprit in this cause did not come from among the worthy citizens of Arkansas, but from the Indian Territory, as you might well expect."

As Merriweather settled back down into his faint cloud of cigar smoke, Evans was on his feet.

"Your honor," he said, "I object to defense counsel's slander of the good people of our neighbors in Indian Territory."

"Mr. Evans," said Parker, "I'm sure the jurors are intelligent enough to understand that such a statement made in openings has no weight in evidence. Now, proceed with your case in chief."

Evans shrugged. "The government calls Miss Jewel Moon."

Parker responded to the general murmur from the spectators with a gentle slapping of his palms on the bench.

Jewel Moon was wearing one of her long, duster-like smocks and a large hat with a brim of artificial flowers. She had removed all the many rings from her fingers, and her lips and cheeks were not rouged. Had anybody not known who she was, she could easily be taken as just another rather buxom Fort Smith matron, perhaps a member of the Methodist Church Ladies' Aid Society or maybe an officer in the Order of the Eastern Star.

After the oath was administered, she testified that she had been unhappy with the tentative nature of the authorities' resolution of her mother's murder and had hired Oscar Schiller to look into the matter further, paying him a handsome fee.

"Then you had made this arrangement some weeks prior to the dramatic events of the night of January 14 and 15, last?" asked Evans.

"Yes."

"Can you describe for the jury what happened on the date I mentioned?"

"Yes. A railroad tank car full of coal oil blew up in the yards, almost in front of my hotel." She spoke with complete calm and in a loud voice, seeming in no way awed by the surroundings. "The coal oil flamed out in all directions and set two buildings afire, two buildings next to mine, and if the wind hadn't changed, my hotel would have burned, too."

"Other than the details of this catastrophe, was there anything else of that time that you recall?"

"Yes. I got a letter through the post office. I think it was the day before the fire."

Now Walter Evans came from behind his desk, carrying what was obviously a torn page from a newspaper. He moved to the witness stand and held it out to Jewel Moon, and she took it in one hand and held it at arm's length and looked at it distastefully, as though it might have been a copperhead snake.

"Can you identify this?"

"Yes," she said. "It's what I got in that letter I said about. It's a piece that was in the paper about my mother being killed."

"What else?"

"There are some things writ by hand on it."

"What does that part say?"

"It says, 'Let it rest in peace or bad things will come.' That's what it says." She passed the tear sheet back to Evans, obviously happy to be rid of it.

"Now, this handwrit part. What color is the ink?"

"Brown."

Evans walked back to his desk, slowly, holding up the sheet of newsprint. Then asked that it be admitted in evidence as prosecution exhibit A, which was done without objection. And again from behind his desk:

"Miss Moon, when you read this and thought of it after the fire, what was your understanding of it?"

"I object," said Merriweather, rising through his blue cloud. "It calls for an opinion."

"There is some doubt here, considering the phrasing of prosecution's question. Sustained."

"Then," said Evans, "Miss Moon, what was your *feeling* at the time?"

"I object, your honor. It's essentially the same question."

"No," said Parker, "it is not. A witness may testify as to how they felt. Precedent allows a person to say they felt threatened in a plea for self-defense, for example. The same holds here. Overruled."

"I take exception, your honor."

"So be it. Note it in the record, Edgar." And the reporter did. "You may answer the question, Miss Moon."

"I felt like somebody was trying to scare me because I had started looking for my mother's murderer," Jewel Moon said. "And that if I didn't stop it, I would have all kinds of serious trouble."

"Objection!" Merriweather was shouting now, although he remained in his seat beside a smiling Muley LaRue.

"Overruled. The jury can consider it."

"Exception, exception, exception," Merriweather said.

"Your exception to this has been noted already but will be so done again. Carry on, Mr. Evans."

"No more questions."

"Mr. Merriweather? Cross?"

"Yes," said Merriweather, up and out of his smoke fog and over to the witness stand. "Miss Moon, isn't it true that on this night you have tried to make seem so dramatically terrible, wasn't there a large party in your so-called hotel, even as the flames were still leaping?"

"Yes."

"How can you say you were distraught over this letter when you are encouraging dancing and drinking and who knows what even as the fire burns your neighbors to the ground?"

"Well, all those folks didn't have no place else to go," said Jewel Moon. "They just come in from the cold at the only place left."

"This feeling of dread you've said resulted from the newspaper tear sheet, didn't you connect that with the fire only after someone else suggested there was a connection?"

"No," she said. "I think I saw it right off."

Merriweather snorted. And went back to his seat.

Evans asked, "Miss Moon, this party. Did you invite people and plan a gala?"

"Good heavens, no. It just happened because of the fire."

"No more questions."

"Recross?" asked Parker.

"No," said Merriweather, and Jewel Moon floated out of the courtroom much like a pale gray tent without pegs, blown smoothly along by a gentle wind.

Evans called the chief office custodian of City Bank, who testified that the bank had made somewhat of a trademark of brown ink, that everybody there used it. He produced a number of memoranda signed by Creighton LaRue, all in brown ink, and one of these Evans asked be entered as prosecution exhibit B.

On cross-examination, Merriweather asked, "Does your bank have a sole proprietorship on brown ink in this city?"

"I beg your pardon?"

"Can anybody else in Fort Smith use brown ink? Besides employees at your bank?"

"Why, of course. They sell it at all the stationery stores."

Evans called Nolan Himes, yardmaster of the Frisco railroad, and called him as an expert witness. Mr. Himes indicated that when the tank car exploded on the night of January 14–15 he had been on the scene within minutes.

"How many tankers pass through your yard in a year?"

"Oh, I'd say average about a hundred."

"Did one ever blow up before?"

"No. They're pretty well built. Pretty good safety record, them tank cars."

"Then why did this one explode?"

"Oh, I'd say an outside charge had to be set against her."

"Object," said Merriweather.

"Sustained," Parker said. "The jury is instructed that the witness cannot state such a thing as fact."

"Very well," said Evans. "As an expert in such things, Mr. Himes, what is your *opinion* of this explosion?"

"It's my opinion that it had to be an outside charge set to it."

On cross, Merriweather asked two questions.

"How many kerosene tank car explosions did you say you'd witnessed?"

"Why, this was the only one."

"Then how can you count yourself an expert on the explosion of tank cars?"

"Objection."

"I withdraw it, your honor," and Merriweather grinned at the jury as he took his seat. And everyone in the room wondered how a man could be an expert on something he had never seen.

Graton Mugley, the yard supervisor for the Consolidated Mining Equipment Company, was called and testified that Creighton LaRue had purchased dynamite, time fuse, detonating cord, and primers some three weeks before the railyard fire and provided a sales slip to substantiate his claim, and it was entered in evidence as prosecution exhibit C without objection. On cross-examination, Merriweather didn't rise.

"Did Mr. LaRue say what he purposed to do with this material?" defense counsel asked.

"Yeah, he said he wanted a water well, a dug well, and he knowed once down a few feet he'd hit sandstone, so he needed blastin' stuff."

"Is this unusual?"

"Naw, folks around here wanta have a dug well 'stead of a drilled one, they gonna need to blast through the sandstone cap. Or maybe limestone."

"So," said Merriweather, leaning back in his chair and holding his cigar, now smoked down to a short nub, like a teacher pointing a pencil, "you didn't think anything unusual?"

"Objection."

"Sustained."

When Oscar Schiller was called, he was glad other witnesses had been excluded from the courtroom, because it meant that he would not be sitting up there having to bear the sharp stare of Moses Masada's gray eyes, like two Damascus sword points, neither Oscar nor the Syrian knowing where all this would lead in the business of Tishacomsie Redstripe. The cookie jar, as Oscar Schiller saw it. And Moses Masada's hand so deep in that jar there was little chance of pulling it out. Well, Oscar Schiller thought, it's not his hand in that jar, either, but a more sensitive member.

Yes, Oscar Schiller said, he had been retained by Miss Jewel Moon, being then a private citizen and not a federal marshal. And Evans guided his witness to the night in the Bamberger brewery, and to the shots fired there, and got a rousing round of laughter from not only the gallery but the bench about a crock of sauerkraut being assaulted. But then Evans produced the slug taken from the kraut and identified by Oscar Schiller, and entered into evidence a .41 caliber bullet. And then:

"Did you later arrest the defendant?"

"Yes."

Evans produced from beneath his small desk a pair of Remington double-barreled pistols and walked with them, one in each hand, to the witness stand.

"When you arrested the defendant, are these the weapons you took from him? These .41 caliber derringers?"

Oscar Schiller checked the serial numbers on the pistols, handed them back to Evans, and said that they were, and the guns were introduced into evidence as a prosecution exhibit. And they lay, silver and gleaming, on the broad railing before the jury where all the other exhibits were.

There was a great squabble over chain of custody on the bullet that had destroyed the kraut crock, but it was resolved by Judge Parker's finally losing patience and all sense of humor and threatening everybody in sight with contempt unless the trial proceeded, and so it did proceed.

"On the night in question, when someone shot at you, what were your feelings?" Evans asked.

"I was like any man shot at and missed. I was scared!"

There was a ripple of laughter among the spectators, hearing a Parker deputy admitting he was scared.

"How long did that feeling of fear persist?"

"Not long," said Oscar Schiller. "I was about two feet from

that window, and I figured anybody trying to hit me with a shot from there couldn't miss. So I figured he tried to miss."

"Objection."

"Sustained," said Parker. "The jury will disregard the last statement."

"All right," said Evans. "Now. In this investigation of the Moon murders, did you have assistance?"

"Yes. Deputy Nason Breedlove from this court. Chief of Police of the Eufaula District in Creek Nation Moma July. A Kansas City detective, in an unofficial capacity, who came to help out. Moses Masada is his name. I also informed Mr. Candy Redstripe of Creek Nation what I was doing. I reckoned a man of his influence over there might be useful."

"How early in your investigation was Mr. Redstripe informed of it?"

"At the very beginning." Sweat had begun to run down the back of Oscar Schiller's neck, feeling like lines of red ants.

Once more on cross-examination, Merriweather did not rise from his seat, as though nothing coming from the witness stand was important enough to require standing.

"You said you enlisted Mr. Candy Redstripe to your service because he was a man of influence. What you meant was that Candy Redstripe was a hardened killer, isn't that how you expected him to be useful?"

"No, I wouldn't call him a hardened killer," Oscar Schiller said. "But he was a man commanded respect from those people over there."

"What you mean is that they were afraid of Candy Redstripe."

"Objection. Calls for an opinion."

"Sustained."

"Tell me, Marshal Schiller, were *you* afraid of Candy Redstripe?"

"No," said Oscar Schiller, and the ants were running down his neck in battalion formations. "But if push came to shove, I wanted him on my side."

"And he certainly was on your side, wasn't he, when he killed three men in Eufaula, men who might have shed much light on this cause in hearing?"

"Your honor, I object," Evans said, and red points of anger showed on his cheeks. "Implying such things to a man with Oscar Schiller's credentials in this court is unconscionable."

"I must agree, Mr. Merriweather," said Parker. "There has been nothing introduced thus far in these proceedings that could lead a man logically to come to such a conclusion. The objection is sustained. And jurors are instructed to disregard the question."

When he was released from the stand, Oscar Schiller stalked from the room, into the main corridor, and out onto the porch of the federal building for gulps of fresh, cold air. He felt that his testimony had somehow been watery, but at least he was glad that Merriweather, when Evans spoke of those credentials, had not brought up the fact that he, Oscar Schiller, had had his commission revoked once for trying to break into the room of a McAlester whorehouse.

"What the hell," he said aloud and went back into the courtroom to stand beside Nason Breedlove at the rear of the spectator section of the room, under the high windows, which now had begun to grow a thin coating of white frost.

By that time, Evans had Mr. Mapes Hanley, owner of Hanley's Gun Shop, on the stand testifying to the fact that Creighton Muley LaRue bought a lot of .41 caliber ammunition for his two belly guns and that often Muley LaRue had brought in turtles he had shot on the Poteau River when he was there catching crawdads.

"Muley liked to target-practice with them little guns," Mr. Hanley said. "He'd brang turtles into my shop so my wife could cook 'em. Me and my wife was never too keen on eatin' such things as turtles, so I'd throw 'em away. They was always shot in the head."

"Why did you take note of these turtles being shot in the head?" Evans asked.

"Them little short pistols wasn't made for exact target shootin'," said Mr. Hanley. "They're more made for ranges about the width of a poker table."

The spectators laughed and nodded.

"So I could see Muley was a crack shot."

"Objection. Opinion," said Merriweather without rising from the cloud of cigar smoke generated by a fresh Havana just lighted.

"Sustained."

"Your witness," Evans said.

"Can we assume from your testimony, Mr. Hanley, that Mr. LaRue was the only one of your customers who ever bought ammunition for the .41 caliber Remington derringer?"

"Why, no."

"How many more of your customers routinely bought this type ammunition?"

"Well, I don't know exactly, but some, I'd say about . . ."

"Very well, Mr. Hanley, thank you. No more questions."

United States Attorney Walter Evans stood now, rubbing his hands, and there was a shining light in his eyes. The jurors could sense a different phase of this trial had begun.

"The government calls Miss Winona Crowfoot to the stand," said Evans, and there was a general murmur among the spectators, all of whom knew, from newspaper accounts, that this woman had been a part of the Temperance Moon Fawley Farm group and that she was now under indictment for her part in the Creek Nation murderers. And knew as well that she was the only one left of the Fawley Farm group, with the exception of Sherman Boggs, the others having been killed in that Eufaula Frisco section house.

ಠ ಠ ಠ "Langston Turtle was my man. He was good to me like no other man had ever been. He never beat me. He never cussed at me. He was a gentle man. He was Temperance Moon's brother-in-law. Langston's older brother had married Temperance Moon, and that's how she come into the Turtle property. Then when Langston's older brother was shot and killed over here in Arkansas, Temperance, she owned the farm all by her own self. But she liked Langston, and he liked her, and so he stayed on at the farm, and then I come and Langston got to be my man.

"Langston was scared of Candy Redstripe. So when Candy Redstripe sent word he wanted to talk to Langston where Temperance couldn't hear, he went and wanted me beside of him. I don't know why. But he did. I was scared of Candy, too. I guess. Everybody in the Nations was afraid of Candy."

"Why, Winona?"

"He'd killed some men. Up in Cherokee Nation. In Choctaw, maybe. In Creek, he never done it, that anybody knew. And he had a lot of big men friends. Some white men, too. Nobody wanted to get crosswise with Candy."

Winona Crowfoot was wearing a new gingham dress, a long dress, neck to ankle, which everybody in the gallery assumed had been bought for her by W. M. Caveness, her attorney. Recently, Zelda Mores, the lady jailer at the federal jail, had cut Winona's hair, docking it shoulder-length, and as she sat on the witness stand it hung straight and black, exposing her ears. And there were two large pearl earrings that accented the high, hard planes of her cheekbones. She was shy and tentative in response to the questions of the United States Attorney, but from the start, she held her head up and she looked back without flinching into the eyes of all the people in that courtroom looking at her.

Later, some of the journalists would describe her as much more attractive than she really was, yet there were some men in the gallery who licked their lips as they watched her well-sculpted mouth phrasing answers to Evans's queries. One correspondent from the *St. Louis Republican* reported that the pearl earrings were large as robin eggs, of a size with Winona's obsidian eyes. Of such prose, Walter Evans observed, are legends made.

She was testifying in English. Never having had the advantage of an education at such places as Mrs. Sawyer's Female Seminary in Fayetteville, Arkansas, Winona had learned the white man's talk from almost thirty years of association with bootleggers, horse thieves, railroad roustabouts, Texas cattle drovers, land specula- tors, Baptist evangelists, pimps, bank robbers, and murderers. In short, as Nason Breedlove said, she was a true daughter of the old Indian Territory.

In what amounted to preliminary stage-setting, Walter Evans had brought from her the hierarchy on Fawley Farm at the time of Temperance Moon's death. Temperance Moon living as wife to Winona's brother Goshen Crowfoot, a wild and very tempestuous coupling; Winona living as wife to Langston Turtle, whose brother had been one of Temperance Moon's legal husbands before he was killed in a bank robbery; Styles Jupiter, the last legal husband, who had run away to California or someplace; various other men wandering in and out, a few maybe one-night lovers for their hostess, others just looking for a place to get drunk or tell tall tales.

And then finally to the meeting.

"If you heard the conversation between Langston Turtle and Candy Redstripe," said Walter Evans, "could you recall it for the jury?"

"I was standin' right there," Winona said. "Candy give my man this little canvas poke and said there was five hundred dol- lars in there and he wanted my man to do a task. And the task was to kill Temperance. And when it was done, Candy would give

another five hundred dollars. And he said that maybe if Temperance Moon was dead, my man would get back the family property
which Temperance had come into when she married my man's
brother."

"When was this, Winona?"

"At night."

"No, I mean what month of the year."

"Oh, it was sickle moon. Along in the midst of August, I
reckon."

"So now, when Candy Redstripe made the proposition, what
did Langston Turtle say?"

"He said he'd think about it. Then Candy and that Comanche
left and we went back into the house and looked in the canvas
poke and there was five hundred dollars there. And my man said
he'd thought of a good plan."

"Did he tell you the plan?"

"Yes. The next day. Temperance was still asleep, because she'd
been stomp dancin' all night. With some Choctaw, I guess. So we
all went to the barn, me and my man and my brother and the
white whiskey man, Sherman Boggs, and my man told his plan.
He said it was a smart plan."

"How was it supposed to work, Winona?"

"Why, my man would tell Toby Jupiter to steal that shotgun
from Mr. Courson's house. Toby worked over there now and then.
Mr. Courson, he's a white man married to a Creek and he raises
cattle and he's got this shotgun everybody was always talkin'
about. It come from someplace else. And everybody said it was
maybe the best shotgun in all of Indian Territory. So Toby was
supposed to steal it while Mr. Courson was off with his family
sellin' spring calves, like he done each year."

"Winona," asked Evans, "who was Toby Jupiter?"

"Oh, just this wild kid," she said. "He didn't like Temperance
and she never liked him neither, I reckon, but he was always
hangin' around because his brother was Temperance Moon's husband that run off someplace, so he just was hangin' around. Temperance was kind of a family woman, so she put up with Toby
'cause he was a brother-in-law, too. Like my man."

"All right," said Evans. "Toby is going to steal the shotgun.
Then what?"

"Why, he'd brang it to the farm and my man would pay him
forty dollars for it. Then Toby could go on a fish-camp trip with

Sherman Boggs, 'cause Sherman Boggs liked fishin' almost as much as Toby and they'd gone off like that before, just them two, and this time Sherman Boggs would buy a lot of whiskey and wine and grub and they could lay out on the Canadian, fishin', until all the whoop and holler about the shotgun being stole had died off, just the two of them, without no women, just stayin' drunk and fishin' like they done before. No women, or nothin', just them two, drunk and havin' a good time fishin'. Toby, he liked that fishin'."

"Now, the plan, Winona," Walter Evans said.

"September 10, that was Temperance's birthday. And she always took grub to the Lurley kids on Saturday. So my brother would take the shotgun and wait for Temperance on the way home and after he shot her, leave the gun on the ground, then come on back to the place. I'd be makin' a birthday cake and my man would be hangin' these paper decorations like you got at Christmas, all for her birthday."

"Did your man pay your brother to do this?"

"Yes, sir. He give my brother a bill he got from Candy and he had some more bills and coins he'd saved, money Temperance had give him, I guess, maybe forty dollars. And right after Candy came over to our place, my man bought me a bottle of wine from a bootlegger in Asbury and paid with one of them bills Candy give him. So my man had a handful of bills, old bills, and coins."

"But Winona what I'm asking, did your man pay your brother to kill Temperance Moon?"

"Yes sir. Seventy-five dollars."

"Winona, did Langston Turtle tell any of the others where the money came from?"

"No sir. He never. He told it was his, saved up. He said Temperance was gettin' mean and was about ready to make us all leave and she was goin' to take up with some of them Choctaws she liked so much. Nobody but me knew any money come from Candy."

"All right, now tell us why Langston Turtle wanted the shotgun left on the ground near Temperance Moon's body."

"Everybody knew whose gun it was and that Toby worked for Mr. Courson and they'd figure he stole it, and when the law found it there, they'd reckon Toby done the shoot."

"But Toby could deny it."

"No he couldn't," said Winona Crowfoot. "That was the plan,

too. Down on the river, at the fish camp, sometime after Saturday when Temperance was done, Sherman Boggs was gonna shoot Toby, and my man give him seventy-five dollars, too, and told him he'd give him a strip on Deep Fork of the Canadian for bootleg thangs."

"You heard all that?"

"Yes. I did."

"The plan worked, didn't it, Winona?"

"Sure. Everybody done what they was supposed to do. Then they found Temperance and the law come to the Fawley place and we was doin' all that birthday stuff but we had to come in here to Fort Smith on the train and tell we was at home on the place all day and that Toby Jupiter had stole the gun, 'cause he'd brought it to the farm and was showin' it off. So after we got done here, my brother went off to Muskogee and it was a long time before I seen him again. A long time after they found Toby dead in the fish camp."

"When did you see Sherman Boggs again?"

"I never seen him since. Since him and Toby taken off to the Canadian fish camp the day before Temperance's birthday. They got him in jail here, ain't they?"

"Winona, the man over there, the defense counsel, he's going to ask you why you're telling all of this now. Why are you?"

"You told me if I didn't tell the whole truth, you might hang me, and my man's not here no more to get hurt by white law anyway."

The fine sculpted lips turned down for a moment, as a whispered murmur passed across the courtroom, turned down as through tears might follow, but they did not, and she was quickly back in control and looking out across the gallery. At the defense table, Ennis Merriweather seemed unperturbed, seemed almost to be asleep.

"Winona, this money Candy Redstripe gave Langston Turtle," Evans asked. "Was it gold or silver or paper?"

"Mostly some fifty-dollar bills, brand-new. The rest old bills."

At which point the United States Attorney produced the money found under the floor at Fawley Farm, in a small, canvas money bag, established chain of custody from then until the moment, and introduced it as a prosecution exhibit. The defense did not object. The defense, in fact, seemed to ignore any part of what was going forward in the case.

"This is the kind of money your man paid to the others, not old, handled money, but this money, is that right, he paid it to Toby Jupiter for the shotgun."

"Yes, he did."

"He paid it to Sherman Boggs for the fish-camp part."

"Yes, he did."

"He paid it to your brother to kill Temperance Moon."

"Yes. He did."

Now Winona Crowfoot lowered her head and her hands went to her ears and took away the large pearls, which she extended toward Walter Evans in one hand.

"My brother done his job. That Saturday morning when he come back from the trail to the Lurleys' he give me these. He said it was a gift for me. When Temperance had left that morning, these is what she was wearing in her ears!"

Now the murmur in the courtroom changed to a harsh whispering babble, and Judge Parker, obviously infuriated, slammed his hands on the bench before him.

"Mr. Evans!" he shouted. "Is this some kind of showmanship you've engineered?"

"Your honor," said Walter Evans, "I am as flabbergasted as anyone."

Only then did he rush from behind his desk and to the witness stand and take the pearls and hold them in the palm of one hand as Winona Crowfoot's head lifted again and in her eyes was a shining not there before and the traces of a smile at the corners of her mouth.

"Goshen give 'em to me," she said. "So I got to wear 'em for a little while anyway."

United States Attorney Walter Evans was flustered, his face furiously red as he came back to his place with the pearls, yet the old-hand courtroom hangers-on took it as obvious that these earrings had no bearing on the cause in question before the court. And Evans knew that. He didn't even place them in evidence but set them gently, as though they were indeed robin eggs, on the prosecution's desk and left them there.

At the back of the room, Oscar Schiller observed that maybe the United States Attorney was even more flustered when defense counsel made no move to cross-examine and Winona Crowfoot was excused. And in fact, Oscar Schiller had seen that throughout all of Winona Crowfoot's testimony Evans had continued to glance over his shoulder, expecting defense to object to this or that, but no such thing had happened. As though Merriweather didn't care about this witness. As though Merriweather had something bigger and better somewhere down the line.

And so Winona Crowfoot departed from the last public life she would ever have, unchallenged, yet leaving behind on that small desk in front of the jury box the two great milky orbs for all to see. And say to their grandchildren that they had seen the pearls Temperance Moon wore in the last moment of her life.

15

There was considerable clanking and bumping when Sherman Boggs entered the courtroom at the door behind the bench and moved to the witness stand. He walked like a web-footed creature of some kind, a few of the spectators observed, and for good reason. At his ankles were heavy iron cuffs joined by a two-foot chain with links of quarter-inch forged steel. He was handcuffed as well, and the bracelets joined by another, smaller chain which was attached by padlock to an iron loop in a wide leather waist belt. The effort of dragging all this metal around seemed to bend his spine, and he looked like a hunchback. His face was pale and his eyes wet and the flesh of his jowls hung loose like bath towels thrown across a fence to dry. This illusion was enhanced by the fact that tears were running down his face and along his neck to blotch his collarless shirt with dark patches of moisture.

After he was sworn in and took his seat on the witness chair, Judge Parker leaned toward him and spoke quietly, but loud enough for the jury to hear.

"Mr. Boggs, you know that you are under indictment by a grand jury for a capital crime?"

"Yes, sir. I do."

"Mr. Boggs, you understand that this case we're trying now is not your case?"

"Yes, sir. I do."

"Mr. Boggs, I instruct you that you need not give any testimony that might incriminate yourself. And further, anything you say here under oath might well be used to that device. Do you understand that?"

"Yes, sir, I do."

"Then understanding these things," said Parker, "you are still willing to testify here?"

"Yes, sir. I am. The Lord has told me."

"Very well," said Parker, leaning back in his chair, "the purpose of the Lord be served. Mr. Evans, you may begin your examination."

Walter Evans began with a complete reworking of the Langston Turtle plan as Sherman Boggs understood it, and there were no contradictions to Winona Crowfoot's story. And from start to finish, there were no defense objections to anything, even though there might have been on hearsay alone, but no objections were made. To anything.

"And how much money were you paid for your part?"

"Seventy-five dollars and promise of a deed on Deep Fork land," said Sherman Boggs, the tears streaming down his face. "My greed and wickedness blinded me to the vision of Jesus."

"Of course," said Walter Evans. "And what happened in that fish camp?"

"Me and Toby had been drunk for two days," said Sherman Boggs. "I liked little Toby. We been fishing so many times, layin' out on the bank, drunk. Pullin' in them fish on trotlines."

"All right, Mr. Boggs. The fish camp now."

"Well, we taken a notion to go upstream awhile," said Sherman Boggs. "So we went to this old corncrib and set out lines along the river, and me and Toby got in that corncrib when it started to rain and et some dried apples and drunk this wine. We never made no fire. We had this lantern. We got drunker and drunker and told stories. And Toby got sleepy. And lay down in the leaves. And the devil told me it was time to kill him."

"Why time?"

"Well, Langston Turtle said it had to be awhile after Saturday when they done Temperance so she could get found and then after that Toby found. You can see why Toby couldn't be done till after Temperance was done, can't you?"

"Of course. So when you decided it was time, what day was this?"

"Why, I don't know. Maybe Sunday. Maybe Monday. It don't matter. The Lord knows. The Lord knows when the sparrow falls."

"Yes, and Toby Jupiter as well, I assume. So what happene then?" asked Walter Evans.

"He was sleepin' so I shot him three times. Then when he go finished jerkin' and thrashin', I seen what a terrible thing I'd done. I looked in his pockets and got that money Langston Turtle had paid him for the shotgun, forty dollars, and then I run out and got the horses and rode off to Arkansas, and it taken me three days to get to Jewel Moon's place up in the hills, and I had a good notion to just keep on ridin' but Satan grabbed me again and I wanted that land on the Canadian River, on Deep Fork, so I never run no farther."

"Why did you go to Jewel Moon's place in Arkansas?"

"Ever since Miss Jewel bought this place, we went there. Sometimes maybe just a few, maybe sometimes a half dozen. Just to lay around and rest and play cards and drink and get away from all the law from this here Parker's court that was always roamin' around the Territory, watchin' what we done. Sometimes Miss Jewel would ride the train up there to see her little daughter Cassie, a sweet little girl, and when she seen us there she never acted too happy about it but she knowed we was her mama's friends and she told us it was all right as long as we never made no trouble. And we never. Made no trouble, I mean.

"So after I done Toby, I went there to stay hid out a while. I was there about two weeks I guess when Goshen Crowfoot showed up and he had the same idea as me. Lay out in the hills for a while and let the dust settle over in the Nations. Goshen said we hadn't ort to be in any rush about going back to Fawley Farm. Just sit still till Langston sent word it was all right to come back.

"So we stayed 'cause Goshen said we ort, him and me bein' the ones who'd done Temperance and Toby. Just winter in, he said. So we hunted squirrels and played a lot of casino and five-card and dominoes. Sometimes at night, we'd stand on the porch and listen to the fox hounds runnin' in the hills. Them men up there liked their fox hounds and night racin'. It's a strange sound.

"But after more than a month, I was gettin' tired of that place. Maybe Goshen knew it. He was watchin' me real close and kept sayin' we couldn't go no place yet. Maybe he was waitin' to get me down in the woods and bash out my brains with a rock so I wouldn't say nothin' about what we'd did.

"Then that Kansas City policeman came. I didn't know then he was a policeman, but it scared me, him comin' and talkin' all

that time to the folks kept Miss Jewel's place. That man comin' made Goshen awful nervous and I reckoned awful dangerous, so I snuck off in the night and come down to Van Buren and that's where Nason Breedlove arrested me."

There was a fresh gush of tears, and Sherman Boggs's nose had begun to run. Walter Evans walked from behind his table and at the witness stand placed a white cotton handkerchief in Sherman Boggs's hand, then returned to his usual place as the witness swiped at his upper lip with the handkerchief.

"Mr. Boggs," said Evans, "this money paid you by Langston Turtle. Where did it come from? Where did he get it?"

Evans braced for an objection, but none came. Even Judge Parker looked at the defense table, but Merriweather remained seated.

"Langston said he'd saved over a long spell so we'd have the money to do what we needed to do," said Boggs. "Ever'body who come around Fawley Farm knew Temperance give Langston money now and again, to buy his drinkin' whiskey."

"No further questions," said Evans.

"Cross?" asked Judge Parker.

"No," said Merriweather.

Watching, Oscar Schiller could see the consternation on Walter Evans's face. And with good reason. Merriweather was completely unconcerned with the testimony of prosecution witnesses, as though none of it had any bearing on his case. As though something would make all testimony from a certain point completely irrelevant to the defense. A very scary proposition.

As Sherman Boggs left the stand, clanking and clanging and thumping, he wiped his nose with the handkerchief and then standing in the center of the pit held it out toward the United States Attorney.

"You keep it, Sherman," Evans said.

And Sherman Boggs laughed, suddenly, jarringly, and wild-eyed looked toward the gallery, where everybody was watching him somewhat breathlessly.

"Why, you know," he shouted, "this ain't so bad. Once you get used to it! They gonna hang me, but I'll go to my Lord cleansed."

Three very large United States Deputy Marshals were suddenly there and escorting Sherman Boggs from the courtroom. And the closer they got him to the door, the louder he proclaimed.

"My Jesus will save me, my Lord will bless this court, we will live forever, I will never do no wrong!"

And finally, he was gone, ushered out by the men with stars on their vests, and everyone left behind in the courtroom bent forward, panting a little, saying to one another that the sooner they hanged that crazy bastard the better. And Judge Isaac Parker was not unaffected.

"Mr. Evans," he said, "do you propose to bring any more witnesses into this court such as that?"

"No, your honor."

"I hope not."

Ennis Merriweather rose and cleared his throat.

"Judge, objection to all these comments you make in the course of hearing."

"Overruled," said Parker.

"Exception," said Merriweather.

"Noted," said Parker. And to the court recorder said, "Edgar, get the exception in the record, you understand, and for the rest of us, let's get on with this trial. Mr. Evans?"

ℤ ℤ ℤ When Moses Masada came to the witness stand, he came proudly and erect. His Kansas City policeman's badge was prominently displayed on the left breast of a flowered silk vest. He wore pearl-button high-topped shoes and broadcloth coat with matching trousers. His mustache was defiantly black and bristling, and his gray eyes were hot and unfriendly as molten lead. When Oscar Schiller saw the Syrian walk into the courtroom, he knew at once that this man would be a fine witness in Kansas City, but here, in Fort Smith, he was a disaster.

In the spectator section of the room, one of the Towson Avenue hangers-on whispered to the man beside him, "Look at this little priss-ike!"

"One of them Hindu people, I'd say."

"Why hell no, just another one of them Greek bastards we been gettin' so many of around here lately. Eight to five you can't understand a word he says."

But everyone could understand Moses Masada as Walter Evans guided him through testimony that placed him at the Redstripe farm when Tishacomsie was arrested, and later, and then was handed a Ceylon tea can and asked to open it and count the money inside, and counting, as everyone leaned forward a little, coming to the sum total of one thousand three hundred and twenty-two dollars. Most of it crisp greenbacks. And Evans emphasized the amount.

"What you found at the time you took the can?"

"Yes."

"Your honor," said Merriweather, sitting in his cloud of blue smoke, "this is absurd. And I object to the whole charade."

"Well, Mr. Merriweather," said Parker, "we have a witness under oath here and I will take what you've said as objection and make note of exception, but we are going to hear the rest of this testimony."

"Well, your honor, I make exception."

"I've already said it will be noted. Now go on, Mr. Evans."

"You were at the Redstripe farm frequently?" asked Evans.

"He's leading the witness," said Merriweather.

"All right, all right. Let's get on with it."

"Yes, I was there a great deal," said Moses Masada.

"Did you see anyone at any time take money from any place other than this can?"

"Oh, for God's sake," said Merriweather.

"No, I did not."

"What kind of money is this?" asked Evans.

"The kind to buy policemen," shouted Merriweather, and laughed, and most of the spectators laughed as well.

"Mr. Merriweather," said Judge Parker, "if you make another such outburst, I will place you in jail and fine you substantially."

"What kind of money is it, Mr. Masada?" asked Evans.

"New money. I would say never in circulation."

And with a great deal of bickering, the can and the money were placed in evidence as a prosecution exhibit. But then Ennis Merriweather rose to cross-examine.

"Mr. Masada, how much are you paid in Kansas City, Missouri?"

"Well, about six hundred dollars a year."

"And Mr. Masada, when you came here to help Oscar Schiller, how much did he pay you?"

"Three hundred dollars at first and another two hundred later on."

"Mr. Masada, when you opened that can in Creek Nation, had you ever in your life seen as much money?"

During the long pause, everyone could hear the wind pitching up to a high note under the courthouse eaves.

"No."

"So what you found in that can was a great deal more than what you have said here, isn't that true?"

"No."

Merriweather turned to the jury, grinning.

"Of course not!" he said. "So much of what you really found was lost in the lint of your fancy pants pockets."

"I object," shouted Walter Evans.

"I withdraw it," said Merriweather. But then, turning viciously and pointing his finger at Moses Masada, "But everyone in this room knows how police officers can afford to buy expensive clothes."

Walter Evans was almost frothing at the mouth. He was almost incoherent.

"He is testifying, he is testifying," Evans screamed. "Let him take the oath and sit on the stand."

"All right," Parker said, tapping his palms on the bench, although the courtroom was deathly silent. "In heat of passion, we sometimes overextend ourselves. But Mr. Merriweather, if you make such a charge again, I will take drastic action against you."

"I apologize, your honor," said Merriweather, standing now in his cloud of blue smoke. "I can't say what came over me."

"Well," said Judge Parker, "if whatever it was comes over you again, it will cost you dearly. Now, let's have a short recess so that the jurors might recreate themselves down the hall in the water closet. Everyone else, stay in your places."

₪ ₪ ₪ There was always in any gallery at Parker trials a certain element who came expecting a circus atmosphere in the famous courtroom, perhaps chief among them being the newspaper reporters from Kansas City, St. Louis, Little Rock, and other civilized places. And these people were usually disappointed and astonished to find that this court, so well publicized as the home of the "Hanging Judge," looked exactly like any other federal court and operated exactly like any other federal court.

And afterward, none of the scribes and pundits ever mentioned in their sensational accounts the fact that Congress had decreed anyone found guilty of murder or rape would suffer the death penalty in this court. Parker, as Oscar Schiller always said, staunch friend of the Indians, respected in his community, member of school board and board of directors at one of the biggest hospitals in town, a leader in charities, a good family man, got all the bloodthirsty credit. And was working himself to death in the process.

It was primarily because of this that Oscar Schiller had always said to his associates, "Boys, don't ever believe a God damned thing you read in a newspaper! Unless it's printed right here on the border."

In the LaRue case, there was one short interval of comic drama, which received much of the attention of the out-of-town correspondents. It was a thing, certainly, that was hard to imagine happening in, say, the Southern District of New York or the Eastern District of Virginia in the federal court system. It was the Comanche.

When Toad walked into the courtroom there was a general babble of conversation and gurgle of suppressed laughter which Judge Parker found so hard to control that he stopped trying. Toad was wearing a hide smock that came to his knees, a hide smock with no decorations except stains and blotches that suggested the butchering of buffalo many years before. There were also extremely long fringes on each sleeve.

Ennis Merriweather did little to calm the situation when he said in a very loud stage whisper that had he known Buffalo Bill Cody's Wild West Show was playing in Fort Smith, he would have brought his children.

Walking to the witness stand with Toad was Moma July, in his usual Union Army overcoat but at least now, in respect for the court, without his hat. It had been Moma July who brought the fringed smock from Creek Nation, at Toad's request, and he was here as official interpreter for the court. No one could think of anybody else who spoke Comanche and nobody wanted the problem of trying to figure out what Toad was saying if he testified in English, despite the fact that Moma July was a police officer who had been involved deeply in the solution of the crimes at cause.

Besides, Toad had said he would not talk to anybody else but

Moma July, perhaps expecting that the little Creek still had a bottle left under the massive Union Army coat. He had told Walter Evans that he would not speak to others even if the white man tied him to a wagon wheel and pulled off his manhood apples with a pair of wire pliers. After all, he'd said, Moma July had saved him from a bunch of crazy Choctaws.

Toad's hair fell loose around his head, all the way to his shoulders and framing his face. As he sat on the witness stand, bent forward, his bloodshot eyes glared defiantly into the faces of all the white men. And one of those whispered to another that he was glad he hadn't lived on the West Texas High Plains a half century earlier when there was a whole tribe of these little bowlegged monsters running around well armed and damned sick and tired of Anglos showing up and trying to take their country away from them.

There was considerable trouble in trying to administer the oath.

"Mr. July," Judge Parker finally said, "if Mr. Toad will not swear on a Christian Bible, what god will he swear to?"

"Your honor," said Moma July, "he says that he doesn't need any of his gods to tell him what the truth is."

Parker was so pleased with the answer that he allowed the trial to go on, and so for the next thirty minutes the people in the gallery leaned forward trying to hear the strange sounds issuing from the mouth of the witness.

One spectator whispered to his companion that it was worse than that Greek who had the café on 3rd Street when the Greek started talking with his wife and kids. There was no intelligible word, like the ones a man could find in the Bible. And if you can't find it in the Bible, he whispered, I'm not sure I trust it!

Walter Evans, through Moma July, guided Toad back to a time of horse racing in Sallisaw in August 1892. There, Toad testified, he had seen Muley LaRue, and he pointed LaRue out in the courtroom. LaRue had come and talked with Candy Redstripe and Candy Redstripe's woman, the Creek witch. And Toad saw LaRue give them a small canvas money bag. Then, back on the Canadian a few days later, Candy Redstripe had taken Toad along, both well armed, to Fawley Farm on a night everybody knew Temperance Moon was attending a stomp dance in Hillabee.

This fat Creek with tattoos on his arms and his woman came outside and talked. And Toad said he saw Candy Redstripe give the fat Creek with the tattoos the canvas bag and he heard Candy

Redstripe say that Temperance Moon had to die and if it didn't happen damned quick, then he and Toad would come back and get the money and break both the legs of the fat Creek with the tattoos. But when it did happen, then Candy Redstripe would give the fat Creek more money.

So, said Toad, Temperance Moon was shot and Candy Redstripe and himself went and gave the fat Creek the rest of the money. Candy Redstripe was very angry because the fat Creek was always drunk and talking too much, and finally, when Toad was in Texas with some of Candy Redstripe's horses, there was this big shoot and Candy Redstripe was killed and so was the fat Creek with the tattoos and two of his friends. When Toad came home, he said, Candy Redstripe's witch sent him away with only two horses and a hundred dollars. He got drunk. When Moma July rescued him from the Choctaws, Toad decided to tell all he knew about this thing, because Moma July seemed interested in knowing and Moma July had been very good to him, and had given him a lot of whiskey and didn't build a fire on his belly or gouge out his eyes as Toad expected Moma July to do just to make him talk about these things.

On cross, Ennis Merriweather's first question was why Toad had not come forward earlier when all this killing was taking place. When Moma July interpreted the question to Toad, the Comanche appeared to be shocked. A number of those unintelligible words tumbled from his mouth.

"Your honor," said Moma July, "he says it was just a usual kind of thing in the Nations. But when the great Candy Redstripe was killed, it became unusual."

Merriweather asked one other question. Had, at any time, Toad seen the amount of money in that canvas money bag? He had not, Toad said.

That was the end of the circus. The United States Attorney called his next witness, Tishacomsie Redstripe.

16 When Tishacomsie Redstripe walked into the courtroom, there was not the usual whisper of sound from the gallery. There was instead a stunned silence followed by a long sigh. As had been the case with Winona Crowfoot, everyone assumed the wardrobe of this witness had been purchased specifically for the trial by attorney W. M. Caveness, defense counsel for both women. But whereas the gingham of Winona was likely a choice of Caveness, everyone was sure Tishacomsie Redstripe had made her own selection. She came to testify in mourning, wearing a long austere dress of black taffeta.

Sleeves came to her wrists and were tightly fastened there with four bone buttons. Patent-leather shoes showed briefly beneath the hem of the dress, black, too, as was the small hat at the back of her head where her hair had been braided and tightly done in a high bun. From the hat a veil hung well below the nape of her neck and in front lay alongside her face. Strikingly incongruous was the deep-red rouge on her high, hard cheekbones. There was no added color on her full lips but in the middle part of her hair the tint of rust ocher.

According to those who saw her, she was in all respects the most beautiful woman who had ever breathed earth's air. In their written reports, the newspaper correspondents rose to orgies of rapturous description. "Glory to Venus of the Wild Border." "Beauty to make Helen of Troy blush with envy." "Stunning Princess of the Savage Aborigines."

At the back of the room, Nason Breedlove whispered to Oscar Schiller.

"She's pretty as a new blacksnake whip, ain't she?"

"Yes. And this may be the wrong time to be that pretty."

As she stood to take the oath, there was no question but that she had the undivided attention of everyone in the room, including his honor.

ℵ ℵ ℵ "If you know the defendant in this case and he is present in the courtroom, would you please identify him and point him out," said Walter Evans.

"Muley LaRue," Tishacomsie Redstripe said and lifted her right arm and held a finger like the barrel of a pistol, and she was looking directly into LaRue's eyes, and he was looking back. Later, court watchers would say it was a look hot enough to set fire to all the furniture.

One of LaRue's children began to cry, and Judge Parker leaned forward.

"Mrs. LaRue, would you like to take the child out?"

The French-valentine face nodded, and as spectators shuffled their feet to allow her passage, she moved, holding a child's hand in each of her own, leading them from the room.

"The marshals will allow Mrs. LaRue back into the courtroom when she desires," said Parker. "Those on the front row, leave her space to be seated when she returns."

Walter Evans, obviously annoyed, said, "Your honor, may we proceed?"

"Please do."

"Mrs. Redstripe," said Walter Evans, "would you tell the jury the circumstances of your knowing the defendant?"

"Last August, in Sallisaw, Cherokee Nation, there were horse races. Three days of horse races."

Unlike Winona Crowfoot, Tishacomsie was not tentative at all. Her words came like small pistol shots. She sat upright, haughty, proud, and her language was not Winona's, learned on the rough side of Indian Territory society, but that taught where she went to school at a ladies' academy in Washington County, Arkansas. She spoke English as well as or better than some of the newspaper correspondents covering this trial, which Nason Breedlove remarked on with some admiration. To which Oscar Schiller said,

"Yes, and that may be as much against her as the shiny black dress and her acting like she owns this courtroom."

"What the hell's the matter, anyway?"

"I got a bad feeling about this one, Nason. A very bad feeling."

"My husband and the Comanche and I went there," Tishacomsie was saying.

"To Sallisaw?"

"Yes. We drove a wagon where we could sleep. On the first afternoon, LaRue came and talked to my husband. I don't know what he said. My husband told me LaRue was a Fort Smith bank man and he said he had helped this man, LaRue, collect some debts in Cherokee Nation before my husband and I were married."

"Your honor," said Merriweather, "this is all hearsay."

"Mr. Merriweather," said Parker, "you know as well as I that a defendant is held accountable for what he says. It only remains for the jury to decide the credibility of the witness. Overruled."

"Exception."

"All right, Edgar, get it in the record. Go on, Mr. Evans."

"But your honor, we're talking here about what her *husband* said."

"Mr. Merriweather, the jury can hear it. Now. Go on."

It was noticed by a number of veteran court watchers that Merriweather was no longer smoking fat cigars. Nor was LaRue. Instead, the Little Rock attorney was bent over his little table scribbling notes with a yellow lead pencil.

"Two nights later, LaRue came again. All the races were done. LaRue came to our camp. We were ready to go to bed and the next day we were going to drive home. This time, when LaRue spoke to my husband, I was there. LaRue said he wanted to talk to my husband alone, and my husband said if he wanted to talk, he would talk to the both of us. It upset LaRue."

"Objection," said Merriweather.

"Sustained," Parker said. "Witness can testify only to what she saw or heard. Not to her opinions."

"So?" said Walter Evans.

"LaRue paced around for a while like a wild horse."

"Objection!"

"Overruled."

"He was carrying a small canvas bag."

Walter Evans moved to the front of the jury box, where, on the wide banister, prosecution exhibits were displayed. He took the canvas money pouch and carried it to the witness stand and held it up, like a bag of dry beans.

"This bag?"

"It looks like the same bag. It was that kind of bag."

Moving slowly, deliberately, Evans replaced the money pouch on the jury-box banister and resumed his place behind the prosecutor's desk, folding his arms, peering over the tops of his pince-nez.

"And then?"

"And then LaRue said the time had come to give poison to a rat in the Indian Nations. He handed the bag to my husband and said there was money there to do it and we could count it, but not out in sight of anybody, and he'd wait while we did. So me and my husband went to the wagon and opened the bag and there was money inside, new, green money, and we counted it. We counted two thousand five hundred dollars. All in fifty-dollar bills."

"Are you sure it was two thousand five hundred dollars?"

"I can count, Mr. Evans," Tishacomsie said petulantly.

Once more Evans left his place and went to the jury banister, taking up the money pouch and the tea can. He approached the witness chair holding these items out before him, then placed them on the court reporter's table, then took them up again one at a time, first the tea can.

"Do you recognize this?"

"It looks like my tea can."

"Take it and open it and tell the jury what you find."

She did so and spread the bills in one hand, like playing cards, and said, "Money. A few small bills but mostly fifty-dollar notes."

"Is this how you recall the tea can the last time you saw it?"

"Yes."

Walter Evans took the tea can and gave her the money pouch, and the process was repeated.

"A few small bills and mostly fifty-dollar notes," she said.

The United States Attorney returned the exhibits to their place on the jury banister and resumed his own behind his desk, still peering over his spectacles like an inquiring schoolmaster.

"And now, Mrs. Redstripe, after you and your husband had counted the two thousand five hundred dollars in the pouch Mr. LaRue gave you, what happened?"

"We went back to LaRue and my husband said for that kind of money it must be a pretty big rat he wanted poisoned. And LaRue said it was. It was Temperance Moon."

Now the gallery raised its loud murmur, and Parker pecked at the bench with his hands.

"Tell us all of it now, Mrs. Redstripe."

"I'm telling it as fast as I can," Tish said. "My husband asked LaRue who it was that wanted Temperance Moon done, and LaRue said it didn't matter, the money spoke for itself."

"Mrs. Redstripe, I ask now that you recall what you've testified to thus far and you *heard* the defendant say these things?"

"With my own ears."

"All right. And then?"

"And then my husband said it was a lot of money and LaRue said he didn't care how it was spent so long as the rat took the poison."

"You recall the defendant's exact words?"

"Yes. It upset me very much. Because when my husband saw all that money, he made up his mind."

"Objection," from defense.

"Sustained," from the bench. "Jury disregard the last part of it."

"All right," said Evans. "Mrs. Redstripe, if you recall that LaRue said it was Temperance Moon to be killed, how did you feel about this?"

"I was angry and put out."

"Why is that?"

"Objection."

"No," said Parker. "We'll take this. Overruled."

"I was put out, I was upset because a white man had come to pay one of us to kill a white woman. Because of the way she married, she was a citizen of Creek Nation. But she was a white woman. And she had brought all the bad things to us that the whites have brought. She corrupted our people. And maybe she deserved to be killed. But I didn't want my husband to do it."

Evans stood for a long time after that, allowing the full impact of it to sink in, Oscar Schiller reckoned. Stood silently with his arms folded, his head bowed as though praying, and everyone in the room leaning forward, waiting for his next question. Finally, it came.

"Tell us all of it, Mrs. Redstripe."

"My husband wanted the money."

"Objection."

"Overruled. Go on, Mrs. Redstripe."

"My husband wanted the money to pay off some of his racing debts, and he told LaRue he'd do it if LaRue wasn't too picayunish about how. And LaRue told my husband he didn't care how. And my husband told him he wouldn't do it, my husband I mean, but would hire it done, and LaRue said he didn't care how. Just do it."

"You personally heard LaRue say these things?"

"Absolutely. I remember it all because my husband and me got into a very serious fuss afterward and it lasted almost all night, and I told him he was foolish. But he had to have the money and so I finally told my husband that whatever he did, I would stand with him. My husband said we could keep most of the money to help pay his debts and hire someone else to do it, and that started the fuss again, but I finally said he could do what he saw best and I'd stand with him."

"You are a woman who stands by her man?"

"Among my people, when the man decides, his wife stands beside him."

"Even if what he decides is a bad thing?"

"Among my people, if a man does a bad thing, he has some reason for it and only he can suffer its pain. All the more reason for his woman to stand beside him."

"Very well, Mrs. Redstripe," said Evans. "Continue."

"Two days after we got home, my husband and the Comanche went to Fawley Farm. At night and heavily armed. They were back by midnight and my husband was laughing and said he knew he could buy Langston Turtle. He said he had given Langston Turtle five hundred dollars to kill Temperance Moon and when it was done, he would give another five hundred."

"So then," said Evans, staring up at the ceiling and counting elaborately on his fingers, "you started with twenty-five hundred dollars from Muley LaRue, and your husband contracted with Langston Turtle for a thousand, which left you fifteen hundred."

"Yes."

"How much of that had you spent at the time of your husband's death?"

"Not much. We went to Muskogee and I bought some clothes and some quilting material and my husband paid off a few of his

"No. There was not."

At the back of the room, Oscar Schiller took off his glasses and wiped them with a cotton handkerchief, although they didn't really need wiping, and in the act rubbed so furiously he almost tore the lenses from the steel frames.

"You sick?" Nason Breedlove whispered.

"Yes," said Oscar Schiller. "I'll never trust anybody again."

"Yeah, well in our line of work that's not a bad policy. Lookee here, Evans got old Moma July comin' to the stand. I wonder what for?"

"I don't know," Oscar Schiller whispered. "I don't know anything about this thing anymore."

Moma July, in his second appearance in this courtroom wearing his Union Army coat, testified that after Tishacomsie's arrest, and after he'd heard about Moses Masada and the tea can, he and three of his men had gone to the Redstripe farm and looked for more money, but had found none. On cross, Merriweather wanted to know how Moma July was such an expert on hidden money, and Moma July said he'd been bred and born in Creek Nation and knew where people hid their cash.

Then with a sly smile, and winks at the jury, Merriweather went to the real meat of his cross-examination.

"Now Mr. July," Merriweather said, "a little finders-keepers is the rule, isn't it? Money you found would end in white man's court, so just keep a bit here and there, right, Mr. July? Besides, hushing about money would feather your nest and help your Indian friend Candy Redstripe. Isn't that about how it was, Mr. July?"

Evans started to object but seeing the impassive Creek on the stand did not.

"Well, my nest has got all the feathers it needs," said Moma July. "And on helpin' Candy, he was never my friend, being a damned Delaware like he was, and for the last ten years I been tryin' to find something I could arrest him on."

Merriweather was too professional in this arena to show that he had been taken aback and as he sat down he winked elaborately at the jury. Some of the court hangers-on argued for years afterward about whether or not some of the jurors winked back.

But for the moment, the United States called Herkimer Warson.

ℤ ℤ ℤ "Temperance Moon came to me last August asking for a loan. To start a business in Eufaula, Creek Nation. I refused it because I assumed it would be a house of ill repute. She was very angry. She threatened to tell things that would damage my reputation."

Herkimer Warson sat on the witness stand as he sat in his seat, his former seat, at City Bank. Stiff and regal, lifting his bald pate, as observers said, toward his god of high finance. What could you expect other than that from an Episcopalian, say all the good members of dissenter churches. Yet, as in his ability to collect voters, his appeal on the witness chair was irresistible and even the Towson Avenue saloon people could not help but lean forward on their seats hoping this man wearing spats might be better than they knew he was.

"Tell us a little more about this request," said Evans.

"It was in my office, Mr. LaRue was there, he was always there when I was dealing with people from Indian Territory, because he was my agent there. The lady asked for five thousand dollars, and when I refused, she became very abusive and made threats."

"What kind of threats?"

"She said she would reveal a thing," said Herkimer Warson, and then his voice seemed to catch in his throat and he looked about the room with a wild glaze in his eyes. "A thing that would destroy my good reputation."

"But then, Mr. Warson?"

"I reconsidered. A few days later. And decided to give her the loan and Mr. LaRue would take it to her." Warson was testifying a little breathlessly and his eyes were darting their glance about the room, yet unseeing.

"Why, Mr. Warson?"

"Because," Warson said, very softly now. "Because. She said she would reveal a thing. . . . So I decided to make the loan."

At this point, the United States Attorney introduced two documents, both obtained by federal subpoena. One was a receipt book of Herkimer Warson showing a duplicate copy of an unsigned receipt for five thousand dollars, the other a copy of his personal bank account at the Sebastian County National Bank indicating a withdrawal of five thousand dollars on August 5, 1892. Without objection, they were entered.

"Mr. Warson," asked Walter Evans, "why is your personal account at a bank other than that where you are an officer?"

"I have always made it a policy to keep my money in a bank other than the one which employs me," Warson said. "It's always seemed to me a good policy."

"So you withdrew this money in what denominations?"

"Fifty-dollar notes."

"And with it?"

"I placed it in a pouch and gave it to Mr. LaRue and gave him the original of that receipt for a loan and told him to get it to Temperance Moon."

"Now, why would you make a loan to a woman of Temperance Moon's reputation?"

"Successful bordello entrepreneurs are good financial risks," Warson said, and the gallery giggled and buzzed and Parker patted his bench. "Because they have enough trouble staying in business at best, and therefore cannot afford to be debtors. And I had assumed from the first that what she wanted was to open a bordello in Creek Nation."

"But Mr. Warson, no one here is going to believe that you changed your mind and made such a loan simply because you expected to get your money repaid. So why did you make the loan?"

Warson's eyes lifted to the ceiling above the heads of all those spectators leaning forward, watching. He swallowed a number of times, his throat contracting.

"Temperance Moon had said she would tell that I had a large interest in her daughter's business here in Fort Smith, the Commerce Railroad Hotel."

The gallery responded to that with such loud babbling that Parker threatened to clear the room. And at that exact moment, Mrs. LaRue returned with her two children, and with the tumult, one began to cry, and she turned and left again, deputy marshals holding the door open for her.

When order was restored, Evans went on.

"Mr. Warson, the five thousand dollars. Please, tell us."

"I put it in a money bag with the receipt and gave it to Mr. LaRue and instructed him to give it to Temperance Moon because I did not want to be blackmailed, and he returned, Mr. LaRue, but with no signed receipt, and explained that it would be forthcoming, the signed receipt, I mean, and then we heard that Temperance Moon had been killed and I assumed somebody had killed her to rob her of the money."

"So actually, it was extortion, wasn't it?"

"Well, I decided to make the loan to avoid something unpleasant."

"So you sent the five thousand dollars Temperance Moon had asked for in the first place, and you sent it by whom, Mr. Warson?"

"Mr. LaRue."

"No further questions," said Walter Evans.

Herkimer Warson had risen and started off the stand when Ennis Merriweather held up a hand and said gently, "Just a minute, Herkimer. I want to ask a few things."

And Herkimer Warson sat back down, looking winded and beaten and defeated, and everyone in the courtroom was aware of his resignation from everything his life had been and even the Towson Avenue saloon people could not help but feel some pang of pity for this man who had done nothing more, so they saw, than being landlord to the best whorehouse in the whole state.

"Hell, they ain't nothin' wrong with that," said one.

"Don't ever say such a thing to my wife," said the other.

"Herkimer," said Merriweather, "Mr. LaRue has been in your employ for some time, has he not?"

"Yes."

"How have you found him?"

"Honest and trustworthy."

"In fact," said Merriweather, "when he came back from Indian Territory without that receipt signed, it was a thing you could accept?"

"I trusted his judgment in Indian Territory."

"When you heard that Temperance Moon had been killed and you assumed someone had done it to steal your money, why did you not report this transaction to the authorities?"

"It would have defeated my whole purpose," said Warson, becoming more and more agitated. "If I reported it, then surely my reason for having made the loan would have been revealed."

"Thank you, Herkimer. No more questions."

Evans rested the government's case with that, and Judge Parker declared an hour recess for supper, court to resume under lamplight.

"Jesus," Nason Breedlove said. "I'm hungry as hell, ain't you, Oscar?"

"No."

"It's really bitin' you, ain't it?"

"Yes, and I think Warson was a better witness for the defense than he was for the prosecution, if Merriweather's headed where I think he is."

"Well, I don't give a damn where Merriweather's headin', I'm headin' for Maria's."

א א א Cantoni's was crowded. Every lawyer in town along with his clerk was there, as they always were during meal recesses in important trials, important trials all these people usually attended in hope of learning something or maybe just from professional curiosity. And any hearing dealing with the Temperance Moon murders was considered an important trial.

The attorneys-at-law community in Fort Smith was a sizable one, because in that small city was not only the federal court and the United States Commissioner's court but the circuit and chancery courts for Sebastian County and a large municipal court besides. Nason Breedlove said that if a man was driving a hack in the streets of Fort Smith and ran over somebody it was bound to be a lawyer because there were so many of them.

As was also usual, the loud conversation in Cantoni's that evening centered on which of Parker's decisions from the bench might be cause for reversible error on appeal. The consensus seemed to be that the judge had conducted a pretty clean trial thus far and that Merriweather couldn't hope for much beyond a favorable finding by the jury.

Oscar Schiller and Nason Breedlove walked past all this legal babble and to the rear of the room, where Moses Masada was alone at a small table, and had been there apparently since his testimony that afternoon. The table before him showed a large number of wet rings where steins of beer had sweated, there was now a half-full stein in his hand, and when he looked up his eyes were bleary and bloodshot.

"How about some company there, Masada?" said Nason Breedlove, and the Syrian waved a hand loosely toward the empty chairs at the table.

Maria Cantoni was there almost at once, without having taken any order, with four pots of beans, a huge stick of rye bread, and four steins of beer. She was sweating and her hair was falling in wet ringlets about her face and she smelled of garlic.

"Little busy, ain't you?" asked Nason Breedlove.

"Honey," she panted, slamming down beans and beer before them from the metal tray she carried, "if they had a Temperance Moon trial in this town every day, I'd pay off the mortgage in a month."

Moses Masada made no effort to eat, and Oscar Schiller picked at his food halfheartedly. Nason Breedlove began a systematic attack on three bean pots at once.

"Masada, you didn't hear any of that trial yet except when you was on the stand, did you?" Nason Breedlove asked, his mouth full.

Moses Masada acted as though he had not heard. He sat with his elbows on the table, staring into his beer stein, blinking and licking his lips.

Oscar Schiller wanted to say something about Tishacomsie Redstripe. But each statement he worked about in his head seemed inappropriate, even hateful. He knew this was because of his own sense of betrayal by Tish and Candy, and to the Syrian, obviously in pain, he wanted to say something helpful. But he didn't know what. He knew Masada had taken a room again at the hotel across the street and that soon he would stagger to his bed there, and Oscar Schiller thought for a moment that he might stay here with the Kansas City peace officer and help him across Garrison Avenue and to his blankets but knew that was a bad idea because obviously Masada wanted neither help nor companionship. Sitting there watching the Syrian slack-lipped, dim-eyed, Oscar Schiller was somehow uncomfortable. Feeling inadequate. Feeling guilty.

It didn't take Nason Breedlove long to finish his supper, and wiping his mustache with his fingertips he suggested a hasty return to the courtroom so as not to miss any of the presentation of the defense case. So they departed, leaving Moses Masada where they had found him. Pausing at the cash register to pay Ed for the beans and beer, Nason Breedlove said, "That's a strange man you got there, Oscar, you know it? Whole time we was sittin' with him, he never said a single word."

"Yes," said Oscar Schiller. "A strange man."

17

"And now, Mr. LaRue, let us first dispense with all this trivial nonsense the government has brought as evidence," said Ennis Merriweather.

"Objection, he's still doing his summation."

"Sustained."

It was all smoke with no fire, and expected, as had been Merriweather's motion that Judge Parker give a directed verdict of not guilty to the jury at the end of the prosecution's case, and the denial of that, and now the defendant on the witness stand.

Creighton Muley LaRue, having been charged with a serious felony, was wearing leg irons. Much lighter, it seemed, than those Sherman Boggs had worn into this courtroom. And LaRue was not handcuffed. He went to the stand erect and showing great confidence and smiled at his wife and two children, now back in the front row of spectators. His olive skin was dry of sweat and his pencil-thin mustache was as finely plucked as a good lady's eyebrows. His hair glistened with brilliantine oil and was parted on the left side. Navy-blue suit, lace shoes, white shirt with a narrow necktie. A picture of solid good citizenship, even if a little French.

"Tell us," said Merriweather, "about your well-digging enterprise."

LaRue confirmed what a prosecution witness had said about his buying explosives and went on to explain that he had thrown all of it into the Poteau River once he had realized that he knew nothing of fusing such things and didn't want it lying about to endanger his dear wife and children. When asked why he hadn't returned it to the seller to redeem his money, LaRue ducked his head and grinned.

"I was a little ashamed to go back down to Jenny Lind and admit I didn't know how to use this stuff."

Some of the jurors smiled and nodded.

Asked about where he had been on the nights of the Bamberger Brewery shooting and the railyard fire, LaRue said he was at home, where he always was at such a time of day.

"I try my best to be at table with my wife and children to have a meal together at eventide," he said.

A few of the jurors nodded and smiled. The ones, Oscar Schiller assumed, who had little children of their own.

Asked about his derringers, LaRue said he had permission, due to his job at the bank, to have them, and that he enjoyed shooting at tin cans, but that any turtle he had ever shot in the head was with a .22 caliber rifle, and he was astonished that anyone could have supposed he was capable of such marksmanship with the pistols.

Ennis Merriweather with his own witness was as immobile as the United States Attorney had been with his, but the counsel for defense did not remain behind his desk. He took his stand four feet in front of the witness chair, thumbs hooked in the great lapels of his coat, one foot advanced as though he were Andy Jackson ready to charge the British, old court hangers-on said. Or maybe, they said, taking the pose he used in the Arkansas legislature when impressing lesser lights. But still aiming his navel at the jury!

"Mr. LaRue," Merriweather said, "tell us about your employer and Temperance Moon."

"My employer is Herkimer Warson of City Bank," LaRue said. "Last August 1, as my journal shows, Temperance Moon came into the bank. It was a Monday, I recall. I showed her into Mr. Warson's office and I remained there. When he was dealing with anyone from the Indian Nations, Mr. Warson wanted me present, because I acted as his agent in the Territory. Temperance Moon asked for a loan of five thousand dollars to start a business in Eufaula, Creek Nation. Although she offered her farm as collateral, Mr. Warson refused. There were some harsh words exchanged. She returned the next day with the same request and with the same results."

"Harsh words, you say," said Merriweather. "You heard these?"

"Yes. I was in the room."

"Good, we'll return to that momentarily. Go on, Mr. LaRue."

"At the end of that week, Mr. Warson called me into his office and he'd reconsidered and would send five thousand dollars to Temperance Moon. By now back in Creek Nation. I advised against it, but Mr. Warson explained his reasons for doing so, reasons of which I was already aware. He had come to the decision. He withdrew the money from his own account and I took it to Sallisaw, Cherokee Nation."

"Mr. LaRue, that money bag on the jury-box banister," said Merriweather, pointing. "You have seen it passed about here and there in this courtroom. Is that the money bag you took to the Indian Territory?"

"It appears to be the same kind, if not the exact one."

"Describe the money Mr. Warson put in the bag."

"It was new money and all in fifty-dollar denomination."

"Why," asked Merriweather, "did you go to Sallisaw?"

"I knew there were horse races at the time and a man I could use to deliver the money would be attending."

Muley LaRue started to cross his legs but was prevented by his leg-iron chains. He laughed and shrugged, and a number of jurors smiled.

"Did you find this man, and if so, who was he?" asked Merriweather.

"I found him as I expected, and he was Candy Redstripe. We had done business together before in the Nations. I spoke to him twice and on the second occasion I gave him the pouch and told him that it was essential it be given to Temperance Moon with the message that it came from Herkimer Warson. I told him I would pay a fee of fifty dollars for his services."

"Fifty dollars is a good deal of money in the Indian Nations, then?"

"Yes."

"How was he to know what was in the pouch?"

"He didn't. Not by my hand. That pouch was never opened from the moment I watched Mr. Warson put the five thousand dollars into it, and I did not open it in Sallisaw. Oh, and there was a receipt for the money, a blank receipt. That was in the bag along with the greenbacks. I paid Mr. Redstripe fifty dollars from my own pocketbook, expecting that Mr. Warson would reimburse me."

"Which?"

"He did."

"Mr. LaRue, why didn't you deliver this money yourself?"

"Why goodness gracious," said LaRue, "I was uneasy about riding about in Indian Territory with that much cash. And where Temperance Moon was, on her farm, it was a rather wild and isolated place. I had confidence in Mr. Redstripe because he had the kind of reputation in the Nations which discouraged anyone from trying to rob him."

"He was, in short, a killer?"

"I object," said Evans.

"Sustained."

"All right, your honor, I withdraw it," said Merriweather. "Now, Mr. LaRue, what happened next?"

"I came home and we heard about Temperance Moon being killed and assumed someone had done it to rob her of the loan."

"The five thousand dollars?"

"That's what we assumed."

"And Mr. Warson decided not to report to the authorities anything about the loan."

"Yes. For reasons he has stated here. But there was a lot more than what he stated. There was a greater secret."

Merriweather blinked. He started to speak, then paused. Every old court watcher in the room could sense that the defense counsel had come to a point where he did not know what his witness was going to say.

"What was that, Mr. LaRue?"

"Why, a thing well known to a few, including myself and Temperance Moon. Jewel Moon, her daughter, has a place in the hills, at Weedy Rough. It was a place Temperance Moon's friends went to now and again for enjoyment of mountain air. But it was mostly a place for Jewel Moon to keep her illegitimate daughter. This daughter was born at the time Jewel Moon was establishing the Commerce Railroad Hotel with the help of Mr. Warson's money. And Herkimer Warson is the father of that illegitimate child!"

After a few seconds of open-mouthed silence, the gallery erupted with giggles, whispers, soft shrieks. Judge Parker made no move to quiet it but called the attorneys to approach the bench and told the court reporter to come close as well. The three men and Parker bent their heads close toward one another and spoke in low tones so the jury could not hear. Nor anyone else.

"Mr. Merriweather," asked Parker, "what is the thrust of this testimony about the child?"

"Your honor, I have no idea. It came as a surprise to me."

"How does it go to the cause except to reinforce what is already in evidence? Besides, unlike the embarrassing fact for Herkimer Warson that he was a brothel landlord, which he himself testified to under oath, this is hearsay. Mr. Merriweather, will you attempt to substantiate Mr. LaRue's statement on the child?"

"I have no intention of doing so," said Merriweather. "It serves no purpose in the defense I have prepared."

"And Mr. Evans, what is your sense of this?"

"Your honor, the statement by Mr. LaRue, if true, would seem to strengthen the possibility of blackmail, but the government is not here to prove blackmail," Evans said. "The only way in which blackmail would play a major part here would be if the government was trying to prove the money was sent specifically not to pay blackmail or as a simple loan, but to hire someone to kill the blackmailer. The government is not trying to prove that. The government believes that if one were contracting a murder in Indian Territory, there would be no need to send so much to have it done."

"To play devil's advocate," said Parker, "suppose Herkimer Warson *did* send the money for a contracted murder and he sent five thousand dollars so that he could claim, if caught at it, he was responding to a request for a simple loan in that amount."

"Your honor," said Evans, "why would anyone get involved in a murder scheme with the expectation of getting caught at it? To do such a thing, to get so involved in such a serious crime, a person would proceed on the assumption that he would *not* be caught. And five thousand dollars is a lot of money in the Territory, so to contract a killing for that sum there would be calling attention to something the involved person wanted to keep hidden.

"Besides, your honor, is it really likely that Mr. LaRue would have such loyalty to Mr. Warson that he would allow himself to take the blame for such a thing, take the blame all to himself, and commit perjury in the bargain?"

Judge Parker drummed on the bench with his fingers. Then

said, "Well taken. It is unfortunate the statement was made. It is inflammatory and serves no one's purpose, apparently. I will strike it as hearsay, of course, but the cat is out of the bag. I only hope it doesn't influence some otherwise clear-headed juror. But regardless of that, I think we can agree it should be stricken. So now, gentleman, back to work."

Once everyone was back in place, Judge Parker instructed the jury to disregard LaRue's last statement and Merriweather proceeded with his case.

"Mr. LaRue, when were you first aware of this so-called investigation into the Moon murders?"

"On the night I was arrested," said Muley LaRue.

"Describe for us what happened."

"I was getting my horse in the bank shed when two federal officers assaulted me, one hitting me with his fist. Shortly thereafter, I became aware of a subpoena issued on my bank account, in which there was less than one hundred dollars, and then a search warrant for my home, where four deputy marshals came and terrified my wife and little children and left my home in a shambles and found no money."

"But Mr. LaRue, it has been testified here that you received a note last November concerning this investigation."

"I never received any such note."

"Let me summarize, Mr. LaRue, to be sure the jury understands your testimony. When you went to Indian Territory, you carried five thousand dollars and a blank receipt in a money bag."

"Yes."

"You passed this to Mr. Candy Redstripe and explained it needed delivery to Temperance Moon and you paid him for his service from your own pocket?"

"Yes."

"I ask you now, Mr. LaRue, did you then or at any time offer to pay for the killing of Temperance Moon?"

"I have never killed anybody in my life and I have never offered money to anybody to kill anybody."

"Your witness," Merriweather said, waving a hand toward Walter Evans.

The United States Attorney stood behind his little table for a long time, head bowed, fingering his eyeglasses. Then looked up and drew a deep breath.

"Mr. LaRue," he said. "It has been testified here that you were a loyal employee. Would you agree to that?"

"Yes."

"Would you agree that your loyalty extended to protecting your employer, in fact isn't that one of the reasons you were his employee?"

"I would say so, yes."

"Would your loyalty extend to looking after his interests whether he knew it or not?"

LaRue looked perplexed. He tried once more to cross his legs, forgetting his leg irons, but this time did not smile and look at the jury.

"I don't know what you mean."

"What I mean is, Mr. LaRue, if someone was threatening to blackmail your employer, would you do what you considered required to prevent that?"

"I think something like that would be handled by him and not me. As it was in this case. He decided to make the loan."

"Mr. LaRue, how much did Herkimer Warson pay you?"

"Why," said LaRue, his eyes suddenly searching about the room and finally finding a point of reference, it seemed, with his wife and children on the front row, "about six hundred dollars a year."

"Isn't it true, Mr. LaRue, that you had told Mr. Warson that you needed more money to maintain your household and support these fine children?"

"We talked about it some," LaRue said.

"The fact that you were always armed indicates that your position with Herkimer Warson might have been dangerous. Was fifty dollars a month adequate compensation for such duty?"

"Well, I never thought so," LaRue said. And perhaps sensing the complete, deadly silence in the room, clamped his lips shut and said no more and glared at Walter Evans.

"No more questions," said Evans.

ℵ ℵ ℵ   In summation, Ennis Merriweather said, "Gentlemen of the jury." Once more standing before them, his thumbs hooked behind the lapels of his legislative coat.

"I may startle you by saying at the outset that defense agrees with everything the government has presented in the way of the crimes committed in Creek Nation last year, in the crimes of the Temperance Moon murders. How money bought the crime, yes, we agreed, yea, indeed. Except on one point, where we do not agree and have shown here before you why so.

"The government has tried to prove that this man," and he paused and pointed to LaRue, "initiated these horrors. This man, a good citizen of your state with this fine little family." He paused again and pointed to Mrs. LaRue in the front row of the gallery with her children, one of whom was sniveling, her mother wiping at her tiny nose with a lacy handkerchief. "The government has failed, gentlemen.

"Because of that one point on which we disagree. Because the government would have you believe this fine man gave to the infamous Redstripes only half the money he started with from your fair city, contracting with them for the killings. When he has told you he passed over to these same despicable characters of a violent society every penny entrusted to him by his employer. On this, gentlemen, we do most assuredly disagree.

"And who does the government bring forward to prove their point? Who, indeed! The very woman involved in this terrible tragedy, self-confessed co-conspirator to the killings, self-confessed supporter of a husband known throughout the Indian Territory as a killer, arrogant, flaunting herself before you as she confesses the part she and her husband played in this whole bloody business. Lying to you about a note sent, according to the government, to alert the defendant to an investigation, lying to you about the amount of money in that pouch she and her husband so gladly took in Sallisaw, Cherokee Nation, last year. Lying to you about the money left from this gory windfall when she was arrested.

"And remember, gentlemen, she was ready to sing any song here to appease the government, because soon the government must try her on many of these serious crimes.

"So *that*'s who the government brought to prove their case. To prove that in Sallisaw when the pouch was passed from Mr. LaRue there was only half of what he had started with, to prove that it was *he* who bought the murder of Temperance Moon. This disreputable woman, this savage, they brought to you to prove their case. And only her.

"Surely, you must not be deceived. Surely, you must find the defendant not guilty!"

ℵ ℵ ℵ   United States Attorney Walter Evans rose for rebuttal. He had taken off his eyeglasses and now he left his position behind the prosecution table and as he spoke walked slowly back and forth before the jury, often rubbing his eyes, often rubbing the back of his neck, often holding his hands on the area of his kidneys, all as though he was very tired. And his voice was low, never rising to fever pitch. Always low. Oscar Schiller at the back of the room thought it was possibly the best argument he had ever heard.

"Gentlemen," Evans began, "I will not dwell on those things that have touched me during the course of this hearing. On that small family of the defendant, innocent of everything, of two brave women from the Territory coming to say the truth before you, on the courage of a man willing to expose his past in the interests of justice, on the persistence of many good men in bringing the Temperance Moon murders finally and at long last to a conclusion.

"I will speak only to the evidence itself.

"Gentlemen, Temperance Moon came to Herkimer Warson asking a loan of five thousand dollars. Refused. On reconsideration, granted. His reasons for changing his mind do not enter into our deliberations here. Only that the money was sent. Five thousand dollars.

"Let us think for a moment about that. Was it extortion? It was. Was it to buy a murder? It was not. There is not one person in this room who doesn't understand that you can buy murder for a great deal less money than that in the Indian Territory.

"So sent by courier to Temperance Moon. Five thousand dollars. But it never reached her. Had it, and had she been slain for it, then wouldn't it be highly improbable that so much money would not have made itself known in the Territory? So no one killed her to rob her of that money.

"By the time Temperance Moon was killed, that money had already been distributed along the line in the conspiracy to take her life. We've seen some of it. A little here, a little there. Among a number of people in the chain, most of whom are now deceased.

"Which means, gentlemen, that somewhere along the line a decision was made to take some of that money and spend the rest on Temperance Moon's death. To have her dispatched, you see, so that she could not say she'd never seen the money. And oh yes, in the event of a loyal employee, to ensure at the same time that she would not, having never seen the money, start telling stories about associations with bordellos and their madams. And gentlemen, at the same time, the source of that money, Herkimer Warson, was sure to remain silent because to have done otherwise would have compromised his reputation.

"But murder will out, so it is written. And people began to look into it all, and that one responsible for the conspiracy saw the danger. And took action against it, but not in the Indian Territory, here in Fort Smith. At least one of those actions was beyond the competence of anyone in the Nations involved.

"So where did the conspiracy begin? Here in Fort Smith, gentlemen. When a man saw the opportunity to make a considerable amount of money and at the same time protect his employer against any bad words that might be uttered against him in future and at the same time still knew that employer would remain silent because to have done otherwise would have compromised his reputation as surely as he had feared from the start.

"Who fits the description in all this, gentlemen? A man with experience in the Indian Nations. A man with experience in banking and handling money. A man with knowledge to do all the things required to make a nice little conspiracy that would supplement his meager income and with little chance of discovery. A man who realized that the death of a so-called bandit queen in the Indian Territory would cause no concern because she was evil, wicked, and who cared if she died?

"All, gentlemen, toward handsome profit, all toward protecting his employer with his employer not even knowing about it, all a shrewd plot for murder with no one the wiser.

"Gentlemen, I give you Creighton Muley LaRue, who is guilty of the charges against him."

፰ ፰ ፰ The least affected person in the courtroom was Judge Parker. Or at least it seemed so. Under the hanging light bulbs his white hair and beard took on the aspect of old snow, the flesh around his eyes like emotionless putty. Everyone waited for his charge, which they expected to be long and involved. But it was not. Court watchers later claimed it was the shortest charge they had ever heard him give to an impaneled body of twelve men.

"Under our system of justice," Judge Parker said, "a defendant may stand mute and offer no defense. He need not prove his innocence. Because the law presumes his innocence. So innocence is not the question. Guilt is the question. And proving guilt is the burden of the government. If, gentlemen, you feel that the government has not proved guilt of this defendant beyond a reasonable doubt, then you must acquit.

"There has been a great deal of circumstantial evidence presented here. Circumstantial evidence is evidence not bearing directly on the fact in dispute but on various attendant situations. From it, you may or may not infer the occurrence of fact in dispute. The weight of this kind of evidence is the jury's province. In order to bring it to the cause, you must deduce actions based on indications a logical man might make.

"As to sworn testimony heard here, the government and the defense have agreed on all except the critical fact of where a conspiracy began. In this regard, two witnesses, Mrs. Redstripe and Mr. LaRue, have given directly opposite views. It is your responsibility to decide where the credibility lies. It is your responsibility to determine which was lying, which telling the truth. I charge you with great responsibility, so think well on it, because in large measure between these two versions lies the decision in this case.

"Now, go and consider your verdict."

뉴 뉴 뉴 By the time the clock on Garrison Avenue struck ten, some of the people still in the courtroom were asleep on the gallery pews. Many of the spectators had gone, drifting out in twos and threes as the time dragged on after the jury had retired. Mrs. LaRue had taken her children into the main corridor, and there was the sound of their laughter and running up and down.

All the popcorn was gone. The red-and-white-striped popcorn sacks lay scattered on the floor under the benches. The court reporter had begun to dust the furniture in the pit, each of the little tables, swiping a cloth across walnut surfaces, moving massive volumes of printed law, humming a hymn. Possibly "Nearer My God to Thee," although those who heard him were not sure. Two of the newspaper correspondents from out of town were playing tic-tac-toe in one corner of the room, near the jury box. A federal jail trusty came in with a basket of wood and coal and a small can of coal oil to stoke the two space heaters. There was the odor of kerosene in the room. Deputy marshals stood around the walls, but looking sleepy now instead of vigilant. They hardly noticed when Mrs. LaRue brought her children back into the courtroom and sat them on the front row of seats and from her purse took two sourballs for them to suck.

At ten-fifteen, the jury trooped in, and there was a general rush of spectators from the main corridor, where they had been smoking and talking while the jury was out. By the time the jurors were seated in the box, the defendant and the attorneys were in their places and the gallery was almost full again. Judge Parker, his black robe flowing out behind, entered the hall, and everyone stood until he had taken his perch in the high-backed chair at the bench, the courtroom doors had been closed, and the bailiff had called, "Be seated." After the rustle of the crowd settling on the benches, the place was completely silent, even the LaRue children making no sound, each sitting wide-eyed, one cheek bulging with a sourball.

"Has the jury reached a verdict?" Parker asked, wearing his steel-rimmed spectacles now and peering from them much as a teacher preparing to examine his students might.

A man on the front row nearest the bench rose, the other jurors in the box looking at his back or at the ceiling or at the judge, but none looking at the defendant, and at the rear of the room Oscar Schiller saw that and whispered, "Good sign, good sign, God, let it be! Please let it be."

The foreman was wearing bib overalls and a collarless shirt, and he had had a haircut before these proceedings were begun, the flesh of his neck between the leathery skin below and the straw-colored hair above showing pale as a catfish belly. In his hand was a long sheet of paper, the usual form given juries on every case, with appropriate wording and blank spaces to be filled. Now, those blank spaces had been filled.

"We have, your honor."

"Bailiff," said Parker, "take the verdict."

The bailiff walked to the jury box, took the sheet of paper, turned and walked to the bench, handed it up to Judge Parker. Every eye in the room, except those of the jury, followed the course of that paper from hand to hand, and in the space of time it took Parker to read it, there was a breathless tension. Parker looked at the jury.

"So say you?"

"On our oath, your honor," said the foreman.

"All right," Parker said, turning in his chair and passing the paper back to the bailiff. "Defendant rise to hear the decision of your peers."

Creighton Muley LaRue rose, and with him, Ennis Merriweather, and behind his own table, so also rose Walter Evans.

"The bailiff will read the verdict," said Parker.

The deputy marshal–bailiff cleared his throat, held the paper at arm's length before his face, and read.

"We, the jury in hearing, for the United States Court of the Western District of Arkansas with jurisdiction in the Indian Territory, in the cause of the government against Creighton Muley LaRue duly charged by grand jury with fraud, conspiracy to commit murder, and murder, find the said Creighton Muley LaRue, of all charges and specifications, guilty!"

With a soft, choked wail, Mrs. LaRue slid from her seat to the floor and lay there as her children began to cry, the sourballs gone now from their mouths. A number of older ladies, wives of City Bank employees who had been asked to come to this trial, by Herkimer Warson, for just such a contingency, immediately surrounded the stricken young woman and her little girls. As Judge Parker dismissed the jury, with his usual comment that they could be proud of having done their duty, the ladies escorted Mrs. LaRue and her children from the courtroom, the children grasping at their mother's skirt, and she, water-kneed, sobbing and being held and almost dragged, and her husband still standing before the bench, Merriweather's arm around him, grinding his teeth, swearing softly. And at the bench, Parker was scribbling notes to himself and consulting a small calendar.

In back of the room, Oscar Schiller was bent over, face in his hands, his hat fallen to the floor. And Nason Breedlove heard him whispering, "He did it! He did it! That God damned Evans did it!"

For a long time, it seemed, Judge Parker consulted his own thinking. Merriweather tried to get his client back into a chair, but Muley LaRue would only stand rigid in the spot where he had heard the verdict, still cursing quietly. The blood vessels on his neck bulged almost to bursting. And Merriweather stroked his shoulder, speaking in to his ear, about appeals, about pardons.

At last, Parker looked up, slipped off his glasses, and spoke from memory of the notes he had just written. Seeing no reason to delay, he explained, the court would pass sentence.

"The crimes of which you have been convicted are all the worse for you having attempted to stand clear of the violence you set in motion. But even from afar, you killed this person in Creek Nation, the Indian Territory, as surely as though you yourself had pressed the trigger on the murder weapon. And I say your crime is greater than that because you have made not only Temperance Moon a victim, you placed the temptation for evil before weak and susceptible men and women, making them victims as well. Your energy in this has resulted in the deaths of two human beings at least, and possibly five more.

"It is the sentence of this court that you be taken to the jail from whence you came, to be there closely kept, and from there taken on Monday, the seventh day of August, 1893, by the United States Marshal for the Western District of Arkansas, to the place of execution and there hanged by the neck until you are dead.

"May God, whose laws you have broken, and before whose tribunal you must then appear, have mercy on your soul!"

As they left the building, stepping out into the cold of a black night, Oscar Schiller and Nason Breedlove could hear behind them the LaRue children crying. They said nothing, and hurried along in the harsh wind. They had reached Rogers Avenue before Oscar Schiller turned aside, bent over with his head against the wall of a building, and threw up.

18

Zelda Mores sat at her duty station on the attic floor of the federal building, her great posterior overflowing the chair, her great arms embracing the small desk before her, a pair of astonishingly delicate hands cupping a platter of roasted beef ribs, half of them already stripped of meat and the other half quickly due the same end. Beside the meat platter was a small crock where baked beans had been and beside that a large beer stein half full of thick buttermilk. All of this having come from Maria Cantoni's café on the Avenue, as it always did each day when the bank clock struck three times signaling a quarter hour before noon. Each day delivered by one of Maria's colored men. Each day consumed as the federal jail kitchen people brought up the tin plates of thin beef stew and corn bread for whatever prisoners were here, ladies in their chicken-wire cells along the long hallway.

As she ate, Zelda listened to the song from far down the attic, from the very end chicken-wire cell, from the place where Winona Crowfoot sat on her steel bunk and sang. Softly. Making a prayer to her pagan gods, so Zelda Mores supposed, different by all odds with her own supplication to the God of Calvin in which Zelda tried each evening to get some hint if perhaps she had been one of those predetermined souls for salvation which the Lord of Hosts had selected a few days before He created the universe and everything in it. So far, she had never been reassured.

Actually, Winona Crowfoot's song was a lullaby having to do with the corn ripening and the crows staying away from it so they could be invited by the tribal elders to the great green corn dance.

So Zelda ate and listened, and occasionally wiped the grease and the white curd of the buttermilk from her mustache. And thought about the great victory yesterday for the forces of law and order, of which by nature of her employment she was a part. A victory in what the old courtroom hangers-on were already calling the Sallisaw Resurrection of Temperance Moon.

Well, she'd known Temperance Moon all right. She'd had Temperance Moon right here in this attic jail a couple of times and had never seen before or since such a parade of lawyers and businessmen and killers and drunk Indians coming up to talk through the chicken wire, and bring so many fried chickens and Jewish black cakes and hot tamales and fresh peaches until the floor around her own desk looked like a 5th Street grocery store.

A new day now, though, she thought, holding the next beef rib with both hands like a slender harmonica and stripping off the meat with her strong teeth. Temperance Moon long dead but not forgot, and lying there beside the buttermilk glass a note from United States Marshal Emory Kimes to the effect that this Kansas City peace officer was coming up to speak with one of the lady prisoners. And the Kansas City peace officer wouldn't even be here, she thought, if it hadn't been for good old Temperance.

Zelda Mores had never seen this Kansas City man. She'd heard a lot about him, but never seen him. So now she would, and it was something to look forward to, because among the things she'd heard was the fact that this Kansas City man carried a British Webley pistol. Just like the one Zelda Mores herself kept in her purse at all times. And in fact had used to shoot an escaping convict back in 1887, a man, not one of Zelda's distaff prisoners, as he was making a run for the nearest gate in the compound, and the shot severed a thigh artery and before a doctor could arrive to stop the flow the man bled to death, thus saving the taxpayers a lot of money to feed and house him until the date he was to be hanged.

But when the Syrian came to the top of the stairs with his little yellow slip from the United States Attorney's office, Zelda Mores was extremely disappointed. The man was handsome enough and wore nice clothes but with one glance she reckoned this was no real man because she outweighed him by maybe as much as one hundred fifty pounds.

"I have permission from the prosecuting attorney to speak with one of your prisoners," he said, handing her the yellow slip of paper.

"I'll see if she's decent," said Zelda, rising massively with a loud grunt and a final swipe of her hand across her hairy upper lip. "Don't pay no mind to that savage singin' from down yonder. It's just another red nigger."

"I'll try to ignore it," he said.

Zelda Mores waddled along the hallway, soon out of sight to him, but was back quickly and said, "She may be asleep. I pulled back the curtain, if you wanta go down there. She's a stubborn one when it comes to talkin'."

"Thank you," Moses Masada said.

꙰ ꙰ ꙰ Tishacomsie Redstripe was lying face to the wall on the narrow bunk bed provided by the government of the United States for its female prisoners. There was a thin straw mattress and one army blanket. Moses Masada thought surely she was sleeping, for no one could have missed the heavy tread of Zelda Mores and then the drawing back of drapes. He lifted one hand to the chicken-wire wall, his fingers hooked in the mesh, and stood silent for a long moment, unwilling to disturb her, but then the decision was taken from him as her voice came, sharp and fully awake.

"Masada?" she asked. "Is that you?"

"Yes. It's me."

She didn't rise from the bunk, she uncoiled. Like a spring, rolling over and rising all in one fluid motion to stand facing him. She still wore the long mourning dress and there was still on her cheeks the rouge and in the part of her hair the ocher, and Moses Masada knew she had slept since the end of the trial yesterday removing nothing but her hat and veil.

Tishacomsie did not approach the wire but stood beside the bunk, her depthless black eyes on him.

"I thought you'd come," she said.

"I have."

Then she came across the short space to the wire but not completely to it, just beyond his reach even had the wire not been there. Her face was somber, hard-boned. But there was no bitter twist at the corner of her lips. From down the hallway came the sounds of Winona Crowfoot singing. Softly. Moses Masada thought there was a slight tilt to Tishacomsie's head.

"You hear that?" she asked.

"Yes."

"It's a Creek song," Tish said. "I remember it, but I haven't heard it in a long time. When I was a little girl, the grandmothers sang it to me."

She listened, head tilted. He had no notion what to say, was not even sure he should have come. She seemed to sense his uncertainty, or maybe, he thought, she designed it.

"When you hear somebody else's song, it's hard to place it in your own heart, isn't it, Masada?"

"Yes."

"If I could hear the songs of your grandmothers in this Kansas City, it would be the same with me." And he had the satisfaction of knowing she was at least trying to put him at ease.

"I have no grandmothers in Kansas City, Tish." He gripped the chicken wire so intently that it cut into his finger. "I have no one in Kansas City. There, all the songs are new songs and each one makes his own."

"That's not good. You need things to hold on to, things that have been there a long time. Family things. Tribal things. Maybe that was the worst part of it when the white man moved my people into a new country. So much had to be left behind, and now it's lost."

She lowered her head and moved a step closer to the wire without seeming to have moved at all. Without looking up, she raised a hand and placed it on one of his, palm to palm, the chicken wire between.

"I am talking like one of my old grandfathers once talked to me, about the Removal. A long time ago. I displeased my family when I married Candy, so they stopped talking to me. Now I have disgraced them and they will never talk to me again."

Before he could respond, still fumbling in his mind about how, her head lifted and there was some of the defiance there that made her eyes shine.

"All those things I told you about this place, maybe I was wrong. Because when I witnessed, those twelve white men believed me instead of one of their own. It is a thing that makes you think maybe justice sometimes does not depend on the color of a person's skin."

"Perhaps," Moses Masada said and then added something he had heard his father say a thousand times and no sooner said it than felt like a fool. "But one egg does not an omelet make."

"Yes, because even so, I will be in this jail a long time. Maybe a year, Evans tells me."

"Tish, with all that happened, you could be in for a lot longer than that, and in a penitentiary, a worse place than this."

Tishacomsie dropped her hand from the wire and looked at the impression made on it as though it were a tattoo. Winona Crowfoot's song went on, and on, softly, sometimes blending with the wind sound from outside. As she looked at her hand, Tish smiled, a sad little smile he thought, one he had never expected to see on her great, delicate lips.

"This Kansas City. You go there now, don't you?"

"Yes. Today. In just a little while."

She moved back to her bunk and sat down, as straight and regal as she had been on the witness chair downstairs in the courtroom. But now her face was not hard and pugnacious but rather soft as she looked at him. Almost smiling. But not smiling yet.

"Would you save a small place for me in this Kansas City and keep it for a year?"

It took him so completely by surprise that he was breathless and open-mouthed, and seeing his expression, she suddenly laughed. But just as suddenly was serious again.

"I'll never go back to the Canadian," she said. "Moma July has said he will sell the horses and bring my clothes here to me and tell my family the land is theirs again. I won't go back."

"I can stay, and help."

"No. Moma July and me, there is no liking there but there is respect and he will do it."

"And then?"

"And then to some small place saved for me."

Moses Masada pressed against the chicken wire.

"No," she said. "I will not come close to you again now because it is too painful with that wire between us. So go on now to your Kansas City. A year. Just a year. Just another spring."

He didn't speak. He wasn't sure he could. He tried to drink in with his eyes the portrait of her sitting there so he might call up the image from memory wherever he needed it. The song of Winona Crowfoot went on, putting a frame around his picture of Tishacomsie Redstripe there in jail. So he turned quickly and started along the hallway, but after two steps, her voice stopped him.

"Masada?"

And he turned, thinking that now she would say it was all a joke, all a cruel joke because he had played a small part in putting her in that chicken-wire cage.

"Masada," she said. "How will I know where to find you?"

"When you walk out of this place," he said, "no matter when it is, I'll be waiting for you with two tickets on a railroad train to the place of many new songs."

ג ג ג After the Kansas City peace officer had gone, Zelda Mores sat at her little desk working slivers of beef from between her teeth with a gold-plated pick given her in 1882 by a condemned violin player from Frankfort, Kentucky, convicted in the rape of a woman in Seminole Nation.

Too bad, she thought, that good Christians like Oscar Schiller had to make friends with such infidel goat herders as this Moses Masada, even if he did carry a British Webley revolver. Now him ready to copulate with a savage barbarian Creek, peopling the earth with criminal children like locusts from the Old Testament who ate all, gave nothing.

All that singing from the far end of the cell hallway was beginning to get on Zelda's nerves. Any moment now, the other red nigger, Tishacomsie, would chime in with her own chorus. Somebody ought to teach these red heathen how to sing "Rock of Ages," Zelda Mores thought.

So time to lay quietus on pagan song. Let them out of their chicken-wire pens one at a time, each carrying her slop jar to be dumped into the tub beside Zelda's desk so the black kid who did such things could come up and carry it all off to the regular prison latrines.

God, Zelda Mores thought, I hate watching over these Indian Territory native savages. Give me a good, honest black nigger or a scaly white woman every time, any day. All this crazy singin' and flint-hard faces, she thought, is enough to bore a person to the simples.

Zelda Mores took the British Webley from her purse and checked the loads. Satisfied, she rose with her usual loud grunt and stood at the head of the hallway.

"All right, ladies," she called. "Get ready to dump out your slop jars!"

刢 刢 刢   Mrs. Clement Hake sat on Oscar Schiller's basement bed with a brown paper sack on her lap. It was so early in the morning that there were no sounds of life from the floors above, the Scissors King and his children still sleeping. Mrs. Hake's normally puffy face was even more spongy than usual, as though she had been weeping, or was about to do so. She watched with mournful expression as Oscar Schiller moved about the room, collecting his things, arranging them all in a wicker suitcase lying open beside her on the bed. Socks and razor and soap and a box of Ohio matches, a handful of .38-40 cartridges and two small bottles filled with white powder, tucked between the folds of long underwear. A duck shirt. Woolen trousers. Everything.

"Mr. Hake and I hate to see you go," she said.

"Assigned back to Creek Nation," Oscar Schiller said. "My old station. Catching a train pretty soon now, with Marshal Breedlove. Going to Okmulgee. But I'll be back often on court business."

"Your room will always be here for you," she said, and sighed mightily. "Everything so sad. And even that thing in the newspaper about Mr. Warson at the bank. I never liked him. But so sad. Resigning his position. Not going to run for the legislature. Mr. Hake and his friends in that political club of theirs all distressed because they have no candidate for the next elections. I hate politics."

"I can understand that."

Oscar Schiller closed the suitcase and buckled the leather strap around it. He took his duster from its wall peg and slipped it on, looking about the room. Then took up the two Winchester rifles that always leaned against the clothes closet, collecting dust, and cradled them awkwardly under one arm and then took up the suitcase.

"I reckon that's it," he said. "Mrs. Hake, would you open the door for me. My hands seem to be occupied."

"Here," she said, leaping up and stuffing the brown paper bag into a pocket of his duster. "Ham sandwiches for your journey. I put in some of my bread-and-butter pickles that you like."

"I thank you, Mrs. Hake."

Then as he stood there somewhat helplessly with both hands full, she kissed him on the mouth, an extremely moist and rubbery kiss, then with a little choking sound ran to the door and opened it. The violent assault had fogged Oscar Schiller's glasses, and he staggered through the door more on instinct than by sight, and out into a gray, snowy morning.

צ צ צ It wasn't easy, carrying all his truck and those two rifles, but Oscar Schiller had made up his mind about a first stop before going to the depot for the ride to Indian Territory. So he walked along B Street to the railyards and across the sidings and the main line toward the Commerce Railroad Hotel. He reckoned it particularly appropriate that when this whole thing started back in November it had been snowing. And now it was snowing again, and just as it had then, the great fluffy flakes drifting down aimlessly with no wind to push them and everything in the early-morning gray taking on a white blanket and the snow muffling the noise of switch engines close by and the farther sounds of the bank clock chimes on Garrison Avenue marking seven and the church bells in the east reminding everyone that it was Sunday. For the Catholics, time for early mass. For the Protestant elders and teachers, time to pull together some sort of Sunday school lesson for the children that should have been done last Thursday.

And Oscar Schiller, stepping over each of the rails of the yard siding, thinking about those bells and this city which he knew better than he knew his own mind. Bells that would waken the considerable community of Jews, even though they were Christian bells, and him thinking that some of them might grumble about being disturbed in sleep on a day that wasn't even the real Sabbath. Bells wakening the English and Welsh laborers from the furniture factories and cotton presses and foundries who cherished this day of no work and late slumber, a thing they could credit to the efforts of old General Andy Jackson over a half century ago when the capitalists had been forced to allow a day of rest in every seven.

And he thought, too, that none of it mattered to him, neither a Jew nor Catholic nor Baptist nor Democrat nor Republican nor fat or thin nor old or young nor rich or poor. So, he thought, let the bells ring or not ring, it didn't matter, as he stepped elaborately over each succeeding set of parallel steel rails on direct course to Jewel Moon's whorehouse.

There it was as it had been that past November, too. Madam of the house at her little table under the window in the front parlor, smoking a black cigarillo, a cup of untouched hot chocolate before her. In the same long, smocklike dress. With the same lines of fatigue on her massive face from the previous night's entertainment of the Society of Bass Anglers or some such thing. And even Nasturtium opening the door for him.

"Come in here, Mr. Marshal, stomp off them feet now, Miss Jewel ain't want no snow on her rugs. Come on, come on in, it's cole out there."

He dropped his traveling duffel in the entry hall beside the tiny table where there was, as always, a four-ounce shot glass full of Jewel Moon's black cigarillos and beside those a vase with holly left over from the Christmas decorations. Some of the berries had dropped off onto the tabletop and lay like little red balls waiting to be picked up by some miniature marble shooter.

"Oscar," Jewel Moon said as he came in and moved to sit with her but without shedding his duster. He dropped his hat on the floor beside his chair.

"Jewel," he said.

From some inside pocket his hand appeared and opened on the table before her, and in his palm were two large, milky pearl earrings. She looked at them for a long time, and he placed them on the table and withdrew his hand.

"Evans said you ought to have 'em," he said. "Your mother's pearls."

"Yes," she said. "The ones she was wearing the day they butchered her."

Then looked away from them, and out through the lacy white curtain and into the railyard.

"Jesus, Oscar, you're in a tough business," she said.

"No tougher than yours, I expect."

She drew a deep breath.

"You want some breakfast?"

"No. Hafta get over to the depot soon. Me and Nason, back to Creek."

"Back to Creek Nation?" she said.

"Yeah, my old territory."

Jewel Moon produced another of her small bottles of white powder and placed it on the table, and Oscar Schiller took it and played with it between the fingers of both hands, as though he were rolling a cue ball.

"I had it ready for a while," she said. "I knew you'd come, sooner or later. You done a good job."

"Much obliged," he said.

"I'm satisfied," Jewel Moon said. "Money well spent."

She was staring out past her lacy white curtain into the rail-yard, where a switch engine was maneuvering boxcars, the whole operation shrouded in a white cloud of steam and snow. Looking at her, Oscar Schiller thought he detected the faint hint of a smile at the corners of her mouth.

"I had a visitor last night," she said.

"I thought having visitors was your business."

"Not this kind of visitor," she said, and the smile was growing. "Herkimer Warson."

Nasturtium appeared with a new cup of hot chocolate for Jewel Moon and a cup of coffee for Oscar Schiller. As she started to turn away from the table, Jewel Moon looked up at her and said, "Here, honey, a little present for you."

And Jewel Moon, using only her fingertips as though unwilling to touch them in any other way, pushed the pearl earrings across the table.

"Oh, my *Lordy*, Miss Jewel, oh my *Lordy*," the girl shrieked. She snatched up the pearls, one in each hand, as though afraid her mistress would change her mind, and with a little mouselike squeal, spun and dashed from the room.

"Well," said Oscar Schiller. "Looks like the girl might enjoy them things. Now what was this Warson visit?"

Oscar Schiller was sprinkling some of the white powder into his coffee. And Jewel Moon began to grin, then laugh. Just a low, controlled chuckle at first.

"You know what he said, Oscar?" she asked. "He said he was goin' over to Guthrie, in Oklahoma Territory, and start a bank. And he thought we could make a lot of money if I came along and we started another hotel, like this one!"

She covered her mouth with one hand, trying to hide the laughter, but it was too much and she had to let it bubble out and she bent over the table, laughing so hard that soon tears were running down her face.

"He wanted to start this thing all over again," she said, gasping for breath, laughing. "All over again. All over again."

Oscar Schiller stared at her, watched her shoulders shaking, watched the tears running down her cheeks.

"Can you beat it?" Jewel Moon gasped. "After all that's happened, that dumb son of a bitch wanted to start it all over again."

Considering the intensity of her spasm, Oscar Schiller reckoned she gained control of it pretty quickly. She daubed at her eyes with a lacy little handkerchief from one of those big pockets in the smocklike dress she wore. And after a few more choking sounds, was back to normal. Oscar Schiller was shocked. He'd never known that whorehouse madams could laugh like that.

"Oh God," she said. "Oh God, can you beat that?"

"Well, about Warson, Jewel," Oscar Schiller said, because it was something he had sworn to himself that he would say, "you should have told me more from the start."

Suddenly, even with some of the tears of laughter on broad cheeks, Jewel Moon's face went crosstie hard and she glared at him.

"I told you enough."

"No, you didn't," said Oscar Schiller. "Me and some of my people were hung out like apples on a limb for somebody to shoot, and I needed to know all of it. I had to worm that business out about Warson's investment in this place, and you never hinted to me about the little daughter."

"My little daughter," she snapped, "was then and now none of your business. It came up because that damned Muley LaRue was trying to gouge Warson. It didn't have anything to do with all the rest."

"The hell it didn't," said Oscar Schiller. "It may have been the very thing that tipped over the slop jar. After you'd told your mama you wouldn't loan her anything and she went to Warson and she tried to blackmail him. Sure, about this place, but more important, about him being daddy to your little girl."

"Oscar," she said, and by now all mirth was gone and her voice was harsh as gravel, "you're beginning to get on my nerves."

"Jewel," he said, "I been getting on my own nerves ever since this thing started. Tryin' to figure what went on. But one thing's for damned sure. Whatever it was that made Warson send that money to Indian Territory, loan or extortion, it don't matter. The money started the whole thing. This man down there on Garrison

Avenue tries to protect his reputation. And as a result, there's two Indian women over there in Parker's jail that will be there a long time. There's a crazy whiskey dealer who'll be tried pretty soon and hanged. Muley LaRue already sentenced to the rope. In Creek Nation, your mother under that tombstone you bought and five men in their graves, and none of them had any notion of what started the whole mess and none of 'em had any control over it because it was about Herkimer Warson's ambition. The only one who knew that was Muley LaRue, and the next time he took a whack at me, he might not have missed."

"All right," she said, looking at him without any flinch. "All right. Everything you say. Plus something earlier. Me refusing to give my mother the money to start a Eufaula whorehouse. Isn't that right, Oscar? Isn't that where it started?"

"I didn't say that," he said. "You said it. And I reckon you been thinking about that."

He expected an explosion, but he didn't get it. Jewel Moon turned her face away, the great, blocky face gone soft again, and looked through her lace curtain at the railyard. She took a number of deep breaths. Oscar Schiller finished his coffee and placed the empty cup very quietly in the saucer.

"Oscar," she said, "I been thinkin' about it for a long time. I never liked my mother much, but it's hard to face it when you think you was the start of her murder."

"Well, you can't do that," said Oscar Schiller.

She waved a hand, one of her hands with fingers heavy-ringed.

"I wanted you to find something else, so I could sleep. And the closer you got, the more I hated you because the more I seen it was true. It was me. If I'd give her the money, it would have been all right. She'd be alive. Poor old Toby Jupiter would be alive. All those others, they'd be alive. And Warson would be still tryin' for the United States Senate, and why not."

"Well, Jewel," he started, but with a look she stopped him, and there was another smile on her face, a different kind of smile.

"And you'd still be a night watchman at the scissors factory."

From the back of the building, Oscar Schiller could hear Clarence making breakfast for the ladies. So they could eat and get into bed and sleep until late evening when customers began to arrive. He could smell the bacon cooking.

"Oscar?"

"Yeah?"

"I know what happened at that trial," she said. "Some thought it was Redstripe started the murder idea. Some think it was LaRue. The jury decided it was LaRue. But do you suppose it might have been Warson?"

"Oh, hell, Jewel, he'd never spend so much money for a shoot in the Nations," Oscar Schiller said. "Besides, Muley LaRue, to save his own butt, would have squealed like a stuck hog if Warson was the man."

"I been thinkin'. I got some more funds for such things. Just for curiosity's sake, maybe you'd like to go over there to Oklahoma Territory and maybe lean up against Herkimer a little and make sure it wasn't him after all."

"No ma'am, no ma'am," he said, jumping up and adjusting his glasses, because his movement had been so violent they very nearly fell off his nose. "No ma'am! I got a nice, steady job with the government in Creek Nation, not Oklahoma Territory, and besides that, I don't want to ever hear of Temperance Moon again. No disrespect."

In the hallway, he took up his gear so quickly that he didn't even bother to pocket a handful of Jewel Moon's black cigarillos. Still at her front-parlor table, Jewel Moon heard him swearing, trying to get out the door, carrying all his truck, and then Nasturtium was there, opening the door, calling after him.

"Mister Marshal, you stay warm now, it's cole out there."

And then Nasturtium was into the front parlor, taking away Oscar Schiller's empty coffee cup, taking away Jewel Moon's untouched hot chocolate cup.

"That Mister Marshal sure taken off like yellow jacket to honey," Nasturtium said.

"Yes," said Jewel Moon. "He's going back over into the Nations."

"Lord, Lord, goin' amongst them savages, I sure glad I don't hafta do them kindsa things."

"It's a brutal world, honey," said Jewel Moon.

"Yes ma'am."

Then Jewel Moon looked up and the willowy black girl was smiling, a great, beaming smile, like sunshine on this snowy day, and at the lobe of each ear was a glowing, milky orb.

"The pearls look real nice, honey," said Jewel Moon.

"Yes, ma'am!"

卍 卍 卍 That walk from Jewel Moon's to the train waiting in the freight yard was as bad a walk as Oscar Schiller ever made. It wasn't just trying to keep the two rifles from slipping from the crook of his arm and into the snow. It was what he kept thinking.

Could it be that Muley LaRue had told the truth and Tish Redstripe lied? Did old Muley have more loyalty to Warson than I thought and was willing to take the fall? Could it be that this conspiracy started in Fort Smith all right, but not with Muley? Could it be that Temperance Moon was still resting uneasy in her grave because he, Oscar Schiller had come close to her killer but not close enough?

For Christ's sake, he thought. He couldn't let himself believe such things. He couldn't even think about it. A jury had decided what justice was here and if you can't believe in a jury there was no longer anything left for belief. This thing had been a bloody mess from start to finish and so far as he could see, nobody had been a big winner. Maybe that's what justice is when there's a bloody mess. No big winners.

Oscar Schiller could see the freight train now and there was Nason Breedlove waiting beside the caboose. In the snow, grinning and waving. What the hell, Oscar Schiller thought. He thinks it's all been done up right. So maybe it has. Just forget about it and get to business!

19 The law offices of W. M. Caveness were much as they had been that day over five years before when Oscar Schiller came and first learned that at the time of her murder Temperance Moon had been trying to borrow five thousand dollars. The massive desk was the same, still cluttered with briefs and scratch pads. And in the pencil tray, an orange. The bookcases were the same and mostly the same books in them as well. And maybe even some of the same dust on them. Everything else, too. The smell of sealing wax and lemon rind, the sound of typewriters clattering from the outer office and from there the frequent jangle of a telephone. And from the street below the clang of trolley-car bells.

Some things were different. On the day Oscar Schiller had come, a portrait of Benjamin Harrison had hung on one wall. Now it had been replaced by a picture of William McKinley. And five years ago the calendar for 1892 had been decorated with a Currier and Ives lithograph of horses, with astonishingly small heads, pulling a sleigh through the snow of Vermont or some such place, the whole thing advertising the public spirit of the Fort Smith Rim and Bow Company. Now the calendar numbered the days of 1897 and there was a steel engraving of a road locomotive pulling an endless line of passenger coaches through a sea of sagebrush and below the picture the emblem of the Missouri Pacific Railroad.

W. M. Caveness sat in his high-backed swivel chair, facing the window, looking down onto Garrison Avenue. He was sucking a lemon. Observing the passage of humanity, as he called it each evening when he went home to his wife and told her in great detail what he had seen as they supped on roast pork or fried wild rabbit or corned beef hash with poached eggs. His hair was completely white now, but there was still plenty of it.

On this day, W. M. Caveness pondered not only the passage of humanity but of time. And the changes time brought. On the street below him were more plate-glass windows in the fronts of Avenue businesses. More red brick facades. More concrete sidewalks. The trolleys were all electric now, running under a web of overhead wires. And the city had begun to replace the old gas streetlamps with electric ones. And only this past summer, he had watched the first gasoline-powered motor car, with a tiller-type steering device, run along the street, leaving a cloud of blue smoke and a lot of terrified horses behind. A vehicle built by a man with a bicycle shop on Grand Avenue who had his inspiration from an *Atlantic* magazine article about such a contraption being designed in Germany by somebody named Karl Benz back in '93.

It was a time for reverie. Brought on by the departure only moments before of the governor, one Ennis Merriweather, who always came by to pay his respects to the best lawyer in western Arkansas whenever his travels brought him to Sebastian County. Ennis Merriweather. Whose political base had been rather broad once, but never broad enough to have won an election for governor until after he became known statewide as the man who acted as trial defense counsel in the Temperance Moon murders.

Even from the grave, that Indian Nations bandit queen was a powerful presence on the imagination and maybe even the loyalties of men, W. M. Caveness thought. He wondered how long the fascination with Temperance Moon would last in this city. Well into the coming century, he assumed. The half-truth, half-legend of her and those who had associated with her went on and on, and no judgment of a jury would end it.

As surely as the sunrise, W. M. Caveness knew that in any saloon in Fort Smith the best way to start a fistfight was to proclaim that in the Moon trial the jury was right, the Indian woman told the truth. Or equally, to proclaim that it had been Muley LaRue who told the truth. And always disputants in such arguments started with the statement "By God, I was *there* that day." W. M. Caveness found it amusing. If everyone he had heard say he was there that day had in fact been there it would have required a hall larger than the main pavilion at Queen Victoria's Golden Jubilee celebration just to hold them all.

It had dragged on and on in the pages of the *Fort Smith Elevator*, each principal in the case receiving newspaper coverage that might have been envied by Henry Morton Stanley when he found David Livingstone in Africa. All of them having their moment of public glory before passing into legend, not because of who they were or what they did, but simply because they had been a part of Temperance Moon.

Even poor Sherman Boggs. Convicted in the shortest capital trial ever held in Parker's court, he was sentenced to be hanged. His case was appealed to the Supreme Court on the basis of his being insane. But the high court sustained Parker in saying that at the time Boggs pumped those three .45 slugs into Toby Jupiter's back, he passed all the tests of legal sanity, which amounted to nothing more than knowing the distinction between right and wrong.

Sherman Boggs had gone to the rope in the fall of 1893. On the scaffold, he had prayed for redemption in a loud, quavering voice. And said, just before they pulled the black hood down over his head, "Boys, remember this. When I looked into my first drink of whiskey, I could see a rope at the bottom of the bottle. That is the rope that will break my neck today."

It had been autumn. All the sugar maple trees along the old fort walls were blood-red in the morning sun.

On that day, Creighton Muley LaRue had been in the federal jail, his appeal pending. The story around Fort Smith was that the head jailer had Muley in a cell on the east side of the building so he could look through one of the high windows and watch the execution.

Then in December, Winona Crowfoot was released two months short of her year sentence. For good behavior, they said. They had other clothes for her but she refused to take them and walked away wearing the gingham dress in which she had been a witness. She went to the railroad bridge, was allowed across without toll, and on the Indian Territory side of the river was last seen walking toward Creek Nation, the cold wind blowing her dress and her short-cropped hair. Nobody in Fort Smith ever heard of her again.

On that day, Muley LaRue was still in the federal jail, waiting his appeal.

In January '94, Mrs. Creighton LaRue, accompanied by her two children and four nuns and a priest from the Catholic church, bought a Missouri Pacific Railroad ticket. It was a long ticket, many varicolored tabs to be torn off by conductors as they went along. To Little Rock, then Pine Bluff, and on to Louisiana, to Monroe and Alexandria, changing there to the cars of the Texas Pacific, then on past Baton Rouge and along the south bank of the Mississippi into New Orleans, another change to the Louisiana Southern for the short ride into St. Bernard Parish, where Mrs. LaRue's parents operated a fleet of shrimp boats. She was finally going back to civilization, where there were real crayfish and not the crawdads of Poteau River.

The LaRue children were crying. Mrs. LaRue was crying, and had difficulty standing. The nuns had to assist her onto the coach.

In only a few weeks, the other Indian woman had served out her term. Tishacomsie Redstripe. And waiting for her was the man from Kansas City, his pale eyes hot and his badge showing on a silk flowered vest. There was a lot of baggage as they boarded a Kansas City Southern passenger train. Her release had been revealed in the *Elevator*, and a number of Towson Avenue rowdies were there to jeer and spit. The ones who thought Muley LaRue had told the truth.

But there was that pale-eyed Arab with her. And there was United States Deputy Marshal Nason Breedlove with her. And there was Creek Police Captain Moma July with her. All obviously armed, as is the nature of peace officers, so the Towson crowd kept discreet silence until the train pulled away in the late glow of day, and only then made a few hisses.

It had been spring. And the redbud along the river not far to the west of the tracks was in bloom. And in its purple haze were the early white buds of the dogwood.

On that spring evening, Creighton Muley LaRue was still in the federal jail. But not for long now.

The Supreme Court decision came down in July of that year, a dreadfully hot year along the Arkansas River. The death sentence of Creighton Muley LaRue had been commuted. He was committed to the federal penitentiary at Moundsville, West Virginia. For life. W. M. Caveness figured that with time already served, Muley would be out, provided he behaved himself and survived the other inmates, in about eight years.

Because they knew a horde of well-wishers and curiosity-seekers would be on hand when Muley was transported, federal authorities had neglected to say anything about the Supreme Court decision until they already had him on the train north. There was a great outcry at this kind of secrecy. Especially from those who were thinking about throwing rotten tomatoes at United States Deputy Marshals.

Of course, W. M. Caveness knew all this intense interest about Muley LaRue was not about Muley LaRue at all. But about Temperance Moon.

The deputy assigned the task of escorting LaRue to his new home on the Ohio River was Oscar Schiller. Not because he wanted the job. But because now there was little else left for him to do. He had been recalled from Creek Nation to serve in the court as bailiff or assistant jailer or to operate the scaffold if required. The jurisdiction of the court had been shrinking, Texas and Kansas judges taking on much of the Territory, and now, finally, courts were being established in the Nations itself, and so the old line of work for Parker's men was going and at last gone.

W. M. Caveness knew part of the reason, too. The Nations would soon be wed to the western Territory around Guthrie, all of it to become the new state of Oklahoma. And Oscar Schiller knew it too, and it had amazed W. M. Caveness that once Oscar Schiller had returned from depositing his prisoner at Moundsville, he had come to this same law office to say good-bye, to say he had resigned his commission.

"It's not my game anymore," he had said.

"Where to, then?"

"Who knows?" had said Oscar Schiller. "Just get to business, wherever."

"Not such a bad philosophy," W. M. Caveness had said.

And when Oscar Schiller left town, nobody knew where he was going, because he didn't take a train. He bought a horse and rode it out with a small duffel tied to the saddle. But people said they'd bet a month's wage that Oscar Schiller still had that big nickel-plated pistol.

W. M. Caveness tossed aside the shrunken hull of the lemon he'd been sucking. And turned from the window. And remembered the day the famous Fort Smith court ceased to exist in the form that everyone had known it. He'd been there, in the courtroom.

In fact, there had been a great many people in that courtroom.

Attorneys. Officials of the court. Maria Cantoni. Max Bamberger. Come to watch the passing of an era. The jury box was empty. The only one in the pit where all the tables were was Walter Evans. When the bailiff marched into the room, everybody rose to his feet. But no black-robed jurist came to take his place at the bench.

The bailiff called, "Oyez! Oyez! Oyez! The Honorable Court for the Western District of Arkansas with jurisdiction in the Indian Territory is now adjourned. Forever. God bless the United States and this Honorable Court!"

ℵ ℵ ℵ Two months later, Isaac Charles Parker was dead. When news of it reached the federal jail, the prisoners held a noisy celebration. But when he was put down in the National Cemetery only a short distance from the infamous gallows, many people gathered. Among those were the principal chiefs of the Civilized Tribe Nations. At the end, one of them placed wildflowers on Parker's grave.

20

There was a resurgence of harangues against sin in Fort Smith. Nobody was sure whether or not this had anything to do with Judge Parker's death. Probably not, because Judge Parker had no jurisdiction over billy-goat proclivities of certain citizens, such things not being an offense in federal law even though there were many who claimed it was an offense against the peace and dignity of the United States of America, not to mention an abomination before good Baptist and Methodist churches and absolutely disgusting to the city's chapter of the Lily White Purity and Temperance League.

One of the leaders in this movement was Clement Hake, who began to appear on various stages to make speeches about the Sodom and Gomorrah kind of thing going on in Fort Smith, and on hearing this, a lot of younger men began looking for it. But the Towson Avenue saloon crowd knew what was happening. They may have been socially indifferent but they were not politically inept, and they all knew that Clement Hake had expressed a desire to run for the state legislature and when somebody was running for office the best thing he could do was get a cause and harp on it until the voters were so tired of hearing about it they'd put him in office just to shut him up.

Clement Hake spoke on various platforms, and almost always when he did, behind him sat his wife looking innocent and bewildered. It was called the Hake Movement, all that screaming about the lust released as soon as any man walked past Commerce Street and came near the infamous Row. Even though the infamous Row had been reduced by fire from a long line of whorehouses to just two, widely separated, one alongside the railyard, the other behind the Frisco roundhouse.

Clement Hake was a very bad public speaker. Yet, sometimes his wife was so moved by his orations that she sat behind him with tears running down her cheeks. This was particularly true in the two weeks after Deputy Oscar Schiller left town. Nobody made any connection, except to think that the Scissors King's wife was distraught that her husband had lost a sure vote when Schiller departed.

It was in this time of frenzied purity that the serenades began. The clergy pronounced them a chorus of angels. The Towson Avenue bunch said they were the howls of dried-up prunes. In fact they were a cavalcade of buggies and hacks, maybe twice a week, that went along B Street to the Commerce Railroad Hotel, where the ladies in the vehicles dismounted, and in a solid body of righteousness sang hymns just outside Jewel Moon's whorehouse.

It was really bad for business, particularly in view of the fact that among Jewel Moon's best customers were the husbands of some of the serenaders outside her windows.

Sometimes there was little to be heard from the throats of these ladies, because the yard locomotives continued to go about their noisy business with pistons and bells and whistles and couplings joining and the yardmen screaming, "Get the God damned hose coupled, you dumb son of a bitch!"

But there was enough. And so after one of her ladies tried to kill herself, which had never happened before, Jewel Moon went to W. M. Caveness and retained him to sell her properties, both in Fort Smith and in Weedy Rough.

"Biloxi, Mississippi," she said. "Good business opportunities, good schools. And on the Gulf of Mexico. My little girl has always said she'd like to see the ocean."

And the hill farm in Weedy Rough would be easy to sell. But the house alongside the railroad tracks might stand empty for a long time. Maybe, W. R. Caveness thought, he could convince the Frisco railroad to use it as a storehouse. But he knew the Frisco railroad would say there were a lot of ghosts there, and lewd ghosts at that.

W. M. Caveness had never seen the breakup of an elegant

whorehouse. He'd never seen the breakup of any kind of establishment such as that, elegant or otherwise, so on the date set for the occasion, he was there in the main corridor of the Commerce Railroad Hotel alongside Jewel Moon and Nasturtium.

"Never seen you much in here," said Jewel Moon.

"No, this is my first time," W. M. Caveness said. "It's a fine building."

Outside there was a collection of hack-taxi vehicles, drivers waiting. To take the Commerce Railroad Hotel ladies and others to railroad stations or wherever. There was some considerable problem holding the dray horses in check what with all the close-by activity in the railroad freight yard. Those whistles and bells and coughings of steam engines and shouts of yardmen, as much a part of Miss Jewel Moon's house as the stained-glass windows.

Inside, there was a slow surge of people in the far end of the hallway, each with a bag or valise or duffel case. And it began to come forward toward Jewel Moon. And the individuals began to detach themselves to say good-bye, the ones behind waiting patiently for their turn. First were the men, Clarence, the cook, and Crutchfield, the bartender.

Jewel Moon shook hands with them like a man. And said to the first, "Clarence, you'll like that job in the kitchen at the Union Hotel. In a year, you'll be runnin' it."

"Yes ma'am," he said.

"Crutchfield, I can still get you a good job right here in Fort Smith."

"No, I think I'll try Oklahoma Territory, Miss Jewel."

"Suit yourself. And good luck."

"Yes ma'am."

Then the ladies. All of them tearful, emotional, as W. M. Caveness had heard only whores can be. They mumbled good-byes and shook hands like the men. Except for a few. Except for the latest Natasha, the Chinese lady.

"Miss Jewel, they take me as number one bumpie at Bear Claw Beth's down behind the roundhouse."

"No, no, no, honey, you go on down to Fort Worth on that ticket I got you and you go to that lady I told you about. Bear Claw Beth's ain't no place for you."

But, of course, Jewel Moon's Natasha cashed in her railroad ticket to Fort Worth and went to Bear Claw Beth's.

Then finally the latest Julip was there, the last in the line, and in tears, youngest of Jewel Moon's charges, wailed, "Miss Jewel, I don't know if I can get along on that Iowa farm."

"Sure, sure you can, honey. That man wants you for a wife. You'll do just fine."

"I don't know nothin' about bein' a wife!"

"You'll do just fine, honey."

And Julip threw her arms around Jewel Moon and then with a great sob picked up her valise and fled through the open door.

They were gone. All of them. And only the old man now sitting at the far end of the hall next the kitchen door, next the kitchen where Clarence made all those breakfasts for the ladies and brewed those endless cups of hot chocolate that Miss Jewel never drank. The old man sitting there, a stranger here, the caretaker who would watch over the place until W. M. Caveness sold it.

Outside, there was the racket of switch engines, with their pistons spurting steam, their bells ringing, their whistles blowing. And through the open door, the odor of coal smoke and cinders.

Jewel Moon looked along the empty hallway, not moving, but W. M. Caveness knew that from where she stood Jewel Moon was seeing all of this place. Top to bottom, side to side. Hearing its sounds. Smelling it smells. Seeing its windows and carpets and peacock feathers and exotic engravings of Toledo, Ohio. Seeing in her mind's eye the polished oak bar, the massive kitchen cookstove, the etched-glass transoms.

"Well," W. M. Caveness heard her whisper, "maybe we made a few people happy."

Then she turned to him and smiled, and with that smile the great, square face seemed almost like a child's.

"Do you know that in all our time here, there was never a shooting, never a knifing, and not many really serious fistfights."

"Miss Jewel," said Nasturtium, the great pearls bobbing at her ears, "she never put up with none of that trouble thang."

"I'll do the best I can for you," said W. M. Caveness.

"I know you will, Counselor," she said and with a great sigh bent to pick up two large suitcases. "Well, come on, honey, time to go to Weedy Rough and pick up Cassie."

And suddenly tears began to run down Nasturtium's cheeks.

"Miss Jewel," she said, "I hate leavin' this nice, warm place. It's such a nice ole place!"

"Yeah," said Jewel Moon, with a one last look along the hallway to where the old caretaker was sitting, smoking a pipe. "It's a brutal world, honey."

"Yes ma'am."

࿔ ࿔ ࿔   It affected W. M. Caveness in a strange and powerful way, which he tried to explain to his wife over supper one night.

The last vestige of the real Temperance Moon gone now. Each and every one, gone. Off to some new place or else hanged. Or shot dead in places as varied as a street in front of a small Arkansas bank or in a Canadian River fish camp or in a Eufaula railroad section house. Gone, indeed, Temperance Moon herself under a cold Creek Nation slab of stone, surviving only in a few fading tintype photographs showing her sidesaddle on her favorite gray horse, the same horse she rode on the day of her murder.

But maybe, W. M. Caveness said, just maybe more real now than ever because she was in the imagination of so many people, people who had never seen her, people who had never known her, yet solid in memories as though they had seen her, had known her. Why, there was hardly a street urchin in Muskogee or a conductor on the Missouri, Kansas, and Texas line or a choir director in Fort Smith who could not recite as authentic a story about Temperance Moon. The kinds of stories passed along through the generations because it is impossible to kill a legend with the appeal of lust and murder at its center.

"Standing beside her daughter the other day," said W. M. Caveness, "I had this astonishing rush of recall. I suppose because I knew those moments were the last I would ever have in direct contact with Temperance Moon. I remembered teaching her numbers in school in Missouri. I remembered representing in court the felons she brought to me, all her lovers I'm sure, all hard men but none so hard as she was. I remembered defending her in Parker's court. And all the while, as I remembered, feeling deeply saddened, for no matter Temperance Moon's wickedness and wildness, there had to have been some quality in her that attracted and held other people. And for this, if for no other reason, she deserved better than to have been slaughtered like a hog by one of those she took in.

"Do you understand any of this, my dear?"

"Of course," said Mrs. W. M. Caveness. "But now enough of

the myth-making business and tell me what it looked like inside that Commerce Railroad Hotel."

"Why, Mrs. Caveness," he said, laughing. "You shock me."

"All right, I withdraw the question. Just eat your cabbage roll."

"I don't particularly like cabbage roll."

"Eat it anyway. And for the moment, at least, forget Temperance Moon."

"Yes, ma'am."

ACKNOWLEDGMENT

Among many sources, the following were most important in fleshing out the mood and music of old Fort Smith, the Parker court, and the Five Civilized Tribes Indian Nations.

Glenn Shirley, *Law West of Fort Smith.*
Grant Foreman, *The Five Civilized Tribes.*
John Morris, Charles Goins, and Edwin Reynolds, *Historical Atlas of Oklahoma.*
Odie Fauck, and Billy Mac Jones, *History of Fort Smith.*
Julia Yadar et al., *Reflections of Fort Smith.*
And many Fort Smith newspapers now long gone.
And members of my own family with their stories of various peace officers in Fort Smith, they and the peace officers as well also long gone.

Thank you.